John Cage

Edited by
Marjorie Perloff and Charles Junkerman

John
Cage

Composed in America

The University of Chicago Press

Chicago & London

Marjorie Perloff is the Sadie Dernham Patek Professor of Humanities at Stanford University. Charles Junkerman is associate director of the Humanities Center and teaches in the Department of English at Stanford University.

The University of Chicago Press, Chicago 60637
The University of Chicago Press, Ltd., London
© 1994 by The University of Chicago
All rights reserved. Published 1994
Printed in the United States of America
03 02 01 00 99 98 97 96 95 94   1 2 3 4 5
ISBN: 0-226-66056-7 (cloth)
        0-226-66057-5 (paper)

Library of Congress Cataloging-in-Publication Data

John Cage : composed in America / edited by Marjorie Perloff and Charles Junkerman.
        p.   cm.
    Includes bibliographical references and index.
    1. Cage, John—Criticism and interpretation.   2. Cage, John—Ethics.   3. Cage, John—Political and social views.   4. Music—United States—Philosophy and aesthetics.   I. Perloff, Marjorie.
II. Junkerman, Charles.
ML410.C24J55   1994
780'92—dc20   93-36325
                                                                                                              MN

Contents

Illustrations

Acknowledgments

O ur first debt is to Herbert Lindenberger who, in his capacity as director of the Stanford Humanities Center for 1991–92, initiated the process that led to the week-long Cage residency and conference which provided the nucleus for these papers. Lindenberger was convinced that a Cage event would do well at Stanford at a time when many others were not, and he proved to be wonderfully right. We would also like to acknowledge the support of Marta Sutton Weeks, whose generosity to the Humanities Center allowed us to invite Cage to Stanford.

At the Humanities Center, we had the able assistance of Sue Dambrau and Susan Sebbard, who made arrangements for the conference; of Margaret Seligson, who put just the right amount of order into the Musicircus; and of Nancy Bjork, who contributed her characteristically fine touch to the entire week of Cage's residency. We are grateful to Laura Kuhn, an accomplished Cage scholar and the advisor to his estate, for her assistance with manuscript material. We also owe our gratitude to Charles Amirkhanian, Karol Berger, Elisabeth Blum, Kathan Brown, Norman O. Brown, Brigitte Carnochan, Matthew Causey, John Chowning, Wanda Corn, Mona Duggan, R. J. Fleck, Betsy Fryberger, David Hahn, Stephen Harrison, Linda Ingram, Mimi Johnson, Caroline Jones, Jerzy Kutnik, Julie Lazar, Michael Ramsaur, Janice Ross, Lucia Saks, Alex Stewart, and Valerie Wade, all of whose abilities were mobilized to celebrate John Cage in his eightieth birthyear.

Finally, our greatest debt is to the late John Cage himself, whose inspiration is present on every page of this book. When revising their essays, many of the contributors, who had never met Cage before, remarked that he had helped them see certain things. At the same time, he did not interfere with our critique—a critique that must have sometimes made him a little uneasy. "I find it hard," he told us one evening, "to hear so many of my works cited. I feel as if the Cage being talked about is not me." He was of course right. The Cage re-presented in these pages is only ours.

Stanford, California, 1993

Marjorie Perloff
Charles Junkerman

×

INTRODUCTION

Marjorie Perloff and Charles Junkerman

[*Richard Kostelanetz*] *Constance Rourke has the thesis that a prime characteristic of American arts is indefinite identity—they don't particularly fit forms we know, like novel or epic.*

[John Cage] That could be like breaking down the boundaries, certainly taking away the center of interest, emphasizing the field.

[*RK*] *These are all American characteristics. This would make Ives your ancestor.*

[JC] I'm flattered to say, yes. But I'm inclined to point out that your comment is a linear one, which is a Renaissance question, which is a European question, which is a non-electronic question.

· · ·

[*RK*] *Does this bother you—the assumption that anyone can be an artist, regardless of his skill?*

[JC] No. No, not at all. Not at all. That's a European question, you know, not an American question, this whole thing of hierarchy—of wanting to make the most the best. And it took us ages, relatively speaking, to get out of that European thing. Many people are now out of it.

[*RK*] *I certainly think that the fact that you live here* [New York], *rather than somewhere else . . .*

[JC] I'm thinking of leaving. Or say I'm not thinking of leaving. I leave anyway, but in this present business I'm so rarely home. This next year I'll be at the University of Cincinnati; but I won't even be there. While I'm there, I'll be going elsewhere.[1]

In January 1992, a week-long John Cage Festival was held at Stanford University. In itself, such an event was not particularly unusual: over the last decade or so, Cage, long regarded as the *enfant terrible* of twentieth-century music, had finally come into his own. In 1988–89, he delivered the Charles Eliot Norton Lectures at Harvard, and for his eightieth birthday (September 5, 1992) celebrations, concerts, symposia, and exhibitions were planned around the world—celebrations that, sadly enough, had to be reconceived as memorial events when Cage died quite suddenly and unexpectedly on August 12.

The Stanford conference differed from most others, however, in that the symposia it sponsored steered clear of the usual "insider" treatment of Cage (anecdote, personal reminiscence, hagiography, exposition of particular works according to the artist's own prescriptions) in favor of a larger consideration of Cage's place in the cultural landscape of the United States in the later twentieth century. What, we asked ourselves, makes Cage, despite all his homage to Schoenberg and Suzuki, such a peculiarly American, indeed peculiarly West Coast American artist? And how does Cage's aesthetic, or, more broadly, what one contributor to this volume calls Cage's "poethics"—the theory that art has ethical and social purposes—accord with the other philosophical discourses of our time? Is what we might call Cage's mystic pragmatism a departure from modernist ideology or can we trace its derivations from modernism more accurately than we might have supposed? And, since so much of the later work was composed according to chance operations, what *is* a chance operation anyway?

There was much discussion of these and related issues at the Stanford conference, but *John Cage: Composed in America* is by no means a straightforward record of the conference proceedings. In fact, even Cage's mesostic lecture "Overpopulation and Art," published here for the first time, is not reproduced as it was delivered at Stanford.[2] First of all, there never was a definitive oral presentation since Cage read the lecture twice during his week in residence, and the two performances were not at all identical ("You can't repeat anything exactly—even yourself").[3] More important, however, is the fact that Cage was in the process of editing the text when he died. Prompted by a conversation with Joan Retallack in the spring of 1992, Cage set about revising the language of the lecture to eliminate its gender specificity, and to bring it into consonance with the lecture's thematic opposition to patriarchy. Because of the rules governing the composition of mesostics, Cage could not simply go through the text substituting "s/he" for "he" or changing "manhour" to "workhour." All the more remarkable, then, that the eighty-year-old Cage wanted to change the text, wanted to "get it right." Because such openness to the new ("I weLcome whatever happens next") was one of the central features of his compositional technique in music and poetry, we publish Cage's lecture as he revised it in August 1992, in the process of becoming something else.

This openness was an equally distinctive feature of his conversation, as his good-natured impatience with Richard Kostelanetz's questions reveals. Cage never showed much interest in answers and always found questions more compelling; a good question can lead to discovery, whereas an answer is inevitably something like a small death. We know from the exchange with Kostelanetz quoted above what a bad question is—one that invokes a linear paradigm (hierarchy, influence, sequentiality), simplifying and falsifying the world in which we live. These are, Cage says, "non-electronic" or "European" questions. But then what would an "American" or "electronic" question look like, and what kind of answer would it elicit? Presumably both question and answer would, as Cage tells Daniel Charles in *For the Birds*, "preserve us from all the logical minimizations that we are at each instant tempted to apply to the flux of events" (*FB*, 80–81).

In composing a volume like the present one, especially so soon after Cage's death, there is the risk of asking all the wrong questions (about status, value, and influence) and answering them with a predictable catechism of superlatives. We have therefore thought it best to be as exploratory as possible in these essays, leaving many questions unanswered. We have not tried to assign Cage a definitive place in contemporary American intellectual life, to fix or categorize him, but to be as responsive as possible to his own omnivorous engagement with the life of the mind. Consequently this is less a book about Cage the composer-performer or Cage the poet than it is about Cage the thinker who, "beginning with ideas," worked and lived his entire life in their constant and intimate presence.

The ten essays in this collection, all of which were written specifically for the Stanford conference or in response to that event, reflect the diverse interests and specialties of their authors. We might note, to begin with, that the contributors don't fall into the usual categories. None of them is a composer or musician. Only one, Jann Pasler, is a musicologist, and, ironically, Pasler, whose recent work deals with the cultural construction of twentieth-century French music, chose to examine Cage's self-invention by studying a verbal rather than a musical text, namely, "Composition in Retrospect." Three of the contributors are trained philosophers: Daniel Herwitz, whose recent *Making Theory, Constructing Art* concerns the way avantgarde art creates the theory by which it is then judged; Gerald L. Bruns, whose readings of modern and postmodern poetry have grown out of his studies of Heidegger, Gadamer, and, more recently, Stanley Cavell; and Joan Retallack, whose work as a practicing poet bears the imprint both of Cage's influence and of her own training in philosophy. Thomas S. Hines is a cultural and architectural historian, whose work on Richard Neutra and Los Angeles architecture provided the perfect background for examining Cage in what we might call his Hollywood avant-garde phase. N. Katherine Hayles's expertise on the interface of literary theory and the new science, specifically chaos, information theory, and cybernetics, provides an understanding of Cage's chance operations that no traditional scholar in any of the humanistic disciplines is likely to have.

The rest of us come to Cage from what is loosely called Comparative Literature, but even here there is great diversity. Herbert Lindenberger has written books on Wordsworth, Büchner, Trakl, historical drama, and opera: the *Europeras* were thus a "natural" for him. Gordana Crnković is a recent graduate of the Stanford Modern Thought and Literature program, whose work on Eastern European and North American writers is concerned with the relation of political to poetic identities. Marjorie Perloff originally came to Cage as a specialist in modern and postmodern poetry; since 1981, when she published *The Poetics of Indeterminacy: Rimbaud to Cage,* she has been making the case for Cage as one of the leading poets and poeticians of our time. Finally, Charles Junkerman, trained as a nineteenth-century comparatist at Berkeley, was introduced to Cage's work in his capacity as associate director of the Humanities Center. It was Junkerman who organized the Musicircus that was one of the highlights of the festival, and his account of that event brings to it a practical engagement tempered by critical distance that more professional Cageans may well lack.

In our initial planning discussions, we posed two broad questions we wanted the contributors to address: (1) How do we assess Cage's national identity, his particular Americanness? And (2) what is the relation of composition to ethics in Cage's work? These issues are, of course, entirely "interpenetrating," to use Cage's own word; the very emphasis on "poethics" in Cage's thinking may be taken as a curiously American phenomenon. The question of an American poethics, moreover, subsumes many of the more specific issues critics have long talked about: Cage's Zen Buddhism, his iconoclasm vis-à-vis traditional methods (whether European or American) of composing music, his relationship to the *Fluxus* movement, his collaborations with Merce Cunningham, and so on. The intersection of an American ethics and poetics provided us with a convenient point of entry into the unique particulars of Cagean composition.

．．．

The genre Cage invented called the Musicircus (first produced at the University of Illinois in 1967) is, as Charles Junkerman describes it, "an urban genre—crowded, noisy, and insubordinate" and distinctly American in the practical and pedagogic ends to which it puts a carnival occasion. In its subversion of traditional aesthetic and social codes, the Musicircus functions not only as carnival but as utopia, providing us with social spaces that, unlike the ones of the cities we live in, are open, safe, free of charge, and interactive. At the same time—and this is where things get complicated—the genuine communality of the Musicircus has been questioned. Isn't it still a performance planned and orchestrated by a single artist, John Cage? And since Cage insisted on performing separately (at the Stanford Musicircus he was in a room by himself, reading *Muoyce*), is the resulting art form really as decentered and non-hierarchical as he would have liked us to believe? It seems, Junkerman writes, "that one needs others to become one's best self, but this need does not necessarily bind one to others in solidarity or sympathy."

This tension between self-creation and solidarity, between "autonomous individualism" and "cultural pluralism," is, Junkerman argues, perhaps the outstanding question in American social culture. Cage has repeatedly made the case for an ethic of community ("Here Comes Everybody"), but he has been equally adamant about guarding his separateness, his right to be *different*. No doubt, as Thomas Hines shows in his study of Cage's Los Angeles years, this ambivalence can be traced back to Cage's childhood, in which his early Protestant training (his grandfather was a minister in the Methodist Episcopal Church) oddly collided with the anarchic and nomadic ethos of his inventor father and his thrice married, curiously unorthodox mother. At one level, young John Cage was the quintessential Californian, attending the local public schools (he was valedictorian at Los Angeles High School), moving from house to house in the then-suburbs of L.A. like Glendale and Santa Monica, participating in Boy Scout activities, and working at various summer jobs. But from the start, Cage was also different. For one thing, he was homosexual—a fact that no doubt contributed to his dropping out of Pomona College during his sophomore year and going to live in Paris where he worked for an architect. This European experience led directly to the artistic preoccupations of the early thirties, when he was living at the Rudolph Schindler commune on King's Road in Hollywood. The lessons of the sometimes programmatic European avant-garde, a number of whose practitioners he met at the Schindlers', were absorbed by a consciousness dedicated to openness, self-invention, and antinomianism. "America," says Cage in "A History of Experimental Music in the United States," "has an intellectual climate suitable for radical experimentation. We are, as Gertrude Stein said, the oldest country in the twentieth century. And I like to add: in our air way of knowing nowness."[4]

Consider Cage's relationship to the artist he considered his most significant precursor, Marcel Duchamp. However much Cage learned from Duchamp about readymades, about the obsolescence of the art object and the consequent Dada identification of "art" with "life," Marjorie Perloff suggests in her essay that the eroticism which permeates Duchamp's art, creating its distinctive puns, sexual double entendres, and witty, scatological (anti-Catholic) representations of the female body, had no place in Cage's more austere, residually Puritan, and (if covertly) homoerotic composition. Emotion, Cage repeatedly tells Daniel Charles, is something to be suppressed, something that removes one from art. "Love," he explains to Thomas Hines (see n. 43 in Hines, this volume), "makes us blind to seeing and hearing." And again: "Once I am doing something 'serious' I don't think about sex" (ibid.). One recalls Gertrude Stein reproaching Picasso for "not ever completely working." *Work*, in this American context, does not mean employment, the nine-to-five job performed for the sake of financial remuneration. On the contrary, Cage looks forward to a time

6

when everyone might be unemployed and get on with the real work to be done, which is nothing less than the improvement of the planet. "Work," as Cage, in his role as "a duchamp unto my self" reconceives it, becomes the perfect opportunity to "do something else," to produce plexigrams, mesostics, and what we might call "poessays" that constitute a de-eroticized counterpart to Duchamp's constructions. At the same time a curious form of re-eroticization takes place, Cage using the sexually ambiguous persona of Marcel (or his female alter ego Rrose Sélavy) as itself a sensuous presence.

In practice, then, "the anxiety of influence" takes the subtle form of inventing a suitable tradition, creating a usable past. Jann Pasler shows that the later mesostic texts (her example is "Composition in Retrospect") present Cage's own tenets as having been derived from his favorite artists, whether or not such derivation actually occurred. For example, "the diviSion of a whole / inTo / paRts," the division of "fouR / foUrs into one two and one (four eight and four)" is attributed by Cage to Erik Satie, even though, as Pasler notes, it is not at all clear that Satie used such a division. Schoenberg, Duchamp, and Rauschenberg function as similar authority figures, invoked by Cage to bolster particular positions that are not necessarily those of his sources. Ironically, both in "Composition in Retrospect" and in the Charles Eliot Norton Lectures, *I–VI*, Cage converts his own originality, his unusually small debt to other artists, into a derivation from the "Great Tradition" of Thoreau, Joyce, Stein, Wittgenstein, Schoenberg, Duchamp, Satie, Marshall McLuhan, and Buckminster Fuller.

We thus have the paradox of the avant-garde artist proclaiming his continuity with a canonical past. And there is a second paradox. American as Cage has always been in his ethos and his aesthetic, his work has consistently had a better reception in Europe and Asia than in the United States. Perhaps like Faulkner's, Cage's very Americanness appeals to foreign audiences. Think of the irony, for instance, of Cage's *Europeras* (1987) being commissioned by the Frankfurt Opera. But perhaps it was not such an irony, "the last remaining refuge of the high style," as Herbert Lindenberger calls opera, became the perfect target for Cagean deconstruction. Every operatic feature: the union of words and music, the fusion of various genres into a larger totality, the cultivation of dramatic progressions, the "sustained effort to express passion and grandeur"—all these are exploded in the plotless, characterless, antimimetic world of *Europeras*. But this amazing work, Lindenberger argues, is not to be understood as parody or send-up; on the contrary, he sees *Europeras* as a serious cultural critique of the High Style and its institutional representations. Ironically, the Frankfurt audience was evidently willing to entertain such critique, made as it was by an American outsider, more willing, perhaps, than we ourselves have been. "Permission granted, but not to do whatever you want."

Cage as cultural critic: in the United States, this proposition still strikes many as dubious. Intellectuals have tended to regard Cage as excessively "soft" and utopian in his thinking, the guru of "purposeless play," who sees art as "a way of waking up to the very life we're living, which is so excellent once one gets one's mind and one's desires out of its way and lets it act of its own accord" (*S*, 12). Cage, the common wisdom has it, takes no stand on political issues; he ignores psychological complexities; he has no sense of human suffering, aggression, or evil. In an exchange with his old friend Norman O. Brown at the Stanford conference, Cage was accused of being excessively optimistic, of making no allowances for the terror and finality of death. Such an accusation now seems doubly ironic, Cage having been just six months away from his own death at the time the discussion with Brown took place. Two weeks before he died, he told Joan Retallack that it was his wish to "disappear without a trace"—a wish that was oddly granted, so far as his body was concerned: he did not become "ill"; there was no time span where he was "dying"; he merely died.

Cage's fabled optimism, in any case, has struck many people, as it must have struck Brown that day in January 1992, as a certain superficiality or shallowness of thought. All the more important, then, to place Cage philosophically, as our contributors have done here. Gordana P. Crnković writes from the perspective of a Yugoslav (she is half Croatian, half Serbian) student of American culture, who reports that in the mid-eighties, before the dissolution of communism in Eastern Europe, visions of a utopian America were common. She herself was skeptical of this idealised vision, but when she read *Silence,* she oddly felt that she had found the utopian "America" she and her friends had been looking for. Totalitarian language, Crnković posits, is "vertically constructed": "its terms are defined by reference to already-established meanings and corresponding material practices." "Vertical construction" is also a corollary of social domination, insofar as its abstractly articulated ideals are unresponsive to potentially liberating material practices and forms of life which diverge from those ideals. "Horizontal" construction, on the other hand, frees words, beings, and thoughts; it is antihierarchical and "opposed to all external ordering systems." Reading key passages in *Silence,* Crnković examines the ways decentering, nonobstruction, and interpenetration work textually.

Cage, as we noted above, has regularly been criticized for his avoidance of "depth," of psychological complexity. Crnković refutes this charge by calling into question the whole notion of interiority, pointing out that "self-expression," far from being an act of resistance to the world of social conformity, is all too often an "insidiously disguised reproduction of the world of power." A similar case is made by Daniel Herwitz. The "very attempt to order sound in the mind's ear as coherent, complete, resolving, elaborative, and formal," writes Herwitz, "is [for Cage] an act of manipulation or possession." If, as Cage puts it to Thomas Hines, he has never learned "to practice the emotions," it is perhaps because he regards subjectivity itself as an authority structure. "To acknowledge sound, like acknowledging people, is for Cage to just let it be." Respect is thus predicated on noninterference. But there is nothing passive about such noninterference: by making music over into poetry, as Cage has done in so many of his more recent works, he has, according to Herwitz, reintroduced reference and hence the world itself into the text.

The contrast Herwitz draws between Cage's anarchic model of a social and musical community and Kant's *sensus communis* casts in sharp relief the tenets of Cage's poethics. For Kant, "the cardinal moral rule is to act so that one's action might be willed as univeral law"; for Cage, in contrast, the deepest freedom is the freedom to be oneself: *difference,* so to speak, is all. Form, in this context, cannot impose moral action; it can only be a means of "artificially organizing the free play of 'whatever happens to happen.'" The need to "demilitarize" syntax, which Cage speaks of so frequently, is thus an "act of passive resistance to the domain of meaning." But resistance, Herwitz reminds us, is by definition resistance to *something;* in Cage's practice of fragmenting texts into mesostic poems, resistance insures that there is authorial choice. The very texts Cage chooses to fragment in works like "Lecture on the Weather" and *I–VI* become all the more important precisely because the fragments send us back to the sources. Indeed, the interplay between the source and its mesostic counterpart (the fragmented, dislocated word groups and asyntactic phrases extracted from the source text) is what produces meaning in Cage's texts.

Cage's poethics thus involves "a self-recognition of one's dwelling within a whole which resists overall determination." Here Herwitz's formulation accords with Gerald Bruns's, although the latter comes to it from a different angle. Bruns locates

Cage's work at the crossroads of two ethical theories: (1) an ethics based on prior "beliefs, desires, values, principles, perceptions, actions, experiences" and (2) an ethics based on "how we are with respect to other people," to the "claims that the other has on us." Bruns associates the former or Kantian view with Martha Nussbaum, the latter with Emmanuel Levinas, and places Cage, along with Stanley Cavell, somewhere in the middle, deriving from both. Like Nussbaum, Cavell begins by positing a knowing subject, but takes the willingness to forego knowing as the beginning of ethical action. The link between Cavell and Cage is provided by their common debt to Emerson and Thoreau, to the notion that Heidegger explored most fully, of "thinking as the receiving or letting be of something, as opposed to the positing or putting together of something."

When Cage insists that music is a listening as much as a playing, that chance operations allow him to produce an art of what Heidegger called *Gelassenheit* or acceptance ("acknowledging the *es gibt* of things"), he is inventing an art of "disturbance" quite different from, say, Mallarmé's. The latter's silence is achieved by excluding the materiality of language; Cagean silence, by contrast, is a way of "opening the doors of music to the sounds that happen to be in the environment." In the same vein, Cage's "noThing" is not Mallarmé's sublime *Néant* but the "nowhere" (or everywhere) where things come from. Music as listening rather than as composing: Cage's openness to the surface and contingency of things, his relinquishment of "categories of deep structure in favor of the singular and irreducible"—here, Bruns suggests, is a poethics highly consonant with our time.

The singular and the irreducible: this brings us to a consideration of Cage's use of chance operations. Of all the facets of Cage's work, this is the one that has been most subject to ridicule. Cage composes music, we read in the newspapers, that is simply random; he doesn't structure his works but merely throws the dice or dreams up some silly mesostic rule: it's all just nonsense, isn't it? In her essay on chance operations, Katherine Hayles puts this sort of talk to rest, let us hope once and for all. She begins with the oxymoronic nature of the term *chance operation,* "chance" pointing to all that exceeds or escapes our designs; "operation," on the contrary, to the reasoned "process by which we put our designs into effect." There are, she says, three interpretations of chance that constitute it "as a concept that can be enacted through an operation." First, as Hayles argues, following Stanislaw Lem in *A Perfect*

Vacuum, "chance . . . is the intersection of independent causal chains. Each is deterministic on its own, but the intersections create unthinkable complexity and inevitable unpredictability." Many of Cage's Zen *koans* in *Silence* illustrate this principle: independent world lines, each having "normal" causality, come together so as to create a wholly unpredictable (and often comic) outcome. "The point," says Hayles, "is not to deny connection, since conjunction is a kind of connection. Rather it is to subvert the anthropomorphic perspective that constructs continuity from a human viewpoint of control and isolation."

Here, as in the essays of Herwitz and Crnković, art is seen as the subversion of control. And yet, because time has directionality, once actions have occurred—no matter how fortuitously they fall into place—their order cannot be undone (Hayles's second interpretation of chance). Chance also involves what is called noncompressibility (Hayles's third interpretation). This is a way of describing the fact that the information generated by chance operations is so random that it cannot be represented in any more compact formula. The "flux of events," in other words, resists the "logical manipulation" the mind is tempted to impose on it. This is the delicate balance, Hayles posits, that Cage has in mind when he speaks of "purposeful purposelessness or a purposeless play" (*S*, 12).

The noncompressibility of Cage's poetry is also Joan Retallack's subject, but her own approach is more intuitive and poetic than straightforwardly analytic. Cage's work, she suggests, "enacts a peculiarly American model of possibility—a pragmatic, philosophical, and aesthetic realism—one which is disruptive of individual and institutional habits of mind while concretely revelatory of the odd and always interesting intersections of whether (chance and choice) and weather (concrete variables)." Retallack's exhibit "A" of such "whether"/"weather" conditions is a short untitled mesostic poem in *X*, which challenges our most entrenched reading habits, containing, as it does, a number of crossed-out lines and phrases and concluding with the word "stet." Not only is the text "problematic in terms of a simple left-right, top to bottom, linear reading," we can't even be sure how many lines it has or what does or does not belong to its ambiguous figure. For Cage, Retallack suggests, again turning to chaos theory, "'noise' is not an interference but a manifestation of the intricate detail that can be noticed with a discipline of receptive attention." Whereas Hayles looks at the mesostics from the point of view of their production, Retallack is especially interested in their reception, what a reader or listener makes of them. The poethics of Cage's little poem, she observes, "invites a practice of reading which enacts a tolerance for, and a delight in complex possibility."

Attentiveness is central to this theory of reading. Cage, Retallack reminds us, believed that such a reading practice "could have real social consequences—that it could, as he has said, change the political climate." We may not all be this sanguine, although it is true that if sounds and words were taken seriously, if their meanings were established by their use, as Wittgenstein, one of Cage's seminal precursors, wanted them to be, we might avoid what Wittgenstein dismissed as "transcendental chit chat"—the making of large and hence questionable generalizations, designed to "explain" the universe. Such explanation is what Crnković refers to as a "vertical" construction of language, whose intention is to control and discipline the world it represents.

Against this perhaps excessively utopian view of Cage's utopian American ethos, one might object that the demand placed on our attentiveness by Cage's compositions can sometimes be excessive. At what point does randomness provoke boredom? Does the use of chance operations always yield the results Hayles finds so interesting in Cage's work? And if not, what sort of operation controls the chance operation?

The discussion of these issues is only now beginning. All that we can hope here is that *John Cage: Composed in America* will help to open the debate, to demonstrate that, far from being a naïve and slightly dotty "inventor" of long, formless compositions that lack harmony and melody or, in the case of the verbal texts, don't "say" anything, John Cage is an artist whose subtle ideas and sophisticated methods will set the stage for a good deal of art discourse in the cyberspaces of the twenty-first century. As he predicted in "Seriously Comma," written as long ago as 1966: "Invade areas where nothing's definite (areas—micro and macro—adjacent to one we know in). It won't sound like music—serial or electronic. It'll sound like what we hear when we're not hearing *music,* just hearing whatever wherever we happen to be. But to accomplish this our technological means must be constantly changing."[5]

"It must change," as Wallace Stevens put it, but how? Perhaps by never taking oneself too seriously. Questioned about his macrobiotic diet in a 1974 radio interview, Cage explained, "Well, as I've gotten older, I've come to feel that I must pay more attention to my health. Now, the macrobiotic diet may not make me live longer, but when I do die, I'll be in perfect condition. And so then I can just die a natural death." And that's exactly how it happened eighteen years later. Chance? Or, in the anagram created by the Brazilian concrete poet Augusto de Campos: **Chance / Change / Cage.**

Notes

1. Richard Kostelanetz, ed., *John Cage: An Anthology* (New York: DaCapo Press, 1968), pp. 25, 12.

2. A mesostic, as Cage has often explained, is an acrostic whose governing letters go down the middle of the text, rather than the left-hand margin. The mesostic rule is that a given capitalized letter does not occur between it and the preceding capitalized letter.

3. John Cage, *For the Birds: John Cage in Conversation with Daniel Charles* (Boston and London: Marion Boyars Press, 1981), p. 48. Hereafter cited as *FB*.

4. John Cage, *Silence* (Middletown, CT: Wesleyan University Press, 1961), p. 73. Hereafter cited as *S*.

5. John Cage, *A Year from Monday* (Middletown, CT: Wesleyan University Press, 1967), p. 27.

Overpopulation and Art

John Cage

O

abOut 1948 or 50 the number of people
liVing
all at oncE
equaled the numbeR who had ever lived at any time all added together
the Present as far as numbers
gO
became equal to the Past
we are now in the fUture
it is something eLse
hAs
iT doubled
has It quadrupled
all we nOw
kNow for sure is
the deAd
are iN the minority
they are outnumbereD by us who're living
whAt does this do to
ouR

way of communicaTing   20

V   mail's rarely frOm people we know

i spend time saVing it

to sEnd it to

wesleyan noRthwestern or santa cruz

for fungi'n'arts a Picture's thus given

Of this moment in history

ePhemera give it

rest of the mail's bUreaucratic fundraising by institutions concerned

with heaLth

And   30

environmenT

human rIghts etc

three cOpies

of the same documeNt   contribution rerequests

bureAucratic

iNefficiency

glaringly exhibiteD

All

thRown away

Triplicate   40

E   stamped envelOpes included   'phone rings

reViving

practicE

whetheR sentient or nonsentient

Practice

Of buddhism   the general outlines of   every being

including the telePhone

is the bUddha

is worLd-honored

is Answered   50

is The

Is
Of
is emptiNessfullness
All of
creatioN
enDless
interpenetrAtion
togetheR
wiTh   60
R   nOnobstruction
of what aVail
thEn the use
of answeRing service
attemPt
tO free oneself from
interruPtion
solitUde for just a moment regained
is utterLy
finAlly   70
lostT
fInding 19th
nOt 21st
iN 20th century
Are you
iN to fax
anD
electronic mAil
aRe you
in Touch hce   80
✿

P   we live in glass hOuses
our Vitric surroundings
transparEnt
Reflective

                    Putting images
                    Outside
            in sPace of what's inside
                oUr homes
everything's as muLtiplied   90
                    As we are
            each momenT
                    Is magic
            we have nO idea
            what's beiNg seen
                or heArd
            the quaNtity
            is beyonD count
            the quAlity is
                    Readymade   100
                arT
O   this demOnstrates
                    Validity
            of thosE
                woRks of art
        in which no Place
                is mOre
                    imPortant than another
                beaUty
                at aLl points   if it doesn't click   110
wittgenstein   tAke a clicker
    from your pockeT
            and clIck it
            transfOrm
        your perceptioN of it
                of whAtever
                    No matter what the name what the artist's name
            no neeD
            for bAlance

haRmony 120
conTrast climax
P   in this situatiOn what's the artist's
proper behaVior
sElf-
expRession
or should artists be Put aside
sO
to sPeak   be changed
asking qUestions
instead of foLlowing 130
lAws
or making an aTtempt
after breakIng them
tO establish
yet aNother or others   getting rid of the principles
of lAw
of coNtrol   increasing
worlD
And life enjoyment
seem moRe radical 140
removal of The likes and dislikes
U   chance Operations   wanting to get a taxi
aVoiding
a gEntleman
on the coRner who was there ahead of me
i seParated
my prOblem from his
by going to the oPposite side of the street
jUst
as i haiLed 150
An
empTy cab

                    I was surprised   the gentleman
        rushed ahead Of me
                aNd
                Actually
            got iN the cab without even a remark
                i Don't know
        whether he hAppened to see
            but anotheR cab picked me up   160
        before he was ouT of sight
                        ❀

L   what are sOme of
                the Various
                        Eventualities in a changed society
            no goveRnment
                keePing
            educatiOn
            in first Place keeping it
            that is for yoU   170
        to give to yourseLf
                increAse
        of unemploymenT
                untIl we are all
            self-emplOyed self-taught
            self-goverNed
                A way
                Not just to say anarchy
            but to Do it
        forget the politiciAns   180
            they aRe
            on The
A   mOon   when they saw we were
        no longer Voting
            thEy left
        not botheRing with money

                    Preferring credit
           credit's electrOnic
                  no Person need be
                withoUt it   190
           but who'Ll do
                 All
                   The work   those who do
                 wIll have pleasure
        seeing their wOrk actually carried out
           robots makiNg robots
                 we hAve
                  the Next war
                  mappeD out for us
                  to mAke   200
                 the woRld
           safe for poverTy
T   viOlation
                   Violation
           of laws madE
                   to pRotect the rich   while there's still
           government Pass laws
                 based On
     the needs of the Poor   give them shelter
                    sqUatting   210
                  priviLeges
                  chAnge
                   The
                  economIc structure
                    Of society
           out of profit'N'ownership into use
           the police wAlled up the doors
                   'N'
                  winDows
           the house is Again not used   220

and the people aRe
sTill
I   hOmeless
mayor said eVict
thE squat
the police did it bRutally
a house was emPty
we restOred it
filled sPace with life
concerts discUssions   230
peopLe's kitchen
librAries
nobody geTs money
for her or hIs
wOrk
a Nonprofit
bAsis
chaNges of behavior
Discussions
About sex   240
oveRcoming
repressive sTructures
O   O
haVing
no nEed
foR art
Pleased with what i see
O
Pleased with what i hear
sUrrounded   250
by muLtiplicity
he sAid he could imagine
a world wiThout art
and that It wasn't bad

O
artlessNess
the sound of trAffic
                aN instance of silence
        the sounD
            of trAffic   260
    the sound of tRaffic
            an insTance
N   Of silence   'phone rings
            reViving
        practicE
        of chRistianity
            sPlit the stick
            O
            sPlit the stick and there is
            jesUs   270
            waLking
    on the wAlking
        on The
        wrIting
            O
        oN
        the wAter
            oN the water as though
    nothing happeneD
the snow the white Animal asleep safely   280
        asleep in the tRee
            no Traces left
A   O
            reViving
        practicE
        whetheR meditation or nonmeditation
            Pleased

                    Or
                    disPleased
              won't bUrn   290
          the metaL ones won't burn
                    is A
                    is The
                    Is
                    Of
              is emptiNessfullness
                    prActicality
          all creatioN
                    enDless
    interpenetrAtion   300
              whispeRed
                    Truths
N   the necessity tO find new forms
                    of liVing
                    nEw
              foRms of living together
          to stoP the estrangement between us
              tO overcome
              the Patriarchal thinking
              the aUthoritarian structures   310
      and the coLdness
              humAn
              noT togetherness
          the necessIty
              tO develop a culture
          that coNsciously opposes the ruling culture
              A culture which we create
    we determiNe   which overcomes the passive consumers
              attituDes
                    And   320

which is not Ruled
   by profiTeering   aesthetic spirit is
D   as thOugh
      Visibility
would not hElp
as though eveRything that is generally understood
   must stoP
     Only
what one Person alone
     Understands
    heLps
     All of us   how
  whaT
    Is
    nOt
    uNderstood
    A mystery
   is Now necessary
something we Don't
of which we cAn't
make head oR
    Tail
A   a music Of
    Variations
without rEpetitions
an intRoduction to
   Pleasure
that has nO need for
    Proof or ideas or feelings
goal withoUt
  goaL
   And
  whaT
   dId i hear

33●

34●

35●

Or see
i caN't be sure
it wAs as if
there was Nothing
on which to Depend
As if   360
theRe was
noThing   but in the presence
R   Of . . . niksa gligo wrote from zagreb to say
the ugly jugoslaVian war is not
bEtween people
it has been bRought about by
that Part
Of government'n'army that's concerned
with serbian Power
let oUr friends   370
and aLl others know the truth   this's not
ethnic nor civil wAr
nor differenT
ways of thInking   this's an imperialist
pOlitical
aggressioN
it's All
happeNing in the heart of europe
at the enD of the 20th century
possibly bringing About   380
the total disappeaRance
of croaTian state and
T   peOple   what did you hear
the pentagon   giVing up
on thE
Radio
soldiers not to be Paid just discharged
seven hundred thOusand   a great boon

for unemPloyment
do yoU think
we'Ll
finAlly see
unemploymenT's
what we've been workIng
tOwards
uNemployment's self-employment
At last
we may be doiNg what we
the human race coulD be doing
All of us   As he said   suzuki said
theRe seems
To be a tendency towards the good

O   even thOugh the future is already here
many are still liVing
in thE past
all goveRnments
are striking examPles
Of what's out of date
and inaPpropriate
to oUr proper business
our evoLution   though there're more
of us   All of us live in
The same place   the planet earth
there Is
nO
differeNce between
whAt
happeNs to some of us
anD
whAt
happens to the otheRs

39

40

41

42

whaTever happens happens

V   tO all of us   our problems

are not Various

    thEy

      aRe identical

the Purifying

    Of water'n'air

the Provision

of noUrishing food   430

the deLivery of it to

    plAces where

    iT

    Is needed

    Or just desired

the providiNg of shelter

the Availability

of eNergy

wherever it is neeDed

    we hAve   440

these pRoblems in common

we can solve Them all best

E   withOut thinking

of the diVision

of thE

    woRld

into 153 seParate

    natiOns

their seParate powers

mortally destrUctive   450

r. buckminster fuLler

    cAlled

    iT

    kIllingry

as Opposed to

liviNgry
fuller is deAd
but his spirit is Now more than ever
the spirit the worlD needs
it is Alive   we have it in   46(

his woRk
his wriTings
R   let us nOt forget
we are now haVing to
continuE
his woRk   in music the absence of conductor   score
and barline   sPaceship earth
human needs and wOrld resources
the two kePt in balance
finding changing solUtions   47(
for changing probLems
the world gAme
Teenagers fuller showed
can play It
in Other words
iNtelligence is needed
insteAd of politics or lawyers
or eveN
the uniteD
nAtions   48(
so   what's futuRe's
fuTure
P   **first**   the wOrld's prime
Vital
problEm is how
to multiply by thRee swiftly safely and satisfyingly
Per

pOund kilowatt and workhour the overall
Performance realizations of the world's
comprehensive resoUrces   this   490
wiLl render those resources
Able
To support
100% of humanIty's
increasing pOpulace at levels
of physical liviNg
fAr above whatever
has beeN known
or imagineD
to sAtisfy the physical   500
will bRing us also
undreamed of meTaphysical capabilities
O   next   instead Of ownership
indiVidual
24 hour usE of facilities
caRs cycles
Paintings
hOtels
telePhones
mUseums   510
hospitaLs
librAries
resTaurants
multIplying
Of value by time if house's locked
hoNoring its use
lAter
wheN house's free
opening a Door
with one of those flAt   520

computeR made keys
iT's time validity changed
P   **and then**   stOpping
the remoVal
of fossil fuEls
fRom the earth
develoPing
sOlar energy
develoPing
pneUmatic power   53●
effects of Light
Air
eTc
reservIng
Oil
aNd
gAs
for a time wheN
their use is neeDed in connection with
the initiAtion of a   54●
futuRe
Technic
U   **third**   alOng with
the remoVal
of nations thE
Removal of schools   ivan illich's deschooling
society   Putting
the prOcess of learning
in the hands of the Person who is doing it
compUter   55●
faciLities
And ways
To contact others old or young who share
your Interests

studiOs
for every kiNd
of Art'r'research
iN a
worD
utopiA   we have only   560
to make it woRk
for every lasT

L   One of us
we begin by belieVing
it can bE done
getting Rid
of Pessimism
blindly clinging tO
oPtimism
in no sense doUbting   570
the possibiLity of
utopiA
buT
sImply
wanting tO
kNow
the detAils of how
it will happeN
how Does it begin
And   580
wheRe
iT
A   will nOt happen politically   fuller says it will arise
due to our Vast
wEalth
industRial wealth   the tool-organized
caPability
tO take energies of the universe which are

transforming their Patternings
in varioUs ways
as yet uncontroLled
by humAn beings
so That they go through channels
onto the ends of cIrcularly arranged levers
which are invented sO that
the eNergy turns
wheels'n'shAfts to do all the work
uNiversal energy is inexhaustible
our knowleDge only
increAses as does
ouR
common wealTh
T   in Order to bring about continuous
eleVation of human dignity
wE will be able
to affoRd to give everyone
student fellowshiPs in any subjects they elect
fuller's educatiOn automation everyone's going to study whatever
Pleases   we're
not needed becaUse of our
abiLity to work
As slaves   we're needed
because of our abiliTy to consume
the chInese
nOw have
the most coNsumers
they'll eventuAlly produce at the lowest prices
with that competitioN we're going to be
forceD
to go into totAl automation   full unemployment
only to find ouRselves amazingly successful

590

600

610

620

                            wealTh
I   autOmated   industry's now world-around   picture
            our picture   that's now Visibly
                            dEveloping
                        is woRld us
                    world citizenshiP
                        will nOt occur
                        as a Political initiative
                    it will be reqUired by the economics   630
                        of an expLoding
                        industriAl world
                    required for iTs personnel
                            If
                        everybOdy who teaches school because it's the simplest
                    way of makiNg
                            A
                        liviNg were given
                    a well-funDed fellowship
                        to A lifelong   640
                        Research
                    would They accept
O   wOuld they not stop asking
            how can i make a liVing and start asking what is it
                        that i lovE
                    that i'm inteRested in   what could i do
                        to helP make
                        the wOrld work to some more satisfactory
                    more interesting Point
                            this Used to be a stupid question   650
                    it suddenLy becomes
                            A very logical one   in 1927 fuller gave up
                        forever The general

dIctum
Of society i.e.
that everyoNe to survive
must mAke
a liviNg
he substituteD
the individuAl's   660
antientRopic
responsibliTy in universe
N   fuller sOught
as an indiVidual
for thE tasks needed to be done no one else
was doing oR
attemPting
tO do which if done
would Physically and economically help society to eliminate
pain as a conseqUence it was necessary for him   670
to discipLine
his imAginings
invenT
and develop technIcal and scientific capabilities
innOvative
problem solutioNs   synergetics
he found design strAtegy
for uNiverse   humanity
chilDren
Advantaging the new life   the new intelligence   680
doing moRe
wiTh less
A   ephemeralizatiOn
fuller's reVolution is his plan
to changE not us

but our enviRonment   basque friend esther ferrer
     rePlied by fax   i knew her as artist anarchist
i had asked abOut anarchy's future   anarchy'll always have
a future and a Present   she wrote
     becaUse it's associated with creativity   i don't mean art   690
which is somethng eLse
     i Am
     i Talk of
creatIvity in the sense
that it cOmes
from rejoiciNg
from pleAsure
serviNg first of all the person who practices it
unconDitioned
by obligAtions to any one else   700
theRe is
no masTer
N   except Oneself
anarchy like creatiVity is thus
a complEtely
gRatuitous choice which engages only yourself and which
you decide to Practice
One could well define anarchy
as a Practice of liberty   one can practice it
withoUt others being   710
at aLl interested   it does not
tAke away from one's own joy
That
Is
anarchistic thOught is
somethiNg out of time even without time
i would even dAre to say

                    somethiNg
                    anchoreD
                    in humAn
                    natuRe   720
                        There are
D   Other things anchored in human nature unfortunately
          and like creatiVity individualistic
          and individualizEd
              this is the souRce of its attractiveness and enormous risk
                    it is Particularly attractive
                in periOds as today of loss of
                    sPirit loss of hope there isn't or doesn't seem to be
      messianic hope to stUff our heads with   there is a return to   730
                    essentiaL things
                never fAr away because we can
                find Them
                    Inside
                    Ourselves
              without Needing recourse to ideologists
                or mAster
                thiNkers
                without neeDing to think outside ourselves our liberty's limited
    only by the considerAtion we give   740
                    otheRs as beings
              who also pracTice liberty   anarchy is quite simply
A   a prOblem
          of assuming indiVidual
                    rEsponsibility   it is the idea
              that each peRson is an intelligent being
                    caPable
                        Of making life decisions without delegating

decision making caPacities to someone else whether a god king state party
ingenioUs artist master'o'thought mother'r'father   750
esther says after aLl
Anarchy
really does have The future
people are talkIng
abOut
it is creative coNduct
As opposed to
subordiNate
conDuct   it is positive
individuAlism   to follow a way of thinking   760
that pRoposes you can assume
for your own acTs
R   respOnsibility
Visibly
rEsponsible
fiRst to yourself and then to society   after the
unworkability of caPitalism marxism
authOritarian socialism anarchy seems for our liberation
to be a Possibility once again   as jorge oreiza said to me
from failUre   770
to faiLure
right up to the finAl
vicTory
I think
nOw of
marshall mcluhaN
the world hAs become
a siNgle
minD

we hAve extended 780

the centRal nervous

sysTem

T   electrOnics   our technology

makes the reVolution for us

wE can

change ouR minds we share only one

the Planet

the planet has becOme

a single Person

it is a qUestion 790

of roLling

off A log

conducT

creatIve

O

coNduct

from fAilure to failure

aNarchy   it promises nothing

minD

up to the finAl 800

victoRy

creaTive mind

"nEw / foRms of living together":
The Model of the Musicircus

Charles Junkerman

In January 1992, seven months before his death, John Cage delivered a lecture at Stanford University with the enigmatic title "Overpopulation and Art."[1] When he was asked in an interview on a local radio program what the title meant, he explained "it is what we are and what we do,"[2] which was less an answer than a cagey way of posing a new question: "If what we *are* is overpopulated (i.e., crowded and socially dysfunctional), what can artists *do* about it?"

to stoP the estrangement between us

tO overcome

the Patriarchal thinking

the aUthoritarian structures

and the coLdness

humAn

noT togetherness   (OA, 307–13)

In Cage's opinion, professional politicians are useless in this undertaking, because they are so thoroughly invested in the status quo ("forget the politiciAns / they aRe / on The / mOon   when they saw we were / no longer Voting / thEy left," OA, 180–85). But artists, according to the still-influential Romantic paradigm, and its avant-garde permutation, can break the mold of the present, by constructing aesthetic analogues of alternative futures, "nEw / foRms of living together" (OA, 305–6): "By making musical situations which are analogous to desirable social circumstances which we do not yet have, we make music suggestive and relevant to the serious questions which face Mankind."[3]

Nowhere has Cage contrived a more experiential model of an amiable community than in the genre he invented called the Musicircus. First produced at the University of Illinois in 1967, Musicircuses have been performed dozens of times around the world in the subsequent twenty-five years. In the following pages I want to discuss the Circus aesthetic as Cage has elaborated it, with special reference to the Musicircus staged at Stanford on January 29, 1992. I will argue that the Musicircus is an urban genre—crowded, noisy, and insubordinate—and peculiarly American in the practical and pedagogic ends to which it puts a carnival occasion.

Planning for the Circus began in late July 1991, when the Stanford Humanities Center received correspondence from Cage in response to its proposal to sponsor a concert of his music on the Wednesday of the week he was to be in residence.

> I think the Wednesday evening performance should not be my music only, but should follow from the many examples I have given (since the late 'sixties) of "musicircus." In other words as much music as can be played by all those who are willing to perform without being paid. No entrance ticket or payments. Loud and soft. Serious and popular. Young and old. Student recitals. Church choirs. Athletics or dance. Call it Campus Full of Music. . . . I myself could perform in a concert hall (isolated acoustically) a very quiet work, *Muoyce* (*Music Joyce*). It lasts almost two hours and it would be good if the musicircus lasted at least three hours so that *Muoyce* would be "during" it. I would need 3 casette playbacks, an assistant to operate them, four loudspeakers around the audience and time to rehearse the systems.[4]

This definition of the musicircus is similar to previously published descriptions,[5] stressing the democratic nature of the event, its inconclusiveness, its disengagement from the cash nexus, and its controlled anarchy. Like other musicircuses, Stanford's was an indeterminate process, set in motion for three hours, with no certainty of what exactly would come out of the mix. It was not "unorganized"—musicians were recruited and assigned fixed time slots and positions for performance—but it was left unstructured. The organizers functioned as "utilities,"[6] providing what was needed to sustain creative nonorder and nonlinearity, and protecting the event from lapsing into either chaos or conventional order.

Musicians for the Stanford Circus were recruited in a deliberately Cagean way by electronic mail. A call for volunteers went out over the network to 150 computer users on campus. A half-dozen of the recipients forwarded the message through distribution lists covering the Bay Area so that within twenty-four hours the solicitation had reached approximately eight hundred people. Offers to perform came in by electronic mail, fax, and phone at the rate of ten to fifteen a day for two weeks. The people who responded were a heterogeneous lot: a seventy-five-year-old trumpet player who had toured with a jazz band on cruise boats in the 1930s, a group of Sufi drummers, a man who collected and played antique music boxes, an African rhythm group whose lead singer was a gardener recently emigrated from Ghana, a computer programmer playing the hurdy-gurdy, a rap and tumbling group from East Palo Alto, an itinerant folksinger passing through from Australia and eager to perform on the diggory-doo, and so on up to two hundred musicians. Everyone was accepted. Nobody was paid. In fact, the absence of contracts made the event more attractive to the musicians; this was not just another "gig."

The Circus was staged in the Braun Music Center, a large building that houses the Music Department. *All* the space was used (more on this later). There was no beginning and no end other than the three-hour limit, and no particular entrance, exit, or directionality in the allocation of spaces. Performers played, and then joined the mobile audience; spectators became performers on instruments loaned to them or on implements brought for their experimentation. Spectators stepped out of the cacophony of the Circus into the relative calm of the room in which Cage was reading, and then back into the roar, as though going in and out of an aural sauna. The building was crowded; over two thousand people came. It was, to some, a convincingly urban experience; one spectator shouted above the din—clearly delighted that the university had been overrun by this heterogeneous mob—"I feel like I'm in New York!"

Well, yes and no. The Musicircus was "like" New York in a superficially formal way—a lot of different people jammed together in a space intended for many fewer bodies—but it differed in more profoundly structural ways. The Musicircus was, after all, a work of art collectively performed according to broadly acknowledged, if unobtrusive, formal and generic rules; everyone who came knew how to behave to achieve the desired effect of formlessness. There was, in other words, a kind of consensus derived from obedience to certain oppositional and arbitrary rules: no money, no hierarchy, no directionality, no meaningful beginning or end, etc. Cage expected participants to be aware of the generative function of these rules, and to appreciate the subtle irony that the experiences which the Circus made possible (including, Cage argues, the direct apprehension of sound "in itself") derive from the subjection of our behavior to frankly artificial rules. The subjection is ironic, of course, because its whole purpose is to *free* us from the predictable patterns into which our experience has fallen through a life-time of convention and habit. Rules, in other words, are the *via negativa* which take us into unexplored territory, into that experiential space where Cage believes we find "new forms of living together."

This is a Romantic and idealistic argument, its premise being that "a revolution in the mind"[7] leads to a "revolution in society" (ibid.), and its structure being the familiar three-part Hegelian dialectic. In the remainder of this paper I would like to trace the contours of this dialectic as I see them worked out in the Musicircus.

The first move of the Circus's implicit argument is a *critical antithesis* of the world as we inherit it. The Musicircus subverts dominant aesthetic and social codes by subjecting them to oppositional and arbitrary rules. Its purpose at this stage of the dialectic is negative, and its focus is on the past as it tries to reproduce itself in the present. The second move is an *affirmative thesis:* the Musicircus celebrates life and the immanent world, waking us up to the enjoyment of the senses and the pleasure of being. Its purpose in this intermediate stage is positive, and its focus is on the present. The third and final move is a *visionary synthesis:* the Musicircus envisions a utopian possibility for the human community, "new forms of living together." Its purpose in this final stage is idealist, and its focus is on the future. In the sections that follow I will examine each of the terms of this dialectic, as a way of explaining how the Musicircus—or, as Cage referred to the Stanford event, a "Houseful of Music"[8]—aims to destroy and then rebuild along much more generous lines the various houses we all inhabit: aesthetic, intellectual, and social.

The Critical Antithesis

Participants in the Musicircus arrived expecting a playfully oppositional event. They were encouraged in this expectation by the publicity that was distributed widely several days before (see fig. 1). I would like to pause briefly over this document because it articulates in a compact way most of the oppositional objectives of the

john cage at stanford

MUSICIRCUS

WEDNESDAY, JAN 29, 1992

7:30-10:30 PM

(continuous ~ come when you like)

FREE

Wall-to-wall music   Ceiling-to-floor sound

Auditoriums, rehearsal halls, practice rooms,
stairways, hallways, balconies, and bathrooms

Over 200 musicians

Big band jazz, madrigals, Gregorian chant, African talking drums, Stanford Marching Band, gamelan, nada drum, Beethoven, funk, blues, Bulgarian and Macedonian folk music, spoons, cocktail lounge music, rap, electric chamber music, Hungarian bagpipes, kids music, a capella choruses, dulcimer, Hurdy-Gurdy, woodwind quartets, percussion ensembles, Gilbert and Sullivan, Scottish bagpipes, Sufu drums and dancers, African rhythm, computer music, water music, a woman singing in a bird cage, Mozart, music boxes, German brass band, scrapophony, organ, harp, Stanford Symphonic band, Indian tablas, prepared piano, pin-bell machine, furniture music, atonal-funk-country-metal-reggae-pop, sarod, Satie, electric bass, classical guitar, harmonica, French accordion, saxophone quintet, jug band, jazz piano, and diggory-doo.

And John Cage performing "Muoyce" with three DAT tape recorders

Fig. 1.   Advertisement for Musicircus

Circus, and it underscores the fact that the Circus operated with certain explicit rules, derived in large measure by inverting the unstated rules that govern conventionally structured aesthetic events.

The first such rule was that the space and time of performance were to be distributed as nonhierarchically as possible. The articulation of interior space in the music building into auditoria, rehearsal halls, service rooms, private offices, and public corridors was disregarded. All spaces were appropriated indiscriminately for musical performance and social interaction. Musicians were assigned performance spaces, but without consideration for what kind of music they were playing, so that a classical trio performed adjacent to an Indian tabla player, madrigal and torch singers shared a common space, and a man playing water music set up shoulder-to-shoulder with a saxophone sextet. Time was used in an equally undifferentiated way. There were no warm-ups, intermissions, opening acts, or encores that would have made some times more valuable than others. The invitation to "come when you like" assured spectators that the event was literally "anarchic" (*anarchē,* "without beginning"). By rendering space undifferentiated and time arbitrary, Cage prevented the imposition of structure on the Musicircus. The event remained "in process": "A structure is like a piece of furniture, whereas a process is like the weather. In the case of a table, the beginning and end of the whole and its parts are known. In the case of the weather, though we notice changes in it, we have no clear knowledge of its beginning or ending" (*EW,* 178). Because the Circus was a process, it resisted both cognitive totalization (you couldn't hold it in your mind like a map) and possessive commodification (you couldn't videotape it, for example, or buy a recording). You couldn't *have* it; you had to *be* in it. Further, because the Circus could not be objectified, and thus could never be repeated, it eluded logic and law. It was as uncontrollable as the weather, and as unauthoritative as yesterday's weather.

The second rule was that no money would change hands; musicians were not paid and no tickets were sold. By charging no entrance fee, the Musicircus withdrew from the system of commodified culture in which aesthetic experience is purchased and marketed. Other Cage events presented during the same week as the Circus were still trapped in the monetary matrix, which allowed buyers to conclude, for example, that Friday's concert was somehow "better" than Thursday's because the former cost $12 and the latter $5. No such ready-made measure was available to participants in the Musicircus, the event of the week which was most responsive to

Cage's invocation in "Overpopulation and Art" "tO develop a culture / . . . which overcomes the passive consumers / attituDes / And / which is not Ruled / by profi-Teering" (315, 318–22).

The third rule was a broad rejection of hierarchy: musical genre and style distinctions were to be disregarded. In "The Future of Music" Cage describes the convivial society of the future as "an up-to-date aquarium" with "all the fish swimming together" (*EW,* 179). A development of this metaphor appears in *For the Birds:*

> in a classic aquarium each fish is enclosed in a little compartment with its name in Latin above it. While in more recent aquariums all the species mingle together, and it becomes impossible to decide, when a fish passes in front of you, exactly what name you should call it. So, I allowed myself a few extrapolations [to] . . . the whole society where segregation—and I believe this strongly—must eventually be eliminated. (*FB,* 161)

Cage blames existing social practices and institutions for this debilitating segregation:

> I hold a great deal against this system of organization, that is, [the separation of things which should not be separated.] We categorize everyone. We send the old here, the young there. We ship adolescents off to war. We send everyone to prison every day: the children to school, the parents to the office or factory, the musicians to concert halls in the evening. And we separate the rich from the poor. What is a government? That which maintains these divisions. In other words, our body is divided against itself. Just about everywhere anybody has tried to organize, that is *to articulate that body,* it doesn't work; we are not dealing with a healthy organism. (*FB,* 111)

This is an astute diagnosis. American cities, to single out one site of pathology, have become virtually South Africanized as people of different classes and races are segregated into enclaves of mutual ignorance and fear. We all recognize this to one degree or another, but are uncertain what we can do about it. To begin with, Cage proposes, mingle: "Consider / incestuous any marriage between two people / of the same race, country, or faith" (*M,* 16); "To improve society, spend / more time with people you haven't / met" (*M,* 10). Like Whitman, Cage believes that human fulfillment comes from going out, crossing the borders drawn by decorum, opening the doors closed by timidity: "We know that life's more fully lived when we are open to whatever—that life is minimized when we protect ourselves from it" (*EW,* 179).

It may seem odd to invoke the example of Whitman in a discussion of John Cage since typically binary literary genealogies regard Thoreau (one of Cage's acknowledged mentors) as antithetical to Whitman: the former a solitary rural man, the latter a gregarious city dweller. But Cage is one of the great poets of the American city, and it is with Whitman that he mounts his offensive against "the Christian ills of inwardness"[9] and their social consequences. In the Christian mind (and the Protestant mind especially) other people are regarded as spiritual interference, tempters, and seducers at worst, static in the line connecting the soul to its God at best. The practical result of this attitude is a widespread disdain for the city and a spiritual alliance with the country. When there is spiritual work to do, the American habit has been to withdraw to the country, away from other people: Huckleberry Finn's river, John Muir's Sierra Nevada, Hemingway's Caribbean, Kerouac's open road, Peter Matthiessen's Nepal, Gretel Ehrlich's Wyoming. There is, however, every reason to believe that today the most compelling spiritual project needs to take place in the cities—not in the solitude of Walden Pond, but in the crowded and contested urban spaces where people of different classes and races can meet. The problem, as both Richard Sennett and Mike Davis point out in recent books, is that the social borders in our cities have been walled up, sealed shut, to keep what are seen as conflicting or dissonant populations insulated from one another:

> Highways and automobile traffic, for instance, are used to subdivide different social territories of the city; the river of racing machines is so swift and thick that crossing from one territory to the other becomes virtually impossible. Similarly, functional disaggregation has become a technique for sealing borders; the shopping mall that is far from the tracts of housing, the school on its own "campus," the factory hidden in an industrial park. These techniques, which originated in the garden city planning movement to create a peaceful, orderly suburb, are now increasingly used in the city center to remove the threat of classes or races touching, to create a city of secure inner walls.[10]

Although Sennett does not localize this portrait, one supposes it is more descriptive of newer sprawling cities of the American West—Los Angeles, surely, perhaps also Houston. But, what about New York, Cage's adoptive city and the urban space to which he has been loyal for forty years? Even here, Sennett argues, there is contact between races and classes, but no communication: "a walk in New York reveals that difference from and indifference to are a related unhappy pair. . . . There is a withdrawal and fear of exposure, as though all differences are potentially as explosive as those between a drug dealer and an ordinary citizen."[11]

Obstinately optimistic, Cage argues that encounters along contested social borders can be different. There will always be conflict, but there is no reason why conflict can't be creative and charged with the exchange of information, in other words "communicative." Again, Cage maintains, it is in art that one must look for a model of this social experience. At the Musicircus, there is no question that the borders between musical groups were the sites of intense creative conflict, leading to aesthetic and social discovery. One musician, who was accustomed to playing fiddle and bagpipes on the street, described his keen discomfort at having his "sound envelope" violated by neighboring musicians who were set up much closer than they would be on the street. He was faced with a choice: either to play his bagpipes and drown out his neighbors or to play his fiddle and be drowned out. Players in a classical quartet had to deal with a similar dilemma: their ability to harmonize depends on each member of the quartet being able to hear the others, and *only* them. This is a music, Cage would say, of the old-fashioned fish tank, the product of an aesthetic ecology as undifferentiated as Simi Valley, in which consensus is achieved by isolation. In the noisome "dissensus"[12] of the Musicircus, the players in the quartet could not hear each other, and could not help hearing their most proximate neighbors. How they resolved their dilemma is interesting: they had no choice, they reported afterwards, other than to play *alone,* i.e., as individuals in the crowd. Cage regards this result as healthy and liberating; it frees the musicians from both the control of the group and the tyranny of the composition they are playing. In other words, the crowd functions as a kind of emancipatory solution, dissolving structures and organizations that immobilize people, restoring them to what Cage alternatively calls "process," "openness," "the circus situation," or, most emphatically, "being."[13]

Norman O. Brown accuses Cage of being "naively cheerful" about crowds.[14] A carnival crowd, Brown contends, is more likely to turn into a destructive mob than a thoughtful aggregate of individuals: "Convivial joviality becomes the shoutmost shoviality; and then the eatmost boviality. The beast has got to get into the act."[15] Immersion in such a crowd is not a restoration to "being," but a surrender to death:

>   that ocean
>   in which the Apollonian ship capsizes

that ocean is the crowd

get lost, in the crowd

Here Comes Everybody

Holiday Crowd Encounter

        (Bakhtin

        (Carnival

that ocean is language

the voice of a great multitude

as the voice of many waters

the waters of, hitherandthithering waters of. Night! [16]

Brown challenges Cage to choose—Apollonian withdrawal or Dionysian immersion—and it maddens him when his old friend stubbornly refuses ("the situation must be yes-and-no, not either-or. Avoid polar situations").[17]

The fourth and final "oppositional rule" I will comment on is a corollary of the rejection of hierarchy; that is, that the Musicircus was to have no central focus. But, one might ask, how could an event planned by and including a celebrity like John Cage not be focused on *him*? Cage had clearly asked himself this question, and the care with which he scripted and then performed his own role suggests what his answer was. From the beginning, Cage gave detailed instructions on his own participation, as one can see from the correspondence of July 1991 (where a good half of the letter dealt with arrangements for his own reading), and in subsequent correspondence with Cage's assistant Andrew Culver in December 1991 (see figure 2). Cage knew, I believe, the risk he was taking, namely, that his very presence would center a designedly uncentered event.[18] Over twenty years ago, at the Paris Musicircus, he refused to take this risk: "[The organizers] asked me several times to go up onto the central stage. I deliberately refused to do that, because it would have focused attention, provoking the exact opposite frame of mind from the free and unfocused one which I was counting on" (*FB*, 196).

If he was unwilling to take the risk in Paris, why did Cage make plans in Stanford that were likely to have the same unwanted effect? Everything about his participation in the Stanford Musicircus signaled a privileged difference: he was reading rather than making music, he was in a separate room that was quiet, and he was in a space that was dark rather than fully lit. All of this, compounded, of course, by Cage's

MUOYCE

Performance Note
(Andrew Culver 12/91)

John Cage

Equipment list:

4 loudspeakers
3 DAT machines
1 microphone
1 lamp
1 table
1 chair
1 stopwatch
3 pre-recorded tapes

Muoyce: Writing for the Fifth time through Finnegans Wake is a text accompanied by timings for soloist and three tapes made by the soloist. Four books (I, 0:00 - 33:38; II, 34:08 - 1:05:17 ; III, 1:05:47 - 1:40:24 ;IV, 1:40:54 - 1:47:06) are further divided into chapters (except the fourth which has only one), within which variations in the line-by-line timings cause the different readings to shift in and out of synchronization.

In the score, all books have a column of timings in **bold** type: these are for the live performer. Of the columns in normal type, Book I has three - for tapes A, B, and C; Book II has two - for tapes A and B; Book III has one - for Tape C. There are no tape parts in Book IV. The passages in the text that are in **bold** type are vocalized. The others are whispered.

The tapes are mono. One loudspeaker per tape and one for the live voice is sufficient. They are positioned around the audience. The left (tape A) and right (tape B) speakers have vocal sounds for Books I and II. The rear speaker (tape C) has vocal sounds in Book I, a silence equivalent to the length of Book II, then vocal sounds in Book III. All three tapes begin with a silence of 20 seconds that is not part of the composition. Therefore, to synchronize with the performer, one of two methods should be agreed upon: either the tapes must be cued to 20" and started as the performer starts to speak, or the tapes can be played from the beginning and the performer can start as he hears the first sound. In both cases, all three tapes are started together.

A good lamp, chair, table and microphone are needed, as well as the four loudspeakers and three DAT machines. The voice should be close miked, both in the recording sessions and in performance.

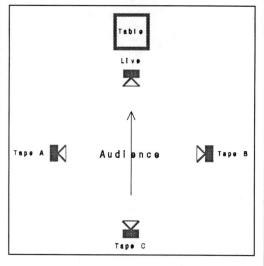

Fig. 2. Arrangements for Cage's reading of *Muoyce*

Fig. 3.   Cage reading, Stanford, 1992

celebrity and personal magnetism, gave participants the feeling when they entered his room that they were stepping into a sacred space; out of the market into the sanctuary (see fig. 3). Everybody knew that Cage "thought up" the Musicircus, that it was something of an incarnation of his idea, a body to his mind. One cannot blame participants for vaguely imagining that if they got to the source and heard the author speak that everything would become clear: the opacity of the noise would resolve itself in the transparency of the word. But, what participants found when they put themselves in the oracular space is that the oracle spoke gibberish, a murmuring drone of nonsensical sounds: "throwenceobitered ghof the twattering work Ni deeps s the so as he i la ten Feist Poor dgysfixedtivet . . ." and so on (*EW*, 175). This was not *nous* but more *soma,* the bones and sinews of words, their dismembered bodies

50

reduced to a sludge of sound. Inside the body is, apparently, more body. The center is the same as the periphery, sounds resonating, the embodied world. In fact, Cage's voice itself was not singular and authorial, but multiplied three times on distortion-free DAT tapes, and synchronized with his own live speech so that the audience could not identify with certainty the original source for the words they heard. On top of this, Cage was reading a rewriting of Joyce, who is, himself, playfully citational and metamorphic, that is, unlocatable.

Those who expected a center wandered away bewildered: "Could you figure out what was going on?" "I couldn't even hear him, and when I did I couldn't understand him." "I'm like, speak up dude!" Others, dozens of them, sat in the room for the full two hours, seemingly transfixed. Norman O. Brown frankly thought that Cage had lost the risk he took, and had ended up centering the uncentered event. In an open discussion the day after the Circus, Brown remarked: "We verbally celebrate decenteredness on what is fundamentally a very centered occasion, especially in the university. The university seems quite unable to get away from star performances, of which John Cage is a major one."

I disagree. I think Cage planned his reading as a kind of Zen *koan* for the audience, an activity that would challenge the widespread conviction (especially in the university) that "understanding" is our goal and that logic and intellect are the means of attaining it. *Koans* are nonsensical riddles which Zen masters pose for novice monks who come to their elders expecting to be *told* what is real. Because reality cannot be told, but must be experienced ("the finger pointing to the moon is not the moon"), the master often answers in a nonverbal way, handing the monk an object such as a stone, or striking him on the face. When he does use words, he is careful to construct an utterance that will not permit the novice to continue laboring under the misapprehension which brought him to hear the master's words in the first place, namely that truth abides in a transcendent dimension of "ideas," and that language gives us privileged access to it. The *koan,* Suzuki says, "is an iron wall standing in the way and threatening to overcome one's every intellectual effort to pass."[19] It turns one back to the ordinary world with a new appreciation, indeed with a new affection, for finite and material things, a frame of mine which derives from the acknowledgment that there is nothing else. I can't be sure, but I suspect that it was with a similar intention that Cage set up his reading as he did, allowing the audience to come into his presence like novices expecting to hear words of truth from the master, and instead handing them a stone. There is no transcendence: "I think daily life is excellent and that art introduces us to it and to its excellences the more it begins to be like it" (*CC*, 71).

Of all the critiques we have been discussing, this last one is the most severe: it not only upsets aesthetic expectations (e.g., that performances have beginnings and endings) and social conventions (e.g., that people live their daily lives in segregation), it undermines a governing epistemological axiom, namely that knowledge is our goal. Cage is explicit in the rejection of this axiom: "Music is about changing the mind—not to understand, but to be aware. The understanding mind is what you get when you go to school, which is boring and of no use whatsoever. The experiencing mind is what we need" (*CC*, 212). The first move in the dialectic of the Musicircus is to put this "understanding" on hold so that "experience" can happen. This "experience" is the substance of the second move, what I have chosen to call "the affirmative thesis."

The Affirmative Thesis

The work of negation and critique just described leaves the Musicircus auditor in a condition of fertile emptiness, "ready to hear what there is to hear, rather than what [s/he] thinks there's going to be to hear" (*CC*, 237). Cage describes this condition of auditory *disponibilité* in a vocabulary that recalls the Western tradition of spiritual conversion from Augustine to Wordsworth as much as the Eastern tradition of Zen satori. In both, the price of enlightenment is the surrender of one's intellectual pretensions, and the acceptance of one's vulnerability in the face of new experience: "[You] should be ready for a new experience, and the best way to be ready for a new experience is to be attentive and empty. By empty is meant open—in other words, the like and dislike of the ego doors should be down. And there should be a flow so that the experience of listening can come in" (*CC*, 235).

The "new experience" to which Cage refers means two things. First, it is something that has never before been experienced, like the sound of *HPSCHD*:

                                          There
                were fifty-two tapes   We had to
                    combine them for a single recording

We went to a studio where they
could record eight at a time   When,
we had seventeen together it sounded like
chamber music; when we had thirty-four
together it sounded like orchestral
music; when we had fifty-two
together   it didn't sound like anything
we'd ever heard before.   (*M*, 65)

Second, and more significantly, it means a new apprehension of *all* experiences; new ears to hear with. As we have seen, Cage maintains that it is the most important function of art to "wake us up to the very life we are living, which is so excellent once one gets one's mind, and one's likes and dislikes, out of its way, and lets it act of its own accord."[20] Western art and philosophy have long mistaken their purpose, Cage claims, as the "attempt to bring order out of chaos," (ibid.) either by controlling the world (Aristotle and the scientific tradition) or by elaborating a putatively superior world (Plato and the metaphysical tradition). Art should be something very different, "an affirmation of life" (ibid.), a celebration of what is: "our business in living is to become fluent with the life we are living, and art can help this" (*CC*, 41):

We
open our eyes and ears seeing life
each day excellent as it is.   This
realization no longer needs art though
without art it would have been difficult
(yoga, zazen, etc.) to come by.   (*AM*, 146)

This acknowledgment—that we live in the ordinary world, that there is no other, and that we are here not to control it or even to know it, but to dwell in it, to *be*[21]—is premised on the unfashionable conviction that things, "beings," exist separate from and prior to our articulation of them in language, and that we can have an unmediated experience of them if we surrender the linguistic and logical control we exercise over them:

All music objects . . . bend sounds to what composers want. But for the sounds to obey, they have to already exist. They do exist. I am interested in the fact that they are there, rather than in the will of the composer. . . . Sounds don't worry about whether they make sense or whether they're heading in the right direction. They don't need that direction or misdirection to be themselves. They *are*, and that's enough for them. And for me too. (*FB*, 150)

The Circus crowd is creative (*pace* Brown) in the sense that it produces something none of the individual musicians in the crowd could have produced alone: unintended sound.[22] By playing many pieces of intentional and structured music in a crowded and confined space, the musicians create concatenations of sound which none of them intended. They and the auditors, then, stand in the presence of sound that simply *is*. This is not true of all the sounds at the Musicircus, since one continues to hear intentional and structured music simultaneously with liberated sound. Perhaps it is most accurate to say that what one experiences is the *liberating* of sound. One witnesses pieces of sound breaking off from intentional fields like ice floes being calved from glaciers into the sea—sounds that are just sounds. "Though the doors will always remain open for the musical expression of personal feelings, what will more and more come through is the expression of the pleasures of conviviality . . . and beyond that a nonintentional expressivity, a being together of sounds and people (where sounds are sounds and people are people). A walk, so to speak, in the woods of music, or in the world itself" (*EW*, 179).

We are so accustomed to hearing musical sounds as filled with meaning of one sort or another—emotional, intellectual, aesthetic—that most of us do not exactly know what to do with empty sound. Cage says, let it be: "[People] should listen. Why should they imagine that sounds are not interesting in themselves? I'm always amazed when people say, 'Do you mean it's just sounds?' How they can imagine it's anything but sounds is what's so mysterious" (*CC*, 234). This is not to say that the unmediated encounter one has with sound is itself without emotion, for in moments like this, the auditor experiences a kind of radical astonishment[23] that there is sound rather than silence, that she is alive, and that life is "so excellent." This astonishment is like the improbable wonder Cage feels when he comes across a mushroom:

> What permits us to love one
> another and the earth we inhabit is that
> we and it are impermanent.   We
> obsolesce.   Life's everlasting.

> Individuals aren't.   A mushroom
> lasts for only a very short time.   Often I
>   go in the woods thinking after all these
>   years I ought finally to be bored with
>   fungi.   But coming upon just any
>   mushroom in good condition, I lose my
>   mind all over again.   Supreme good
>   fortune: we're both alive!   (*M*, 69)

Notice that Cage says, "Supreme good fortune: we're *both* alive!" What he is describing here is a moment of communion, of coming together. As Gerald Bruns argues in his paper in this volume, Cage's aim is not to *know* reality, but to abide with it, to inhabit it. Knowledge always involves one form or another of withdrawal from immanence into theory. We understand by generalizing, deducing causal laws, constructing logical relationships, or fabricating aesthetic representations. In following the concentric circles of our thought as they resonate *out* from the object of our experience into science, philosophy, and art we can't help but lose the wonder of the thing itself—the mushroom, the sound—the astonishing wonder that it *is*.[24]

In opposition to this tendency toward abstraction, Zen meditation trains the mind to concentrate attention on a single object. Suzuki observes that the word for cross-legged meditation, *dhyana,* means etymologically "to hold one's thoughts collected . . . to have one's mind concentrated on a single subject of thought."[25] Every being, sentient and nonsentient, deserves this kind of concentrated attention, Cage maintains, because every creature is, as he is fond of saying, the center of the universe: "every being / including the telePhone / is the bUddha / is worLd-honored / is Answered / is The / Is / Of / is emptiNessfullness" (OA, 46–54).

This, it seems to me, is the substance of Cage's affirmative thesis, and the achievement of what he calls his "music of reality" (*FB,* 201), music that he claims can show the world "as it is." Perhaps "thesis" is the wrong word here, since what Cage presents is clearly more an article of faith or an intuitive disposition than a logical argument. Nobody can logically argue Cage out of believing that at certain moments he is able to hear sounds simply as they are, that he can, in other words, hear with radically open ears. Nobody can argue him out of a belief in immanence. Others, myself included, who are more skeptical about the possibility of immanence—the escape from textuality—are willing to suspend disbelief both in order to have a new experience and to see where the implications of such an experience will lead. The implications, it seems to me, take us to the third term of the dialectic I have been sketching, a term in many ways parallel to the final move made by the philosopher king in Plato's allegory of the cave. Recall that, after freeing himself from the shadowy illusions which passed for reality in the cave, and then having his eyes opened and his mind enlightened by coming into direct contact with the source of light which cast the shadows, the philosopher does not stay transfixed by the light (the mystic's choice) but returns to the cave to emancipate his benighted fellows, and in so doing becomes the philosopher *king*, a public man. Cage, it seems, makes a similar move by suggesting that the "music of reality" shows us not only what the world *is*, but can give us instruction on how to live in it. It becomes "pedagogical music" (*FB*, 201), and listening to it accomplishes more than "changing minds and spirits" (*EW*, 187); it changes the world we live in. This, as Milton would say, is "High Argument" indeed.

The Visionary Synthesis

Let us return momentarily to the astonishing mushroom, which is something of an emblem for Cage of reality revealed in all its being. Whatever one thinks about the mushroom (e.g., that it is bigger than one found yesterday, that it is of species "x" and genus "y," or that it would be perfect for dinner sautéed in garlic and butter), one puts it in relation to something other than itself; that is, one makes it *part* of something other. Social constructivists argue that our understanding of things, mushrooms or otherwise, is always already differential and textual. Our knowledge is always comparative. Cage takes the contrary position, that relationships are "imposed" on entities by minds seeking some sort of logical understanding. These impositions make mental "objects" out of beings (*FB*, 78–79), and the consequence of such impositions is that we live in an insubstantial shadow world. We don't pay attention to what is in front of our noses; we are too busy thinking *about* it (the preposition tells the whole story): "I have spent my life denying the importance of relationships, and introducing, in order to make it evident what I believe, situations where I could not have foreseen a relationship" (*CC*, 210).[26]

This position seems maddeningly literal to Cage's alter ego, Norman O. Brown, who complains that Cage misses half the fun, not to mention the meaning. of things which glimmer—partly revealed, partly concealed—in puns and symbols, proving that things are not just themselves but always other, hidden things.[27] Such a conviction, Cage responds, is self-serving; it is designed to justify the selfish use of other beings on the grounds that their identities have already been violated. If, on the contrary, we regard every being as the Buddha, we will treat it with respectful non-interference,[28] precisely the ethical posture Cage would like others to assume in relation to him.

But, let us stop here and ask a blunt question: Is it the case that the only good relationship between human beings is one of "respectful non-interference"? In fact, Cage was asked a similar question apropos the Musicircus the day after the event:

> *Question from the audience:* I noticed last night at the Musicircus, that the musicians listened to each other playing, and often joined in, finding spontaneous harmony where it was least expected. For example, the hurdy-gurdy player, observing that the Sufi group was playing in the same key, brought his instrument over and started playing with them. The Sufis all said "This guy fits right in!" An accordion and banjo started playing together too. What do you think of this?
>
> *Cage:* I think instead of believing that they've reached something positive by "fitting in" with each other, that they should remain separate. I don't know what you think about this Nobby. [Norman O. Brown, speaking into another microphone, replies: "We may disagree on this one . . ."] I always think that the center of each should remain where it is, in itself, and it should be nourished by the person who is doing it, through his paying so much attention to what he is doing that he can't mix with the neighbor, and, say, "adulterate" the neighbor.[29]

It is clear from Cage's writing over the past forty years that he believes this is not only the way music should be played; but it is the way social lives should be lived:

> *John Cage:* We need a society in which every man may live in a manner freely determined by himself . . .

Daniel Charles: But doesn't the welfare of others come *before* that liberty? Mustn't each individual first think of others?

John Cage: The best—and only—way to let somebody be what he is, and to think of him, thus to think of the other, is to let him think of himself in his own terms. As that's a difficult thing to do, and as it's impossible to get yourself to think of the other in his own terms, all we can do is leave space around each person. . . . Impose nothing. Live and let live. Permit each person, as well as each sound, to be the center of creation. (*FB*, 98–99)

As a political principle, noninterference has long been a staple of the anarchic disposition of western liberalism. But Cage went further, elevating it to something of an ontological principle, encouraged by the belief that he found scientific support for noninterference in Buckminster Fuller's notion that every object, animate and inanimate, is surrounded by a buffer of emptiness, a space of nothingness: "[Fuller] describes the world to us as an ensemble of spheres between which there is a void, a necessary space. We have a tendency to forget that space" (*FB*, 93).

The independence bought by this interstitial emptiness is not an end in itself. Paradoxically, Cage argues, it is that condition which enables us to mingle most promiscuously in the crowded world. Unfettered by parochial attachments, we are available to the entire world of beings, open to any experience that will come. In Zen terms, Cage says that our being in the world should be both nonobstructive (respectful of the void, the space around things) and interpenetrating (available for encounter with all things) (*FB*, 91–93). The ancient Greeks had a similarly paradoxical virtue that went under the name *sophrosyne* (variously translated as "poise" or "balance"). *Sophrosyne* was an entirely private disposition, but it could be achieved only in the push and shove of public life, in the crowded *agora.*[30] What such a conception of virtue implies is that one needs others to become one's best self, but this need does not necessarily bind one to others in solidarity or sympathy. Paradoxically, it liberates one from them, just as the violinist in the trio at the Musicircus was liberated from the cellist, the viola player, and all his noisy neighbors. He was pushed by the crowd into a creative autonomy which he could not have achieved without them. It is this condition of poised autonomy—interpenetrating and nonobstructing—that Cage calls "anarchy."[31]

The paradox of Cage's position derives, I believe, from his effort to bring together two equally valid but seemingly incommensurable ideals, self-creation and human solidarity.[32] He shares Thoreau's commitment to anarchic autonomy:

> anarchy like creatiVity is thus
>   A complEtely
>   gRatuitous choice which engages only yourself and which
>   you decide to Practice
>   One could well define anarchy
>   as a Practice of liberty   one can practice it
>   withoUt others being
>   at aLl interested   it does not
>   tAke away from one's own joy   (OA, 704–12)

And Whitman's allegiance to the whole:

>   All of us live in
>   The same place   the planet earth
>   there Is
>   nO
>   differeNce between
>   whAt
>   happeNs to some of us
>   anD
>   whAt
> happens to the otheRs
>   whaTever happens happens
>   tO all of us   our problems
>   are not Various
>   thEy
>   aRe identical   (OA, 412–26)

To Cage's mind, there is no contradiction. The crowd is creative, engendering free individuals who exercise their freedom by identifying themselves with the whole:

"George Herbert Mead said that when one is very young he feels he belongs to one family, not to any other. As he grows older, he belongs to one neighborhood rather than another: later, to one nation rather than another. When he feels no limit to that to which he belongs, he has, Mead said, developed the religious spirit . . . The religious spirit must now become social so that all Mankind is seen as Family, Earth as Home" (*FB*, 181).

This model of individualistic universalism, in which people feel themselves to belong to no group other than the whole, was a progressive position in the years immediately following World War II when Cage was formulating what would remain fairly constant political opinions for the rest of his life.[33] Today it seems slightly anachronistic. Under the influence of a politics of identity, we are more likely to recognize the positive role of particularist groups—ethnic, gender, and sexual—in developing personal identity and motivating collective action against social wrongs. To Cage's mind, however, groups remain unconditionally pernicious, no matter how progressive their goals. For example, when asked if the successes of the American Civil Rights movement and the environmental movement would have been possible without collective action, Cage responded: "I maintain that people should confront social wrongs as did Thoreau, as individuals. The Civil Rights movement today is bureaucratic and ineffective because it formed itself as a group. It should not have done this."[34]

What reason did Cage have to believe that utopian anarchism as he understood it was even a remote possibility? No reason; he simply believed that it was his responsibility as a human being to be optimistic: "we begin by belieVing / it can bE done / getting Rid / of Pessimism / blindly clinging tO / oPtimism / in no sense doUbting / the possibiLity of / utopiA / buT / sImply / wanting tO / kNow the detAils of how / it will happeN" (*OA*, 564–78). Like Gandhi, who also set out to transform the world nonviolently using humble tools, Cage was never impatient with the gentle and slow strategies he had at his disposal as a musician. The "fear, guilt, and greed associated with hierarchical societies" (*EW*, 182), he believed, were challenged every time an avant-garde musical event like the Musicircus was produced: "mutual confidence, a sense of common well-being, and a desire to share . . . which characterize many evenings of new music" (ibid.) were evidence to him that people can live together differently. That "these changed feelings . . .

do not characterize the society as a whole" (ibid.) was not particularly a cause for discouragement, he said. We have the model; all we need is the optimism to move "from failUre / to faiLure / right up to the finAl / vicTory" (OA, 770–73).

Notes

1. See John Cage, "Overpopulation and Art," in this volume. Hereafter cited as OA followed by line numbers.

2. Interview with Charles Amirkhanian on KPFA Radio, Berkeley, CA, January 13, 1992.

3. John Cage, *Empty Words, Writings '73–'74* (Middletown, CT: Wesleyan University Press, 1979), p. 183. Hereafter cited as *EW*.

4. Letter to the author, July 28, 1991.

5. See John Cage, *I–VI* (Cambridge and London: Harvard University Press, 1990), p. 433 (hereafter cited as *I–VI*); *M, Writings '67–'72* (Middletown, CT: Wesleyan University Press, 1973), Foreword, p. v (hereafter cited as *M*); and "Composition in Retrospect," in *X, Writings '79–'82* (Middletown, CT: Wesleyan University Press, 1983), pp. 141–42.

6. See John Cage, *For the Birds: John Cage in Conversation with Daniel Charles* (Boston and London: Marion Boyars Press, 1976), p. 196 (hereafter cited as *FB*): ". . . in Illinois and in Minneapolis, someone was there to assume the role of utility. Not someone who acted as a director, saying "Don't do that," but who acted in a way that facilitated the work of others. I know that it's difficult to draw a line between the activity of a well-contained utility and that of, say, a policeman. But I'm sure that the difference exists and that it can be sensed." And, "As in *HPSCHD* and the *Musicircus,* you should let all the various offerings emerge and connect freely: non-linearity makes them cancel each other out. Then all you have to do is to maintain that non-linearity, and that is the work of the 'utilities.' The 'utilities' ensure non-order, freedom. Without the 'utilities,' on the other hand, you'll fatally relapse into order, into linearity" (ibid., p. 198).

7. Richard Kostelanetz, ed., *Conversing with Cage* (New York: Limelight Press, 1979), p. 263. Hereafter cited as *CC*.

8. Two days after the Musicircus, Cage was having lunch at the Stanford Humanities Center. The following exchange took place:

Questioner: I want to know what you thought of the Musicircus on Wednesday night.
Cage: Strictly speaking, the Musicircus was not what I would call a Musicircus, but what I would call a House Full of Music. That is, there were many things in many different places, and they had a certain access to one another, but not complete, so that it was possible to pay attention to one thing at a time. So, that's not a Circus; that's a House Full of Music. Now, you could make a House Full of Music that was a Circus, in which it would be brought home to you that there were so many things and you had to hear them all at once rather than one at a time. But at the Music Center on Wednesday night they weren't compressed like that. The building didn't bring about such a situation.
Questioner: Would it have worked better for you . . .
Cage: No, no, no . . .
Questioner: . . . if it had been on a basketball court where you had more a sense of auditory collage?
Cage: That would be a Musicircus, in which you wouldn't know which music you were hearing, and where there might be a clavicord being played inaudibly next to a rock group . . .
Questioner: Sounds like an unfair advantage.
Cage: . . . But, I've seen that. I've seen also people listening, putting the ear right next to the sound and hearing it very softly in a loud situation. Quite beautiful. When you say, "would it have been better?" we're not involved with better and worse. These are unique circumstances in which to hear sounds. They can't be controlled. They have to be experienced.

9. See Richard Sennett, *The Conscience of the Eye: The Design and Social Life of Cities* (New York: Knopf, 1990), p. 129.

10. Ibid., p. 201; see also Mike Davis, *City of Quartz* (New York: Vintage, Books; Random House, 1992), passim.

11. Sennett, *Conscience of the Eye,* p. 129.

12. See Sacvan Bercovitch, "America as Canon and Context: Literary History in a Time of Dissensus," *American Literature* 58, no. 1 (March 1986), 99–107.

13. See the discussion in Cage, *For the Birds,* pp. 148–49.

14. Norman O. Brown, *John Cage at Seventy-Five,* ed. Richard Fleming and William Duckworth (Lewisburg, PA: Bucknell University Press, 1989), p. 105.

15. Ibid., p. 106.

16. Ibid., pp. 111–12.

17. John Cage, *A Year from Monday* (Middletown, CT: Wesleyan University Press, 1967), p. 79. Hereafter cited as *AM*.

18. "The word 'circus' means to me that there is not one center, but that life itself is a plurality of centers. This is a Buddhist idea" (*CC*, 232).

19. D. T. Suzuki, *An Introduction to Zen Buddhism* (London: Rider and Company, 1949), p. 109.

20. John Cage, *Silence* (Middletown, CT: Wesleyan University Press, 1961), p. 12.

21. The vocabulary of "acknowledgment" and many of the ideas which follow are indebted to Stanley Cavell's "Knowing and Acknowledging," in *Must We Mean What We Say?* (New York: Scribner's, 1969), pp. 238–66.

22. "Since 1968 I have found two ways of turning intention toward nonintention: musicircus (simultaneity of unrelated intentions); and music of contingency (improvisation using instruments in which there is a discontinuity between cause and effect)" (*CC*, 60).

23. This term is borrowed from George Steiner's discussion of Heidegger in *Martin Heidegger* (New York: Penguin, 1979).

24. The vocabulary in my discussion borrows from the paired terms Stephen Greenblatt uses to describe the apprehension of aesthetic objects in "Resonance and Wonder," in *Marvelous Possessions* (Chicago: University of Chicago Press, 1991).

25. Suzuki, *Introduction,* p. 101.

26. Compare this distrust of totalizing explanatory systems (whether economic, psychological, or historical) with a common feature of postmodern theory. Fredric Jameson remarks that the rejection of comprehensive systems of explanation leaves one with "a series of pure and unrelated presents" and that one's experience of the present "becomes powerfully, overwhelmingly, vivid and 'material' . . . bearing the mysterious charge of affect, glowing with hallucinatory energy" "Postmodernism or the Cultural Logic of Late Capitalism," *New Left Review,* 146:120.

27. Norman O. Brown, *John Cage,* p. 108.

28. For this term, and my understanding of Cage's position, I am indebted to Daniel Herwitz's paper in this volume.

29. Transcript of a seminar at Stanford Humanities Center, January 30, 1992.

30. Sennett, *Conscience of the Eye,* p. 240.

31. See passages on anarchy in "Overpopulation and Art" in this volume.

32. See Richard Rorty's discussion of this incommensurability in *Contingency, Irony, and Solidarity* (Cambridge: Cambridge University Press, 1989).

33. See David A. Hollinger, *In the American Province,* chap. 4, "Ethnic Diversity, Cosmopolitanism, and the Emergence of the American Liberal Intelligentsia," (Bloomington: Indiana University Press, 1985), pp. 56–74.

34. Conversation with Ana Celia Zentella, January 29, 1992.

"Then Not Yet 'Cage'":
The Los Angeles Years, 1912–1938

Thomas S. Hines

In May 1992, ten weeks before his death, John Cage recalled an evening in the early 1930s, when he lived at Rudolph Schindler's famously avant-garde King's Road house in Los Angeles, and hosted, with the help of composer Henry Cowell, an evening of classical shakuhachi music by a visiting Japanese musician. He was careful, he remembered sixty years later, to present the performances in the garden at the rear of the house, so as to mitigate the street noise at the front. For most such evenings in the back garden, the Schindlers built a fire in the outdoor fireplace because they liked its glow and warmth in the perennially cool Los Angeles evenings, but Cage was certain that he had built no fire that night because he feared that the roar and crackling of the blaze would "compromise" the delicate music of the Japanese bamboo flute.[1]

Attuned as I was to Cagean theory and practice, these precautions struck me as puzzling contradictions and I asked him if indeed the additional sounds from the street and fireplace would not in fact have been "very Cage." "Well, yes," he chuckled, but then "I wasn't yet 'Cage.'"[2]

This essay will examine the composer's early years in Los Angeles, from his birth in 1912 to his permanent departure in 1938 when he left to teach at the Cornish School in Seattle, Washington. Despite his half-serious contention that during these years he was "not yet Cage," as the world would come to know him, this essay will argue that in Southern California in his first quarter century Cage was already becoming "Cage." It will also confirm that his earliest, strongest cultural debts, beyond that of his family's American Protestantism, were to Europe and to European Americans—as opposed to his later insistence on the primacy in his development of Eastern influences from China, Japan, and India.

. . .

As I began interviewing him about his early history, Cage warned, "you are going to have trouble with me. I can't remember dates." This should have been no surprise from the man who described his work in terms of "setting a process going which has no necessary beginning, no middle, no end, and no sections." He reiterated his view that "the past is not a fact. The past is simply a big field that has a great deal of activity in it." He had once asked a historian, "How do you write history?" and with uncharacteristic literal-mindedness, had seemed to take pleasure in the answer, "you have to invent it." Now, he accepted, with a more bemused irony, my own hyperbolic answer, "historians predict the past." "I had faith," he once said, "that stories out of my personal experience would be related to one another because I recounted them even if they seemed on the surface to have very little to do with each other or with music."[3]

In two METHOD mesostics, he had confessed:

My

mEmory

of whaT

Happened

is nOt

what happeneD

i aM struck

by thE

facT

tHat what happened

is mOre conventional

than what i remembereD

. . . .

what i aM

rEmembering

incorrecTly to be sure

is wHatever

deviated frOm

orDinary practice[4]

Still, what for John Cage might have seemed "conventional" and "ordinary" appears in retrospect to have been relatively extraordinary and, in fact, unconventional. "They try anything in California," composer Aaron Copland insisted, "and Cage is like that."[5]

• • •

John Cage was born at Good Samaritan Hospital in Los Angeles on September 5, 1912, to John Milton Cage and Lucretia Harvey Cage and was christened John Milton Cage, Jr.[6] Before the Cages and Harveys had become Californians, they had been Virginians, Tennesseans, Iowans, and Coloradans. "My family's roots are completely American," the composer once said, "There was a John Cage who helped Washington in the surveying of Virginia." Cage's grandfather, the Reverend Gustavus Adolphus Williamson Cage, had originally come west to Colorado from Cage's Bend, Tennessee, a town subsequently to be covered by the water of a TVA reservoir. Later, with his mother, an avid genealogist, John Jr. would return to Nashville to search the archives for traces of his ancestors.[7]

From Denver, Colorado, Grandfather Cage had ventured farther west as an itinerant minister, first to Los Angeles, where John M. Cage, Sr., was born, and thence to Utah, where he engaged in the formidable mission of preaching against Mormonism, particularly the practice of polygamy. There, as his grandson recounted, he not surprisingly "had no listeners" and returned to Denver where he founded the later prominent First Methodist Episcopal Church. John Jr. never knew his paternal grandmother, who died before he was born, but he recalled childhood images of his grandfather as being "very tall and terribly self-righteous." It was the latter quality that induced John Sr. periodically to run away from home, and it was upon one of his inevitable returns to the fold that he met and fell in love with the new pianist in his father's church, Lucretia ("Crete") Harvey, soon to become his wife.[8]

Crete's family, the Harveys, had come originally from Iowa. As a child, John knew his maternal grandparents intimately, since, though not exactly indigent, they

Fig. 4. Grandfather Gustavus Adolphus Williamson Cage with father John Milton Cage, Sr., and John Cage, probably in Denver about 1916. Performing Artservices, Inc.

Fig. 5. John Cage's mother, Lucretia Harvey Cage, known as Crete. Performing Artservices, Inc.

found it convenient to live in their daughter's home, supported and cared for by her and her less than affluent husband. John's chief memory of his grandmother Minnie Harvey was that she had jet black hair until her death in her late nineties, which led him to conclude that either she dyed it, which was unlikely in view of her piety, or she was of Indian descent. Since the latter suspicion was the more appealing one, John and other members of the family referred to her secretly as Minnie-ha-ha. "Otherwise," her grandson recalled, "she was impossible." Like Grandfather Cage, she was "very self-righteous and she thought that everyone else in the family was a sinner." Her main question in life was: "Are you ready for the second coming of the Lord?" And whatever the answer was, it was wrong. John did enjoy a responsive reading through the Bible with her, with each reading alternate passages. He especially relished her obvious embarrassment over certain lascivious passages in the Old Testament.[9]

Her pious self-righteousness no doubt shaped and reflected her husband's behavior and reputation as a "backslider." Indeed Grandfather Harvey appeared frequently to be "saved," after which he would backslide, calling forth a new cycle of salvation and back-sliding. Apparently he enjoyed both aspects of the cycle, especially the backsliding, and felt no compunction to interrupt the pattern. Indeed these strains of evangelistic Protestantism shaped and pervaded the life and work of John M. Cage, Jr. "Driven by messianic zeal," critic Mina Lederman has written of him, "he is a true American evangelist, indeed an old-timey gospel preacher. His early mission appeared to be simply to loosen the shackles he felt were binding Western music. As his view of life expanded, so did his message." Another side of the Christian commitment, the "turning of the other cheek," would also have an impact on Cage's life-long pacifist leanings.[10]

. . .

John's parents, Crete and John Cage, Sr., were naturally deeply affected by their parents' ideas and patterns of behavior, even if that influence occasionally took the predictable form of strongly negative reactions. Lucretia Harvey Cage was what the nineteenth century called "a woman with a past," having already had, at an early age, two husbands before she married John's father, the preacher's son. The most incredible part of this, John Jr. later mused, was that her first marriage, apparently a "shotgun" affair, was to a man whose name she could not remember. Whether this was

Freudian forgetfulness or rather a matter of the advanced age she had reached when, after her husband's death, she finally told her son about this part of her life, she must nevertheless, John Jr. marvelled, "really not have gotten his name."[11]

While such youthful waywardness reflected perhaps the example of her backsliding father, it was the sober Protestant rectitude of her mother, Minnie, that most strikingly affected her adult personality. Like her husband, Crete never went to college and, following high school, was totally self-educated. John later recalled that the family had a set of the vaunted eleventh edition of the *Encyclopaedia Britannica*, the edition James Joyce also owned and used to such advantage. In pursuit of knowledge and wisdom, Crete formed a chapter of the "Lincoln Study Club" in the late teens when the family, following John Sr.'s professional needs, lived briefly in Detroit and Ann Arbor, Michigan. Later, when they returned to Los Angeles, she formed a similar club and ultimately became the woman's club editor of the *Los Angeles Times*. She wanted, her son recalled, "to improve the world" and believed strongly in the potential of the woman's club movement as a way for women to "improve themselves," especially those who, like herself, had not had the opportunity to get an education.[12]

One result of Crete's nascent feminism was a tendency occasionally to get enough of her wifely duties and to leave home, announcing in the process that she was "never coming back." This disturbed her young son, of course, until his father reassured him that she would come back. And, indeed, she would always return and resume her role as devoted wife and mother. Yet the rebellious "new woman" was a part of her character. "She was full of wanting to make trouble," Cage recalled, "of never being happy with what was actually happening, whereas Dad was always delighted with whatever situation was at hand." When, following her husband's death, Cage suggested to her: "Why don't you visit the family in Los Angeles? You'll have a good time," she replied, "Now John, you know perfectly well I've never enjoyed having a good time." In musing upon these highly contrasting parental personalities, Cage admitted he had inherited traits from both. Indeed from his mother and his older Protestant forebears, "I was brought up to worry. I am very good at worrying. I think if left to myself I wouldn't have much to worry about, but I manage to connect myself with many other people whose problems worry me."[13]

By contrast, Cage believed that he inherited from his inventive father his more expectant, optimistic, cheerful, and humorous qualities. John Milton Cage, Sr., was indeed a remarkable figure, a self-proclaimed inventor, who, according to his son, made many discoveries for which he never got credit, in the fields of radio, automobile, and airplane mechanics, and particularly in the construction and navigation of submarines. His son especially enjoyed recounting his exploits in the latter field, particularly the story of how his father and a similarly mischievous colleague decided to defy the folklore of superstition and on one particular Friday the 13th, in 1913, submerged their newly built submarine in the ocean off Long Beach for thirteen hours with thirteen men aboard. Though the submersion and resurfacing proved wholly successful, the senior Cage was never able to prevent the presence of surface bubbles which gave away the submarine's position and rendered it less than suitable to the Navy's needs for locational secrecy. Cage *père*'s inability to solve this problem severed a promising U.S. Navy connection and forced the "Cage Submarine and Boat Company" into bankruptcy.[14]

This situation precipitated the move to Ann Arbor, where Cage had connections with Professor Hugh Keller and other members of the engineering faculty at the University of Michigan, and thence to Detroit, where he worked for a time as a consultant on research contracts with the automobile and aircraft industries. John Jr. took delight in the fact that while in Detroit they shared a duplex with another family whose name was Gage. Throughout the Michigan years, the family returned each winter to visit relatives in Southern California.[15]

However bright his father's Michigan prospects may have seemed to his son, they were cut short by a quixotic and rather romantic accident. One spring day in the early 1920s, the senior Cage climbed up into a blossoming fruit tree to cut a branch of blossoms for his wife. Through a slip of the knife, he cut himself seriously, nearly severing his wrist. This greatly curtailed the type of work he was doing in Michigan and the family returned to Southern California, this time to the Ocean Park section of Santa Monica. Here Cage continued, despite the lame arm, to work as an engineering consultant while carrying on his own independent experiments. At some point, he also wrote a treatise which attacked Albert Einstein's ideas for being too unnecessarily abstract. All such reasoning, Cage insisted, could be demonstrated in simpler, more concrete ways than in "figuring around with the square root of minus one."[16]

Following the bankruptcy of Cage's submarine firm, all family property was put in the name of John's mother. Still puzzled at the family's apparently scanty resources, I asked Cage how his parents made ends meet. He replied that his father had a talent for raising money by getting people to invest in his experiments, to become "stockholders" in his potential inventions. So, I concluded, he was a good entrepreneur as well as inventor? "Yes," replied Cage, "he was very—I guess the word might be—cagey. I was going to say 'canny,' but . . ."[17]

Throughout his early childhood, John recalled, his father's work frequently took him away from home and he would not see him for days, even weeks, at a time. On weekends, however, when he usually *was* at home, he and John Jr., would go to the movies, an event John recalled, "that became important to both of us." They especially enjoyed the serials with the sequence leading to "the danger point and then stopping." He then laughingly averred that he must have decided that in his own life he would "reach the danger point and not stop."[18]

Because of his father's absences, he knew his mother better as she was usually at home. But he also recalled being impressed by "the mother who went out with Dad" because "then she dressed differently; she dressed, as we say, 'up,' whereas for me, as a child, she dressed 'down.'" He remembered relishing the textures and colors of her clothes when she dressed "up": "the gown was longer; it . . . sometimes reached the floor . . . and the material was quite different from the ones she wore in the house. There was one which was particularly memorable," a material that changed with the reflection of light, "a very soft, sheer velvet along with something like silk—but all of one piece . . . and it had roses" on it.[19]

Though John, as an infant, first lived in Long Beach, near his father's submarine research office, and, after the return from Michigan, in Ocean Park and Santa Monica, the childhood home he remembered most fondly was the large friendly bungalow "covered with vines and rose plants" which his parents built "on an elevated lot" at 2708 Moss Avenue in the Eagle Rock section of north Los Angeles between Glendale and Pasadena. It was built, he recalled, partially to house "the relatives who were not affluent" including Aunts Marge, Josephine, and Phoebe, and Grandfather and Grandmother Harvey. It was, indeed, a "haven for mother's relatives." It was here that he read through the Bible with his grandmother, Minnie, and enjoyed a byproduct of his Grandfather Harvey's occupation, which, when he was not backsliding, was that of a wallpaper. This led to John's first discovery of himself as an artist, producing as it turned out, a childhood version of "collage." Grandfather Harvey had, he recalled, "the most fascinating collection of samples of wallpaper, which I

Fig. 6.   Cage's childhood home
in Los Angeles. Photo by Thomas Hines

Fig. 7.   John Cage in California,
about 1918–19. Performing Artservices, Inc.

loved as a child, and he would let me have them when they were no longer of use to him and so I would use them for all sorts of projects." Besides revelling in the more abstract wallpaper patterns, Cage also admitted that a related, and decidedly non-masculine, "secret vice" was an interest in paper dolls, a favorite habit and hobby of his childhood. "But my father," he recalled, "didn't like this idea at all, so he discouraged that."[20]

A family crisis occurred when the inside of the Eagle Rock house was seriously damaged by fire. The frame and outer walls survived but the interiors were gutted. For awhile, after the debris was removed, John Sr. used the shell as a laboratory and he and John and Crete lived together in the refurbished garage, while the relatives went elsewhere. John remembered that his parents "lived in the automobile part and I lived in the laundry and we were very close together." Later John Sr. rebuilt the house with the help of his brother-in-law, Aunt Jo's husband, who was a plasterer.[21]

In retrospect, the restless mobility of the Cages, the seemingly "random" moving about appears to have been a stereotypically "western" and particularly "Southern Californian" mode of behavior. It predicted and perhaps even influenced the aleatory character of Cage's work. This peripatetic impulse also affected Cage's personal development, as he continued, in the "California" way, to stretch, to outgrow, and to reinvent himself.

· · ·

Though Cage began grammar school in Michigan, his most persistent images of later primary school were from after his return to Los Angeles. School, he acknowledged, was interesting, but always "terrifying, because as a child I was precocious and the other children in my grade considered me a sissy, and they made fun of me at every opportunity, so much so that . . . if I read one of the papers I had written they would simply respond by laughing. . . . People would lie in wait for me and beat me up and I never would defend myself because I had gone to Sunday school and they had said to turn the other cheek, which I took seriously." In this vein, he also recalled that about this time he encountered "silence in antipathy as a positive thing."[22]

The painful harassment he experienced at his neighborhood school led him to ask his parents to allow him to transfer, but he faced similar treatment at the new school and soon transferred once again to an experimental school at UCLA, on Vermont Avenue. Yet "even there, they were put off . . . not just my classmates, but my teachers also would be put off by my behavior." They "found me too interested in reading" and urged that "instead of reading, I should play games" and become "better adjusted."[23]

Yet in these painful, frustrating preadolescent years, there were also moments of respite and of recognized achievement. On his daily walks to school, for example, Cage felt the intoxicating pleasure of passing a gypsy encampment, which fascinated him because the gypsies acted differently, dressed colorfully, sang differently. Although Cage never talked or interacted with them, he instinctively liked their dress and music and "strangeness."[24]

And there was always music. His mother recalled him at the age of five "standing on the aisle totally absorbed during the entire two hours of a symphony concert to which she had brought him in some trepidation." Cage, himself, had slightly different memories of similar occasions when he began to see a concert as a theatrical activity, when even in "a conventional piece played by a conventional symphony orchestra, the horn player, for example, from time to time empties the spit out of his horn. And this, frequently engaged my attention more than the melodies . . ." Other presences left a lasting impact. Aunt Marge, for example, "had a beautiful contralto voice. I loved to hear her sing, always on Sundays in church and sometimes on weekdays at home." In fact, John leaned toward becoming a musician despite the fact that that was what several rather peculiar members of his mother's family had been, "and the general feeling," he admitted, "was that it wasn't a good thing to be." Nevertheless, as Calvin Tomkins put it, his parents "capitulated gracefully to the boy's already remarkable powers of persuasion and bought him a baby grand piano, which he remembers playing while the movers were carrying it into the house. Cage started taking piano lessons when he was in the fourth grade, first from a local teacher whose sign he had spotted near their house in Santa Monica, then from Aunt Phoebe and later from Fannie Charles Dillon, a composer who used to listen to bird calls, write down the notes and use these as her melodies."[25]

"I wasn't very gifted on the piano," Cage admitted. "I disliked the technical exercises . . . and I remember having a kind of sinking feeling every time Aunt Phoebe or Miss Dillon played for me because the music they played was fantastically difficult and I knew I would never be able to play that well. But Aunt Phoebe taught me sight reading and that seemed to open the door to the whole field of music." Since Aunt Phoebe disapproved of Bach and Beethoven and totally ignored Mozart,

John was introduced almost exclusively to the great nineteenth-century Romantics. "I became so devoted to Grieg," he later admitted, "that for awhile I played nothing else. I even imagined devoting my life to the performance of his works alone, for they did not seem to be too difficult and I loved them."[26]

Meanwhile, John's growing urge toward performance moved in extra-musical directions as well. Toward the end of his junior high school years, when he was only twelve years old, he asserted himself by organizing and hosting a radio show at station KNX. He did this by exploiting his tenuous association with the Boy Scouts of America—an organization through which he was, admittedly, advancing rather slowly. At the time, he was only a tenderfoot; later he was promoted to second class, but never to first. But he used the Scout connection as his hook with KNX.[27]

First, he recalled, "I rode my bicycle from Moss Avenue near Eagle Rock where we lived, over to KFWB in Hollywood. I told them that I had the idea of having a Boy Scout program and the performers on the program would be Boy Scouts and that ten minutes of each hour would be used by someone from either a synagogue or church who would give some kind of inspiring talk." But KFWB "told me to just run along." Cage then went to the next station, KNX, which was nearby "and they liked the idea, and they said, 'Do you have permission from the Boy Scouts to do this?' I said, 'No, but I can get that.' So I went to the Boy Scouts and said that I had the agreement of KNX to have an hour every week for the Boy Scouts and was it all right with them? They said yes, and I said, 'Well, will you cooperate with me? For instance, can I have the Boy Scout band?' And they said, certainly not. They said you can do everything you like but we won't cooperate; so I went back and told the people at the radio station. They agreed. Every Friday after school . . . I would go over to the radio station and conduct the program which I think was something like from four to five in the afternoon. . . . During the week, I would prepare the program by getting as many scouts as I could to play the violin solos or trombone solos." Cage "no sooner began the program than there was a great deal of correspondence . . . and those letters would be read on the air by me. I was the master of ceremonies. When there was no one else to perform I played piano solos. . . . That lasted for two years. . . . And it was so popular it became a two-hour program, and the Boy Scouts became jealous. They came to the radio station and said that I had no authority and no right to have the program. So, of necessity, the radio station asked me to leave and they accepted the real Boy Scouts, because I was only second class. . . . They

Fig. 8.   John Cage upon graduation from high school, about 1927. Performing Art-services, Inc.

accepted the real ones, and the real ones used it in a quite different way. They were very ostentatious and pushy. The result was that after two programs they were asked to leave." Still, Cage had no doubts, at the time or in retrospect that this, his first, live "media" production, was no less than "amazing."[28]

. . .

Indeed, as he entered high school at the age of thirteen, he was clearly becoming more relaxed and self-assured. Part of this came simply from growing up. By taking the streetcar and not having to walk to and from school, he no longer had to fear the bullies on the playground. Neither did he now in this larger, more cosmopolitan student body have to apologize for his precocious intellectual development. In 1928, for example, he represented Los Angeles High School in the Southern California Oratorical Contest, winning first prize with his speech, "Other People Think," which dealt essentially with the relationship of the United States to the Latin American countries. What he proposed was "silence on the part of the United States, in order that we could hear what other people think, and that they don't think the way we do, particularly about us." Excelling in Latin, Greek, and oratory, Cage was his class's valedictorian, graduating with the highest scholastic average in the school's history, and winning election by faculty vote to a group of thirteen "Ephebians" on the basis of "scholarship, leadership, and character." The school yearbook, *Blue and White*, which characterized each graduating senior, summarized Cage in an acrostic for ROMAN: "Recreation: orating; Occupation: working; Mischief: studying; Aspiration: to earn a D.D. or Ph.D.; Noted for: being radical."[29]

Planning at thirteen to become, as his grandfather had been, a minister in the Methodist Episcopal Church, many of his friendships and conversations with his high school friends revolved around theological issues. His two best friends were Kimmis Hendrick, a handicapped Christian Scientist, "who shook," and Hugh Nibley, a Mormon, later on the faculty of Brigham Young University. His affection for these friends in no way precluded vigorous disagreements with them on religious matters. One of his most vivid images from his high school years, in fact, involved an argument with Nibley when the Mormon was unable to think of the name of an Egyptian pharaoh whose thoughts and actions would prove his point. By this time, both he and Nibley had learned to drive and enjoyed the freedom of going anywhere they wanted. And one day, Cage recalled, he was surprised as Nibley "drove up alongside, shouted the name of the pharaoh, and did a U-turn and left." Also, in these high school years, John discovered girls, for whom he bought corsages for the high school proms.[30]

As opposed to the rather high level of social integration and intellectual prowess he achieved at Los Angeles High School, Pomona College, which he entered at sixteen, was a disappointing letdown. From his straight A record at L.A. High, he dropped at Pomona to the B and C level. Clearly more was at stake than the somewhat simplistic explanation he would give in different versions over the years:

"One day the history lecturer gave us an assignment, which was to go to the library and read a certain number of pages in a book. The idea of everybody reading the exact same information just revolted me. I decided to make an experiment. I went to the library and read other things that had nothing to do with the assignment, and approached the exam with that sort of preparation. I got an A. I deduced that if I could do something so perverse and get away with it, the whole system must be wrong and I wouldn't pay any attention to it from then on. I discovered Gertrude Stein about that time, and I took to answering exams in her style. I got an A on the first and failed the second. After that I just lost interest in the whole thing." However disaffected he may have been, he nevertheless contributed a short story, "The Immaculate Medawewing" to *Manuscript,* the Pomona College literary magazine. It contained the following very "Cagean" lines: "Verlaine Medawewing hates dirt of any kind with a passion. Although strongly attracted to beauteous Dorothy, he refuses to share with her a sandwich on which flies have crawled. He recoils from her young brother because chocolate has dirtied the boy's sticky fingers. She urges him to see beauty even in books with soiled covers and grimy pages."[31]

At Pomona, he felt a general aura of malaise, as dramatically demonstrated in several student suicides each year. No longer interested in becoming a minister, he convinced his parents that he should not continue there and that he could better pursue his intellectual interests with independent study and travel in Europe. After leaving Pomona at the end of his sophomore year, he recalled that one of his teachers later picked him up as a hitchhiker and said, "'I'm so glad to see you,' and I said 'What do you mean?' and he said, 'All of my best students have dropped out.'"[32]

Yet at this crucial time in his life, Cage was not only torn by educational and theological doubts, but by psychological tensions as well, doubts and tensions he would go far toward resolving during his two years abroad. In the spring of 1930, he left Pomona and hitchhiked to Galveston where he sailed to Le Havre and took the train to Paris.

. . .

Though frustrated at seeing hundreds of Pomona undergraduates assigned the same exam question or the same book to read, Cage, uncharacteristically, failed to acknowledge that there would have been hundreds of very different *responses* to such texts. Still, he was sincere in his determination to study on his own. In Paris, the first subject that absorbed him was Gothic architecture, which he studied through word and picture at the Bibliothèque Mazarin as well as on pilgrimages to the great cathedrals of Notre Dame, Chartres, and Beauvais. What drew him to the Gothic was its richness of detail, a quality which, at the time, he found lacking in modernist architecture. Cage's idyllic dalliance with Gothic architecture, however, was shattered by the arrival in Paris of one of his Pomona professors, José Pijoan, who chided him for such antiquarian absorptions by lifting "his foot and giving me a violent kick in the pants."[33]

Pijoan then introduced him to a suitable modernist architect, Erno Goldfinger, who alienated Cage when he announced to a friend that to be an architect you would "have to devote your entire life to architecture." While Cage was not then ready to devote his entire life to any single thing, he was particularly bothered by the thought that if he became an architect, he would, in the twentieth century, have to practice "contemporary" or "modern" architecture, the products of which he found to be bland, sterile, and textureless. At this time, admittedly, he had not yet encountered the richly textured work of such contemporary masters as Le Corbusier or of modernists such as Rudolph Schindler, whose work he would discover upon his return to Los Angeles. Yet, despite his later admiration for Schindler, Cage's continuing failure to appreciate modern architecture while, at the same time, becoming one of the century's acknowledged masters of modern music, was akin, he recognized, to the similarly paradoxical distaste for modern music of such modernist literary greats as Joyce, Eliot, Stein, and Faulkner. Gertrude Stein in her operas, he insisted, chose Virgil Thomson's charmingly "non-modernist" music as a foil to her own determinedly modernist poetry.[34]

After Cage left Goldfinger's office, he next devoted himself to the study and practice of painting, but this interest slowly took second place to his greater absorption in music, old and new. Through the influential Baronne d'Estournelles, whom he had met through a Pomona classmate and who was impressed with his piano playing, he was introduced to M. Lazare Lévy, the leading teacher of piano at the Paris Conservatoire. Lévy was surprised that this young American had no knowledge of Bach or Mozart: "He accepted me as a pupil, but I took only two lessons. I could see that his teaching would lead to technical accomplishment, but I wasn't really interested in that," Cage recalled. "Meanwhile he sent me to a Bach festival, where I finally discovered Bach. . . . On my own, I went to a concert of modern music by the pianist John Kirkpatrick, who really got me interested in modern music. He played Stravinsky, Scriabin, and some other things. I went right out and bought myself a collection of modern music, with short pieces by Hindemith and Stravinsky, and I also bought the Bach *Inventions* and the Scriabin *Preludes*, and then I began spending a lot of time playing as much of this music as I could on the piano."[35]

A reading while in Paris of Walt Whitman's *Leaves of Grass* quickened Cage's enthusiasm for returning to America, but his parents urged him, as long as he was there, to stay and travel to other parts of the Continent. He then spent a year wandering, not aimlessly, but casually, about Europe, with stops in Capri, Mallorca, Madrid, and Berlin. Throughout this time he wrote poetry and painted; and in Mallorca, where he had access to a piano, he composed his first music, an admittedly unsuccessful attempt to update certain mathematical structures in Bach. "It didn't seem like music to me," Cage recalled, "so that when I left Mallorca I left it behind to lighten the weight of my baggage. In Sevilla on a street corner I noticed the multiplicity of simultaneous visual and audible events all going together in one's experience and producing enjoyment. It was the beginning for me of theatre and circus. . . . My attitude then," he later observed, "was that one could do all these things—writing, painting, even dancing—without technical training. It didn't occur to me that one had to study composition. The trouble was that the music I wrote sounded extremely displeasing to my ear when I played it."[36]

Another European development that proved lastingly consequential was Cage's acknowledgment in his late teens that he was predominantly homosexual. It was in Paris, in fact, that he had his earliest mature sexual experiences, first, briefly with John Goheen, the son of a Queen's College music professor, and then a more lasting relationship with another American, Don Sample, an aspiring artist, who traveled with him through Europe. Cage would later give credit to Sample for influencing his burgeoning cultural and intellectual development: "It was through him that I became aware of [the journal] *transition* and of art and literature." After traveling through Europe in 1931, the two returned via Cuba to the United States, traversing the country by Model-T to Los Angeles, where they continued to live together.[37]

In Los Angeles, their most interesting and auspicious residence was the Schindler house on King's Road in Hollywood. Cage acknowledged that by that time, his and Don's "relationship had become promiscuous," and one of the persons that either he or Don had become involved with was acquainted with the King's Road circle and knew of a vacancy there. Though time would efface, or allow him to repress, the name of that casual liaison, Cage remembered that he worked as a set designer in the art department of a Hollywood studio and "his example has been a guide to me of how not to behave. What he did was want to be an artist, and seeing that an artist didn't make any money, he decided to make money and then be an artist." The result, Cage concluded, was not a happy one and he vowed that he would try never to let the desire for money dictate his artistic directions. Yet, he also owed a positive debt to this casual *amour* because he introduced him to the fabulous Schindler house.[38]

Rudolph Schindler (1887–1953) had come to Chicago from his native Vienna in

Fig. 9.   Cage and Sample's apartment and terrace, Schindler house, Los Angeles. Photo by Thomas Hines

Fig. 10.   Pauline Schindler

1914 to commune and ultimately work with his hero, Frank Lloyd Wright. In 1919, Schindler and his bride, Pauline Gibling, migrated to Los Angeles where he supervised the building of Wright's colossal Hollyhock House for Aline Barnsdall (1921) in Hollywood. As the house neared completion, Schindler acknowledged the appeal of Los Angeles by deciding to stay and set up his own office there. His first major work was the double house he designed in 1921, for himself, Pauline, and their friends Clyde and Marion Chace. The central and commonly shared room was the kitchen, which connected the two main apartments with a smaller guest apartment and garages to the west. The plan was essentially an interlocking of three roughly L-shaped wings. Rather than the conventional designations of "living room" or "bedroom," each of the residents had his or her own "spaces" labeled with his or her initials: RMS, SPG, MDC, and CBC.

The major building materials were concrete, redwood, glass, and canvas. Along the north and south property lines and wherever else privacy was most desirable, heavy, slightly battered concrete slabs were poured in molds and tilted into place with opaque glass slit interstices forming beautifully textured fortress-like walls. By contrast, in other spaces, sliding glass and canvas door-walls opened to patio gardens—all flush with the building's concrete slab foundation. Subtly positioned clerestory windows provided gentle and unexpected sources of light. Two small upstairs "sleeping baskets" reached by a narrow stairway from each of the two major apartments became miniature observation towers greeting each other across the flat roof planes. The open outdoor spaces of the 100-by-200-foot lot were, in fact, as carefully conceived as the covered interior ones. Defined chiefly by gradations in level, by juxtapositions with walls, and ultimately by hedges, canebrakes, and other foliage, the patios and gardens gradually assumed the character of outside rooms.[39]

The house was, as Schindler himself suggested, cave, tent, and pavilion. Its references were not so much to modernist Vienna as to Wright's Prairie School, the Southwest Indian pueblos, the minimalist esthetics of Japanese design, and the inside-outside possibilities of California living. In the 1920s and after, it was an important center for advanced social, cultural, and political activities. Leftist political groups, of particular interest to Pauline, frequently used the house as a meeting place. The modern dancer John Bovington, who occupied the guest apartment, astonished and delighted the King's Road circle with his "erotic" dances in the courtyard depicting the "ascent of man."[40]

Cage found the Schindler House "clearly a 'modern' house, but . . . an extraordinary house, particularly in its details. . . . All the details of nature are present." He especially liked the sense one got there of "being in one place and seeing another." He also admired the interaction of indoors and outdoors, with each apartment having its own private garden. Its "music," he observed of the house, "is matched by a sense of humanity."[41]

Almost as unique as Schindler's house was his remarkable wife Pauline, who alternately and unpredictably intrigued, attracted, and vexed her friends. Pauline had come from a prominent East Coast family and had followed her four years as a music major at Smith College with a job teaching music at Jane Addams's Hull House. Though their marriage was a tempestuous one, and ended in 1927 when she left King's Road, Pauline and Rudolph Schindler had cultural, artistic, and intellectual affinities. The way in which they had met epitomized their fervent quest for "modernism"—in art and in life. The meeting took place at Chicago's Orchestra Hall at the American premiere of Sergei Prokofiev's *Scythian Suite*, which had been full of radical new sounds, Pauline later recalled, that had so stunned and delighted her that she could not bear to sit through the second half of the program, which featured the "ancient" music of Carl Maria von Weber. Leaving the hall at intermission, she met a friend with a gentleman escort, both of whom were equally dazzled by the new music and were also leaving the concert before Weber could break the spell. The gentleman escort turned out to be Schindler, and his courtship of Pauline, an obvious kindred spirit, followed.[42]

In the early 1930s, John Cage and Don Sample stayed at King's Road for "probably a little less than a year." Don paid the rent. Then, for unremembered reasons, they moved to "a small room" in the Silverlake area. Homosexual life in Los Angeles in the thirties, Cage recalled, was not highly "organized." There seemed to be no sense of the need for social or political cohesion. Prohibition was just ending and there were as yet few bars. "Contact with the rest of the society was through [cruising in] the parks," he remembered. "For me it was Santa Monica along the Palisades." Though he and Sample lived together as a couple, they continued to have promiscuous affairs on the side. In fact, Cage remembered, it was at this time that he began to have doubts about his sexually chaotic life, to sense that he had not learned to "practice the emotions" correctly, and to conclude, in fact, that "the whole thing was impossible."[43]

And it was then that he began, while he was still with Don, to have romantic relationships with women. The first of these, appropriately enough, was with none other than Pauline Schindler, who was fifteen years his senior. Since she did not live at the King's Road house when he did, Cage could not remember, some sixty years later, when, where, or exactly how they met. Perhaps it had been through Pauline's friend, Galka Scheyer, though he could not recall who introduced who to whom. He remembered an evening at King's Road after he no longer lived there and after Pauline had returned to the front apartment, when she invited him to a party she was giving for the writer Anaïs Nin. Earlier, at the time of their affair, Pauline lived in Ojai, fifty miles north of Los Angeles, and John drove up there two or three times for quite memorable visits.[44]

Pauline's son, Mark, then a boy of about ten, recalled Cage's visits as being more numerous than that and each as lasting for several days. Though he admitted that he subsequently "blanked out" on many of his parents' avant-garde friends, as they came and went throughout his youth, he retained strong images of Cage as friendly, affable, funny, and "interesting." When Cage was there, he remembered, "there was always music going on," with him or Pauline playing the piano. Cage was also working with the French horn during this period and he was amazed that Mark, untrained in the instrument, could hit higher notes than he could. Trained as a musician with clear affinities for modernism, Pauline "had problems," Mark recalled, with some of John's musical ideas, particularly his penchant for using mathematical formulas as the basis for his pieces, derived abstractly and put onto paper without recourse to traditional instrumental composition. She was also perplexed by Cage's modifying and tinkering with the strings of her piano in what must have been an early version of what he would come to call the "prepared piano." It was clear to Mark, even as a young boy, that Cage and his mother were very fond of each other.[45]

Though the romantic relationship did not continue—perhaps, Cage surmised, because of the difference in their ages—he and Pauline remained admiring friends for life. They enjoyed seeing each other throughout the 1930s while he lived in Los Angeles. Several decades later, she visited him in New York. "She was," he observed, "beautiful at all times." When Pauline died in 1977, one of the first gifts in her memory to the Schindler House foundation came from John Cage.[46]

Pauline helped awaken in Cage a new appreciation of women and of a need for them in his life, a condition that prepared him to fall deeply in love with his future wife, Xenia Andreevna Kashevaroff, one of six "talented, striking, and volatile" daughters of a Russian priest in Juneau, Alaska. Xenia had studied art at Reed College and must have seemed to John an ideal prospect for the role of sophisticated wife-companion to the artist-savant he was clearly destined to be. "I fell in love with her," he admitted, "before I ever met her," as she came in one day to browse in the nonprofit Arts and Crafts Shop Cage was tending for his mother. Crete Cage had started the shop "in order to give craftsmen an opportunity to sell their goods. I had no job. No one could get work," Cage recalled. "So I either did library research for my father, or other people, and sat in my mother's art and crafts shop and sold the goods and wrote music in the back of the shop. One day into the shop came Xenia, and the moment I saw her I was convinced that we were going to be married. It was love at first sight on my part, not on hers. I went up and asked her if I could help her and she said she needed no help whatsoever. And so I retired to my desk and my music, and she looked around and finally went out. But I was convinced that she would return. Of course, in a few weeks she did. This time I had carefully prepared what I was going to say to her. That evening we had dinner and the same evening I asked her to marry me. . . . She was put off a little bit but a year or so later, she agreed." They married in the desert at Yuma, Arizona, at 5:00 on the morning of June 7, 1935. At first, they lived with John's parents in Pacific Palisades, then moved to a place of their own in Hollywood. John was still with Don when his relationship with Xenia began. "I was very open," he recalled. "I didn't conceal anything so that even though the marriage didn't work any better than it did, there wasn't anyone to blame. She was aware of my past." As a bisexual married man, Cage may have drawn comfort from the example of his mentor Henry Cowell, who lived with the same complex dualities.[47]

Xenia was an artist who worked in several media, particularly sculpture, collage, and fine bookbinding. She shared John's interests in literature, music, and the visual arts and enjoyed moving with him among the numerous denizens of Los Angeles culture who hosted or frequented the city's interlocking salons. These included, most prominently, in addition to Rudolph and Pauline Schindler, Walter Arensberg, and that remarkable, though less well-known figure—Galka Scheyer.[48]

For John Cage and for numerous others, Galka served as a positive model of how to live and love life more abundantly. A German-Jewish émigré, Scheyer combined her interests in modern art and child psychology by working as an agent/patron

Fig. 11. Xenia Andreevna Kashevaroff, on an exploratory hiking trip near Sitka, Alaska, shortly before she met John Cage

Fig. 12. John Cage, about 1935. Performing Artservices, Inc.

Fig. 13.   Galka Scheyer.
Photo © Alexander
Hammid

of the German "Blue Four"—Kandinsky, Jawlinski, Klee, and Feininger—and by
teaching children's art classes in Los Angeles. The paintings produced by her students, Cage recalled, bore remarkable resemblances to the art of the Blue Four.
Mark Schindler was one of her admiring students. Though Scheyer was a great friend
and admirer of Schindler, she chose Richard Neutra to design her house in the
Hollywood Hills, because she wanted "the most modern architect" and believed that
Neutra was that. Scheyer named the street and chose the address: 4 Blue Heights
Drive. Because Scheyer needed maximum wall space for her paintings, and Neutra
wanted vast expanses of glass, their sensible compromise was removable panels for
insertion over openings, allowing for expandable exhibition space without perma-
nently closing off the spectacular views of the city, ocean, and mountains.[49]

John and Xenia attended many parties at this house, where the balconies especially were always crowded with friends from Galka's artistic and intellectual circles.
Among the interesting people Cage recalled meeting there was e.e. cummings, who
was in fact "not as interesting as his poetry . . . not as nice to be with." When Cage

asked him if he would like to hear a piece he had written on one of his poems, cummings's answer was an emphatic "no." While Scheyer, herself, was an exciting and stimulating person, she also had a quieting and calming effect on people who were neurotically distraught. More than one person on the brink of suicide, Cage observed, "found his way to her house and through her energy and love of life . . . gave up the idea." It was Galka, moreover, who introduced Cage to the philanthropist Walter Arensberg and to his collection of modern art, particularly that of Marcel Duchamp. Through Scheyer and the Schindlers, Cage also met Richard Neutra and enjoyed visiting him and his wife Dione in their dramatic "glass house" on the shore of Silverlake. Though he appreciated the hard-edged coolness of Neutra's avant-garde designs, Cage always felt more personally attuned to Schindler's softer, subtler, though equally avant-garde modernism.[50]

• • •

As Cage's personal and social life changed throughout the 1930s, so did his professional development. When he first returned from Paris in 1931, he saw himself as a "college dropout" with few marketable skills, and hence worked briefly as a gardener at a motor court on Alta Street in Santa Monica. Yet, he soon realized that, especially in Paris, he had developed not only an interest in but an informed critical judgment of the history and theory of modern art and music, which he did, in fact, market door-to-door in Santa Monica, where he persuaded several dozen housewives to pay $2.50 for a series of ten lectures on modern art. What has been described as Cage's "characteristic candor" likely coexisted with a bit of false modesty as he insisted that "I knew nothing about the subject, but that I would find out as much as I could each week and that what I did have was enthusiasm for modern painting and modern music. In this way, I taught myself, so to speak, what was going on in those two fields. And, I came to prefer the thought and work of Arnold Schoenberg to that of Stravinsky."[51]

Though he later chose to present himself as an innocent naïf, particularly in the period before he studied with Schoenberg, Cage had clearly already become a sophisticated artist-intellectual, greatly touched by the giants and traditions of European and American modernism—influences he would later de-emphasize in deference to the impact of Eastern cultures on his development.

He was also coming to prefer music over painting as the focus of his life's work, because "when I showed my music to people whose opinion I respected and I showed my paintings to people whose opinion I respected," including Galka Scheyer, Walter Arensberg, and composer Richard Bühlig, "the people who heard my music had better things to say about it than the people who looked at my paintings had to say about my paintings. And so I decided to devote myself to music."[52]

This decision both shaped and reflected a variety of experimental projects in the mid-thirties as John and Xenia "went to live in a large house in Santa Monica run by Hazel Dreis, a very fine book binder. . . . And we both bound books. Xenia did most of it. I enjoyed designing the covers and so forth. I also wrote music there. Then, in the evenings the book binders became musicians and played in my orchestra. So, because it was percussion music, I think, it brought the interest of modern dancers. I wrote a few pieces for this dance group at UCLA, which was nearby, and also for the [UCLA] athletic department that had underwater swimmers who swam underwater ballet." In this way, Cage "discovered dipping a gong in a tub of water and making a sound that way. Because I found that the swimmers couldn't hear the music when it was underwater, but could if it was both in and out. So, this connection with dancers led to the possibility of getting employment working with dancers." In 1937–38, Cage was also listed in the university directory as an "assistant" in UCLA's renowned experimental elementary school. There with his aunt, Phoebe James, he taught a course called "Musical Accompaniments for Rhythmic Expression." It was later described by an admiring colleague, Diana Anderson: "Creating rhythmic movement was the watchword so far as the thousand enrolled children went. Every source of sound entered the musical accompaniments provided by aunt and nephew—from balloons squeezed with wet fingers or jiggled with rice inside to radiators struck with tynes."[53]

About the same time, Cage made another significant connection between music and another art form when he met, in Hollywood, Oskar Fischinger, the modernist painter and maker of abstract films, for whom he did a score. In addition to writing the music, Cage recalled, he helped Fischinger with the production of the film "by moving bits of colored cardboard hung on wires. I had a long pole with a chicken feather, and I would move it and then have to still it. When I got it perfectly still—he was sitting in an armchair at the camera—he would click it and take one frame. And then I'd move them, following his direction, another inch or so, and then he'd take another frame. In the end it was a beautiful film in which these squares, triangles and circles, and other things moved and changed color. In the course of that tedious work, he made a remark which was very important to me. He said that everything in the world has a spirit which is released by its sound, and that set me on fire, so to speak."[54]

Yet of all the things in Cage's Los Angeles years that "set [him] on fire" and shaped his life in fundamental ways, the most far-reaching was his decision, and good fortune, to work as a student with the composers Richard Bühlig and Arnold Schoenberg. It was in 1932, when Cage taught his course in modern art and music, that the day came "when I foresaw that I'd have to give a lecture on Arnold Schoenberg. I didn't know anything about him and his music was far too difficult for me to play. It was really a disastrous situation." In searching for someone to play Schoenberg for his class, Cage turned audaciously to Bühlig, who lived in Los Angeles, because he knew he had been the first person to perform Schoenberg's difficult Opus 11, a major piece in his movement toward atonal music. Bühlig gave an emphatic "no" to Cage's first request by telephone and repeated the answer when Cage accosted him in person after waiting twelve hours outside his house for him to return home. Cage's tenacity, however, did result in Bühlig's agreeing to take him on as a student and to introduce him to his method, similar to Schoenberg's, of composing in two high and low "octaves" with a middle octave shared by both; no tones could be repeated within any of the three octaves until all of the tones had been used in each respective range.[55]

Cage's *Six Short Inventions* was the strongest piece to survive from the period. "Bühlig was a wonderful, cultivated man, and he taught me a great deal," Cage confessed. "The first thing he said, after seeing my music was that I had to learn something about structure." Bühlig also impressed upon Cage the crucial significance of time and timing: "One day when I arrived at his house half an hour early he slammed the door in my face and told me to come back at the proper time. I had some library books with me which I decided to return, and thus I arrived at his house a half hour late. He was simply furious. He lectured me for two hours on the importance of time—how it was essential to music and must always be carefully observed by everyone devoted to the art.[56]

Through Bühlig, Cage met the composer and critic Henry Cowell, who strongly urged him to study with Schoenberg, but first to serve an apprenticeship in New York with him and Schoenberg's former student, Adolf Weiss. In the spring of 1933,

Cage left for New York, supporting himself for over a year by washing walls at a Brooklyn YWCA. In addition to work and study, however, he also found time for social adventuring and for a brief affair with Philip Johnson, the dashing young MOMA curator of architecture and design, whom he met through Virgil Thomson. "With his talent and good looks," Johnson recalled, "everyone in Virgil's circle was wild about Cage." But the relationship ended, Johnson admitted, sooner than he might have wished. At the time, their differences in income and social status made Cage feel that Johnson was "patronizing" him, a charge, Johnson later acknowledged, that was probably and unfortunately true. Nevertheless, the year in New York gave Cage the confidence and the background he needed to return to Los Angeles in the fall of 1934 and to approach Schoenberg about studying with him.[57]

"I went to see him in Los Angeles," Cage recalled. "He said, 'You probably can't afford my price,' and I said, 'You don't need to mention it because I don't have any money.' So he said, 'Will you devote your life to music?' and I said I would. . . . When I was studying with Schoenberg in the thirties, Stravinsky came to live in Los Angeles, and an impresario who was our local Hurok advertised a concert of his music as 'Music of the World's Greatest Living Composer.' I was indignant and marched straight into the impresario's office and told him that he should think twice before he made such advertisements in a city where Schoenberg was living. I was *extremely* partisan. I was like a tiger in defense of Schoenberg."[58]

Cage believed that "Schoenberg was a magnificent teacher, who always gave the impression that he was putting us in touch with musical principles. I studied counterpoint at his home and attended all his classes at USC and later at UCLA when he moved there. I also took his course in harmony, for which I had no gift. Several times I tried to explain to Schoenberg that I had no feeling for harmony. He told me that without a feeling for harmony I would always encounter an obstacle, a wall through which I wouldn't be able to pass. My reply was that in that case I would devote my life to beating my head against that wall—and maybe that is what I've been doing ever since. In all the time I studied with Schoenberg, he never once led me to believe that my work was distinguished in any way. He never praised my compositions, and when I commented on other students' work in class he held my comments up to ridicule. And yet I worshipped him like a god." Cage was in fact, especially pleased to learn that the critic Peter Yates had once "asked Schoenberg about his American pupils, whether he'd had any that were interesting, and Schoenberg's first reply was

Fig. 14.   John Cage and Merce
Cunningham, about 1948. Performing
Artservices, Inc.

to say there were no interesting pupils, but then he smiled and said, 'There was one,'
and he named me. Then he said, 'Of course he's not a composer, but he's an inventor—of genius.'"[59]

• • •

In 1938, after Cage completed his studies with Schoenberg, he was offered a job as
a composer-accompanist for Bonnie Bird's dance classes at the Cornish School in
Seattle, Washington, where he and Xenia lived for two intense years. There they
met, among other intriguing individuals, a teenaged dancer named Merce Cunningham—to whom Cage became deeply attached. Ultimately Cage's relationship with
Cunningham far superseded his waning commitment to Xenia. As the marriage
ended in the mid-1940s, the association with Cunningham—in love and in work—
became a guiding force in the lives of both men.[60]

The rest—as the saying goes—is history.

While New York remained the center of his world from the mid-1940s until his death in 1992, Cage retained a nostalgic affection for Los Angeles, the city that had sheltered and shaped him during his first quarter century.[61] There, especially among its vaunted European émigrés—Schindler, Neutra, Scheyer, Bühlig, Fischinger, Schoenberg—Cage imbibed the culture of avant-garde modernism that shaped and permeated his thought and work. These influences from the 1930s merged in his development with the culture of another Los Angeles from the teens and twenties—that of his family's Protestant America, as transplanted from Iowa, Tennessee, and Virginia. Even though he later insisted that in his Los Angeles years, he was "not yet Cage," both his memories and the harder evidence of "history" suggest that the Cage who emerged in the City of the Angels was indeed already becoming "Cage."

Notes

1. Thomas S. Hines, Interview with John Cage, New York, May 21 and 23, 1992 (hereafter cited as Hines Interview with Cage). This five-hour interview, most of which was taped, took place in Cage's apartment over part of two days. For encouraging me to write this essay and for introducing me to Cage, I am especially indebted to Marjorie Perloff. Others who provided crucial logistical and intellectual assistance include: Arthur Cobin, Alan Onoye, Taylor Hines, Jon Mochizuki, George Rand, David Sanders, Brian Knott, Richard Smith, Harris Saunders, Peter Lowenberg, and Robert Stevenson. In addition to the taped interview, there was also interesting, if more random, conversation before and after it and during pauses for lunch. A copy of the interview, transcribed by Brian Knott, is on file at the Stanford Humanities Center, Mariposa House, Stanford University, Stanford, California, and the Library of the UCLA Department of Music, Los Angeles, California.

2. Hines, Interview with Cage.

3. Ibid.; quoted in Marjorie Perloff, "'Unimpededness and Interpenetration,' the Poetry of John Cage," in Peter Gena and Jonathan Brent, ed., *A John Cage Reader, in Celebration of His 70th Birthday* (New York: C. P. Peters Corp., 1982), p. 6; Alan Gillmor, "Interview with John Cage," [1973], *Contact* 14 (Autumn 1976), in Richard Kostelanetz, ed., *Conversing with Cage* (New York: Limelight Press, 1988), 38 (hereafter cited as *CC*); John Cage, "An

Autobiographical Statement," *Southwest Review* 76, no. 1 (Winter 1991): 59; "Cage," quoted in Calvin Tomkins, *The Bride and the Bachelors: Five Masters of the Avant-Garde* (New York: Penguin Books, 1976), p. 130.

4. Quoted in Jann Pasler, "Inventing a Tradition: John Cage's 'Composition in Retrospect,'" in this volume.

5. Aaron Copland, quoted in Tomkins, *The Bride and the Bachelors*, p. 75.

6. Ibid.; two previous sons had died in infancy whose names, Cage believed, were also John, Jr. Birth records indicate, however, that their names were Gustavus Adolphus Williamson Cage, III, and IV.

7. Ibid. Jeff Goldberg, "John Cage Interviewed," *Transatlantic Review* 55–56 (May 1976), in *CC*, p. 1.

8. Hines, Interview with Cage.

9. Ibid.

10. Ibid.; Mina Lederman, "John Cage: A View of My Own," in Gena and Brent, eds., *A John Cage Reader*, p. 153.

11. Hines, Interview with Cage.

12. Ibid. Crete Cage, as she signed her by-line, began writing for the *Times* in the middle 1930s. A typical article extolling the importance of "hobbies" for women, began: "They are cured—scores of Los Angeles clubwomen—cured of depression ills!" "The Hobby-Horse Changes His Fodder," *Los Angeles Times Sunday Magazine* (April 7, 1935), p. 8. As early as 1928, however, Crete had gained sufficient renown for her club work to be listed in the biographical dictionary, *Women of the West*. This and other significant biographical data have been collected by UCLA music historian Robert Stevenson, in "John Cage on His 70th Birthday: West Coast Background," *Inter-American Music Review* 5 (Fall 1982): 3–17.

13. Stevenson; Cage, "An Autobiographical Statement," p. 59; Cage, quoted in Moira and William Roth, "John Cage on Marcel Duchamp," *Art in America* (November–December 1973), in *CC*, p. 194.

14. Hines, Interview with Cage; the obituary for John M. Cage, Sr., in *The New York Times* (January 5, 1964) noted that he, "invented the hydraphone during World War I and the sonobuoy in World War II, both . . . devices for detecting submarines." His "many patents included an inhaler for treating colds, a radio using alternating current, and a lightning protection system." Robert Stevenson has discovered that Cage's thirty-four patents recorded in the *Official Gazette of the United States Patent Office* began in 1906 and extended to 1957. See Stevenson, "John Cage on His 70th Birthday," p. 4.

15. Hines, Interview with Cage.

16. Ibid.

17. Ibid.

18. Ibid.

19. Ibid.

20. Ibid. Cage admitted that he had trouble recalling the dates and sequences of his family's residences. The stays in Santa Monica, Ocean Park, and Pacific Palisades were apparently short ones. The Los Angeles City Directories for the pertinent years list the Cages addresses as follows:

1912–1914: no listing

1915: Long Beach, no address

1916–1918: no listing

1919: no directory published

1920–1922: no listing

1923–1924: 2708 Moss Ave.

1925: 4604 Los Feliz Blvd.

1926–1932: 2708 Moss Ave. (1931: John Cage, Jr., also listed)

1933–1934: no listing

1935–1936: 1207 Miramar

Stevenson has made heroic efforts to sort out the Cage's residences and addresses in "John Cage on His 70th Birthday."

21. Hines, Interview with Cage.

22. Ibid.

23. Ibid.

24. Ibid.

25. Ibid.; Tomkins, *The Bride and the Bachelors*, p. 77.

26. Ibid.

27. Ibid.

28. Cage, quoted in Richard Kostelanetz and John Cage, "A Conversation about Radio in Twelve Parts" [1984], *Bucknell Review: John Cage at 75*, 33, no. 2 (1988).

29. Hines, Interview with Cage; Cole Gagne and Tracy Cara, "An Interview with John Cage," *East West Journal* (May 1979), in *CC*, p. 218; Stevenson, "John Cage," p. 6.

30. Hines, Interview with Cage.

31. Cage, quoted in Tomkins, *The Bride and the Bachelors*, p. 78; Stevenson, "John Cage," p. 7.

32. Hines, Interview with Cage.

33. Hines, Interview with Cage; Tomkins, *The Bride and the Bachelors*, pp. 78–80.

34. Ibid.

35. Ibid.

36. Ibid.; Cage, "An Autobiographical Statement," p. 60.

37. Hines, Interview with Cage. Other accounts have suggested that Cage returned and lived with his parents in Pacific Palisades, but this was not the case. No record exists of his parents' attitudes toward his homosexual identity. This was one of several questions I intended to ask him in a telephone conversation scheduled for the week he died. One can conjecture that, on the one hand, they would probably not have asked questions to which they did not want answers. On the other hand, it is likely that in a family full of "eccentrics," they would have seen this as a forgivable eccentricity in their extraordinary son. Don Sample later adopted the variant of his surname: "St. Paul." Stevenson discovered that on Cage's Pomona alumni card he was listed as having had with Don Sample an exhibition of "modern paintings," though no date was given ("John Cage").

The actor and early gay activist, Harry Hay, a friend of Cage's from Los Angeles High School days, later recalled that Don Sample had "bright, mischievous eyes in a scholarly looking face. He wore little glasses and had a shock of lank hair that kept falling over his lenses; he looked very boyish." In his relationship with Cage, "the insatiably cultural Sample took the role of instructor," introducing his friend to, among other things, the modernist architecture of Schindler and Neutra. "Back home they checked the Bauhaus catalogue Sample had brought back from Europe for commentary on furniture and design detail." Hay assisted Cage in preparing his art course for Santa Monica housewives, and in the mid-1930s, sang in several small public concerts of Cage compositions, claiming, convincingly, that he was "probably the earliest stage performer of Cage's music." For more on Cage, Sample, and Hay, see Stuart Timmons, *The Trouble with Harry Hay: Founder of the Modern Gay Movement* (Boston: Alyson Publications, 1990), pp. 40, 56–59, 72, 75, 85.

38. Hines, Interview with Cage.

39. See Esther McCoy, "Schindler," in *Five California Architects* (New York: Reinhold, 1960).

40. Ibid.; Hines, taped interviews with Pauline Schindler, February 9, 1972 and July 1, 1976, Los Angeles.

41. Hines, Interview with Cage.

42. Hines, taped interviews with Pauline Schindler, February 9, 1972; July 1, 1976. Years later, Cage, himself, would have virtually the same experience, as recounted by Tomkins: "Leaving a Philharmonic concert early one evening—he had come to hear Webern's Symphony Opus 21 and had been so overwhelmed by it that he did not want to stay for the

Rachmaninoff that followed—he met a large man in the lobby who was leaving at the same time and, as it turned out, for the same reason. This was Morton Feldman, a composer several years younger than Cage." The two then introduced themselves and began an "immediate friendship"; Tomkins, *The Bride and the Bachelors,* p. 107.

43. Hines, Interview with Cage. In this interview, I asked Cage if he had stayed in touch with Don, and he replied that he regretted to say that he had not. He wondered, in fact, whether he was living or dead, and explained his failure to stay in touch with such crucial people in his life as a failure "to practice the emotions" properly. As he phrased it, somewhat eccentrically: "I don't think I'm capable about my emotions." In a related context, he mused further on the relationship of art and sexuality, particularly homosexuality. He acknowledged the growing contemporary interest in "gay composers," such as Franz Schubert, a reassessment, he averred, "which takes the relationship between art and sex very seriously. I do not. Once I am doing something 'serious,' I don't think about sex." In another part of the interview he stated, "I'm entirely opposed to the emotions . . . I really am. I think of love as an opportunity to become blind and blind in a bad way . . . I think that seeing and hearing are extremely important; in my view they are what life is; love makes us blind to seeing and hearing."

44. Hines, Interview with Cage.

45. Hines, Interview with Mark Schindler, Los Angeles, August 17, 1992.

46. Hines, Interview with Cage.

47. Ibid.; Paul Cummings, "Interview: John Cage [May 2, 1974]" (manuscript at the Archives of American Art), in *CC*, pp. 7–8. The data on John and Xenia's marriage in Yuma and early addresses come from David Revill, *The Roaring Silence, John Cage: A Life* (New York: Arcade Publishing, 1992), which appeared after this essay was written and already in press.

48. Hines, Interview with Cage.

49. Ibid.; Hines, Interview with Lette Valeska, March 12, 1980, Los Angeles. See also, Thomas S. Hines, *Richard Neutra and the Search for Modern Architecture: A Biography and History* (New York: Oxford University Press, 1982).

50. Hines, Interview with Cage.

51. Ibid.; Gillmor, "Interview with John Cage," in *CC*, p. 4.

52. Ibid.

53. Cummings, "Interview: John Cage [May 2, 1974]; Stevenson, "John Cage," p. 9.

54. Joel Eric Suben, Interview with Cage, in *CC*, p. 8.

55. Tomkins, *The Bride and the Bachelors,* pp. 81–84. Since Cage's relationship with

Schoenberg has been analyzed extensively elsewhere, I treat it here somewhat sketchily, but crucially, as the culmination of his Los Angeles journey.

56. Ibid.

57. Ibid.; Cagne and Caras, "An Interview with John Cage"; Hines, Conversation with Philip Johnson, New York, June 24, 1993.

58. Goldberg, "John Cage Interviewed," in *CC*, pp. 8–9; Tomkins, *The Bride and the Bachelors*, pp. 84–85.

59. Ibid.

60. Hines, Interview with Cage. I regret that I turned off the tape recorder when Cage and I reached the point in our interview when he left Los Angeles for Seattle. He continued to talk without pausing and to tell me that in his and Xenia's "open marriage," she and he were drawn to Cunningham and he to them, resulting in a ménage à trois. It was in that situation, Cage stated, that he realized he was more attracted to Cunningham than to Xenia. After their divorce, Cage told me, earlier he found it difficult to communicate with Xenia and that their later relationship had not been particularly friendly. Xenia, he explained, had a rather "barby" wit and "so if I telephone her or write to her, I take my life in my hands." When I asked him if he regretted not having had children, he replied, "no," though he acknowledged that Xenia had once become pregnant and upon the advice of her doctor, "though it was illegal at the time," had had an abortion.

61. It was, in fact, Cage's roots in, and long identity with Los Angeles that prompted me to ask him in May 1992 what his reactions had been to the "horrible events" of the previous weeks when he and the world had watched televised images of L.A. erupting in flame and violence. "I don't think they are 'horrible,'" he replied, "I think it is part of the present necessity which results from too great a division between the haves and the have-nots. And we will have, if you wish, more 'horrible' things until we come to an understanding and care for the whole. We only have it, so to speak, coming to us. That it should come to us in Los Angeles . . . is simply meaningless . . . It's coming to us throughout the entire country . . . It's painful here but we pay no attention . . . But you listen to the news anywhere in the United States or anywhere in the world [and] you are daily shocked. Shocked to the numbness that we all don't care for. The things that happened in Los Angeles brings us, so to speak, to life, but what *is* that life?"

"A duchamp unto my self":
"Writing through" Marcel
Marjorie Perloff

> A family resemblance pleases when there is a cessation of resemblances.
> —Gertrude Stein, "Next: Life and Letters of Marcel Duchamp"

questions i Might

hAve

leaRned

to ask Can

no longEr

receive repLies[1]

When asked what artist had most profoundly influenced his own work, John Cage regularly cited Marcel Duchamp. In the Preface to "James Joyce, Marcel Duchamp, Erik Satie: An Alphabet" (1981), for example, Cage explains:

> I happened one year to see a large exhibition of Dada in Düsseldorf. All of it had turned into art with the exception of Duchamp. The effect for me of Duchamp's work was to so change my way of seeing that I became in my way a duchamp unto my self. I could find as he did for himself the space and time of my own experience. The works signed by Duchamp are centrifugal. The world around becomes indistinguishable. In Düsseldorf it began with the light switches and electric outlets. One day after he had died Teeny Duchamp was taking me to see the *Etant Donnés* when it was still in New York before it went to Philadelphia. We were walking east along 10th Street. I said, needing

some courage to do so: You know, Teeny, I don't understand Marcel's work. She replied: Neither do I. While he was alive I could have asked him questions, but I didn't. I preferred simply to be near him. I love him and for me more than any other artist of this century he is the one who changed my life.[2]

Why Duchamp? The obvious answer is that Duchamp's subversion of causality and psychological depth, coupled with his predilection for chance operations and his larger refusal to distinguish between "life" and "art," a refusal epitomized by such readymades as the *Tzanck Check* and the *Bottle Dryer*, prepared the ground for Cage's own aesthetic of "unimpededness and interpenetration."[3] Picabia, Arp, Schwitters—all these "had become artists with the passing of time"; only Duchamp's work "remained unacceptable as art" and hence perpetually new and challenging.[4] Which is the light switch, which the art object? These are the kinds of questions Cage poses in his own work.[5]

Yet he refrained from asking Duchamp any questions about his work, preferring, he tells us, "simply to be near him." Such deference to a living artist is quite un-Cagean: neither in his relationship with Pierre Boulez nor even with Arnold Schoenberg was Cage so willing to accept the other's word. The forebearance is doubly odd when one stops to think that, however ardently Cage admired Duchamp's fabled indifference, his incorporation, say, of the cracks in the pane of window glass he was working on, along with the dust that covered it, into the design of the *Large Glass (The Bride Stripped Bare by Her Bachelors, Even)*, there was a side to Duchamp's art that Cage could never really assimilate. That side, or more accurately center, of Duchamp's work is its preoccupation with eroticism, with sexual punning and double entendre, with the display of men and women as perverse machines or machine parts, bumping and grinding against one another. The upside-down urinal turned vagina shape and called *Fountain*, the *Bicycle Wheel*, whose rod penetrates the hole of the stool beneath it, the french window called *Fresh Widow*, whose upper right-hand pane has skin-like texture and what looks like a nipple—these belong to a different discourse from Cage's, which is, after all, an American—more specifically, a Californian, evangelical Protestant-cum-Zen Buddhist, and (however veiled) homosexual discourse.

Ironically, the real appeal of Duchamp for Cage ("I love him and he . . . changed my life") may have had less to do with Marcel's work than with his enticing pres-

Fig. 15. *Marcel Duchamp as Rrose Sélavy*, 1924, by Man Ray. Philadelphia Museum of Art, the Samuel S. White III and Vera White Collection

ence—the exotic image of the man smiling enigmatically over the chessboard or appearing in drag as *Rrose Sélavy* (fig. 15). But this image was as troubling as it was seductive. During their summers at Cadaqués, for example, Cage found himself dismayed by Duchamp's expressed admiration for Salvador Dali:

> I was furious that all the postal cards in the local post office had photographs of Dali, and there were no cards of Duchamp. Poor Marcel. . . . And the moment I entered [Dali's] house, I just didn't feel at home. We sat in a large circle, and Marcel sat next to Dali. . . . And they served the pink champagne, and Dali talked all the time. Marcel never took his eyes off him. . . . Finally, Dali asked whether we wanted to see his painting. Marcel said, "Oh, yes." And we went into his studio, and here was this huge painting, oh, four times the size of that wall; and Marcel proceeded to admire it. And it was vulgar and miserable. (*CC*, 183)

"Vulgar and miserable," from Cage's perspective, because Dali's hyperrealistic, sensationalistic, and quasi-pornographic canvases represented an exhibitionism that ran wholly counter to his own aesthetic as well as to what he took to be Marcel's. Nevertheless, after Duchamp's death, when he again met Dali at Cadaqués, Cage recalls "searching . . . to see if I could find in Dali something that might have attracted Marcel; and I happened to notice his eyes were very beautiful" (ibid.). Rather, perhaps, like the moist eyes of Rrose Sélavy, which attracted Cage in spite of himself. But in keeping with his own commitment to the renunciation of the ego in art, he shifted the parameters of the discourse so that the making of "a duchamp unto my self" (note the lower-case *d* and the division of "my" and "self") involved the transformation of the erotic into the ideational, the sexual into the textual. It is this transfer, producing as it does a textuality which is itself sensuous and erotic, that was to become Cage's own signature.

Work/Play Ethic

What, to begin with, was Cage's understanding of "purposeless play" (*S*, 12), a concept central to Duchamp's own aesthetic? Here is Cage recalling his first meeting with Duchamp:

I'd come from Chicago and was staying in the apartment of Peggy Guggenheim and Max Ernst [in 1943]. Peggy had agreed to pay for the transport of my percussion instruments from Chicago to New York, and I was to give a concert to open her gallery, "The Art of This Century." Meanwhile, being young and ambitious, I had also arranged to give a concert at the Museum of Modern Art. When Peggy discovered that, she cancelled not only the concert but also her willingness to pay for the transport of the instruments. When she gave me this information, I burst into tears. In the room next to mine at the back of the house Marcel Duchamp was sitting in a rocking chair smoking a cigar. He asked why I was crying and I told him. He said virtually nothing, but his presence was such that I felt calmer. . . . He had calmness in the face of disaster. (*CC*, 11)

"Calmness in the face of disaster": it is an odd attribute to apply to Duchamp, the artist who regularly declared that he believed in "nothing," that indeed "the word 'belief' is an error . . . like the word 'judgment,' they're both horrible ideas, on which the world is based."[6] How could there be "disaster" when what happened was a matter of perfect "indifference"? Only in playing chess, so Duchamp would have it, was winning worthwhile. Cage, who admits that "I was using chess as a pretext to be with" Duchamp (*CC*, 11), recalls that when they played, "Every now and then [Marcel] would get very impatient with me. He complained that I didn't seem to want to win. I was so delighted to be with him that the notion of winning was beside the point" (*CC*, 25).

Duchamp, on the other hand, took *winning* to be important, provided that there was nothing at stake. To win for the sake of winning, that was genuine play; to work in order to attain something, quite another. "He was not ever completely working," Gertrude Stein remarked of Picasso; in Duchamp's case, she might have said that he was not "working" at all or, as she observed cryptically in her portrait "Next: Life and Letters of Marcel Duchamp," it was his method "to interlace a story with glass and with rope with color and roam. How many people roam. Dark people roam."[7] The artist as roamer or *flaneur*—the notion would have appealed to Duchamp. "I consider," he tells Pierre Cabanne, "working for a living slightly imbecilic from an economic point of view. I hope that some day we'll be able to live without being obliged to work" (PC, 15). And again, "Deep down I'm enormously lazy. I like living, breathing, better than working" (PC, 72).

Why work, moreover, when life was so consistently *amusing* (*amusant*)? Putting a mustache on the Mona Lisa and calling the new "art work" *L. H. O. O. Q.* was, he tells Cabanne, "very amusing." Bringing a glass bulb labeled "Physiological serum" to Walter Arensberg in New York as a souvenir of Paris was "amusing" (PC, 63). The pun "Fresh Widow"/"French Window" was amusing. The Picabia auction at the Salle Drouot was "an amusing experience." Making insignias bearing the four letters D A D A was "amusing." And even New York during World War II was "amusing," so Duchamp remarks, "because Peggy Guggenheim had also returned" and "then all the Surrealists arrived. . . . There was lots of activity" (PC, 83).

"Amusing" is hardly a recurrent word in Cage's lexicon, there being, in the nature of things, so much important work to do. Like Duchamp, Cage rejects work-as-employment, the nine-to-five job performed routinely for the sake of financial remuneration. In this sense, he looked forward, even as did Duchamp, to a day when everyone might be unemployed. But for Cage, freedom from employment spells the opportunity to get on with the real work to be done, which is nothing less than the improvement of the planet. Indeed, the work ethic, as applied to the making of art, had been central to Cage's life from the time when he was twelve years old and organized Friday afternoon concerts, conducted by himself and performed by Boy Scouts, for the radio station KNX in Hollywood (see *CC*, 2). "I can work in the society as it intolerably structured is," Cage remarks in the foreword to *M*, "and I can also work in it as hopefully unstructured it will in the future be." Or, as he puts it in "The Future of Music": "The first part of a new text by Norman O. Brown is on work. . . . In our polluted air there is the idea that we must get to work. Somehow, recently, in New York and in other cities too, the air seems less polluted than it was. Work has begun." And he adds, "People frequently ask me what my definition of music is. This is it. It is work. That is my conclusion."[8]

A very unDuchampian comment, even though on the same page Cage talks of those who, like Duchamp, go underground "to get the work done that is to be done." A further difference between the two artists has to do with work and war, which is to say, warwork. Duchamp spent most of the World War I years trying to find a neutral country that would harbor him: first the United States, then in 1918, after the United States had entered the war, Argentina (see PC, 59). "I left France," he tells Cabanne, "basically for lack of militarism, for lack of patriotism." Cage similarly "never had to go to war," but, as he tells Alcides Lanza, "Had I been drafted, I would have accepted and gone into it; I would not have refused. There are so many examples of people who were able to continue their work in the Army. The first I think of is the philosopher Ludwig Wittgenstein, who wrote his *Tractatus* in the trenches in Italy. . . . In other words, I believe in the principle of Daniel in the Lion's Den" (*CC*, 10).

This emphasis on obligation and good works ("one does what must be done") may well reflect Cage's childhood training: his father, after all, was the inventor of "useful" (if sometimes failed) objects in the fields of automobile, airplane, and submarine mechanics, and his paternal grandfather, the Reverend Gustavus Adolphus Cage, was an itinerant minister and founder of the Methodist Episcopal Church. Not surprisingly, in any case, when Duchamp died in 1968 and Cage was asked by a magazine to "do something for Marcel," he decided to follow the lead of their mutual friend Jasper Johns, who told the magazine in question, "I don't want to say anything about Marcel" (*CC*, 184). Not "saying" but "doing": this became the impetus for Cage's first full-scale visual art work, which he made in collaboration with Calvin Sumsion—a four-panel construction (125 copies were produced) made of plexiglass and lithograph paper, called *Not Wanting to Say Anything about Marcel* (fig. 16).

Unlike Duchamp's erotically charged readymades (the *Bottle Dryer* with its circular bands bearing phallic rods, or the bird cage containing sugar cubes, a cuttle bone, and a thermometer, called *Why Not Sneeze Rrose Sélavy?*), *Not Wanting to Say Anything about Marcel* is curiously chaste. In *For the Birds*, Cage describes the piece's genesis:

> It's a tribute to Marcel Duchamp. But I didn't want to say anything about Duchamp, as the title indicates. So I subjected a dictionary to the *I Ching*; I picked words, then letters from those words, and finally their arrangement in space by chance operations. I distributed these words according to a typography likewise based on chance, on sheets of plexiglass. I put the eight sheets of plexiglass parallel to each other on a wooden base. Thus the letters appear in depth, they are superimposed and combined as we look at them. There are four bases, each holding eight sheets. The whole thing comes from chance, including the colors. It is an object that has no meaning and which cannot be said to refer to a text. And yet, it seems to me that Duchamp would have been, as he used to say, "amused" by that object.[9]

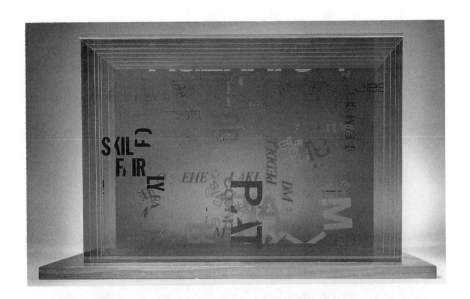

Fig. 16. *Not Wanting to Say Anything about Marcel*, 1969, two parts of a plexigram multiple by John Cage and Calvin Sumsion. Stanford University Museum of Art (1973.25), gift of Prof. and Mrs. John H. Merryman

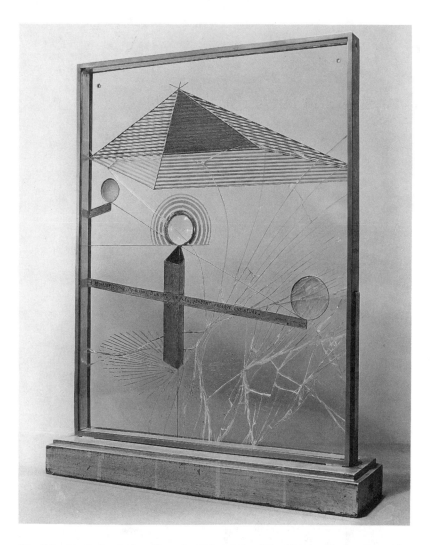

Fig. 17. *To Be Looked at (from the Other Side of the Glass) with One Eye, Close to, for Almost an Hour,* by Marcel Duchamp. Oil paint, silver leaf, lead wire, and magnifying lens on glass (cracked), mounted between two panes of glass in a standing metal frame of a painted wood base; overall height 22 inches. The Museum of Modern Art, New York, Katherine S. Dreier Bequest

The last sentence suggests that Cage took himself to be producing a kind of ready-made, but it is doubtful that Duchamp would have regarded the plexigrams in this way or that he would have found them especially "amusing." For *Not Wanting to Say Anything about Marcel* is a formal construction, not a found object, like, say, the playful cracked-glass construction *To Be Looked at (from the Other Side of the Glass) with One Eye, Close to, for Almost an Hour* (fig. 17).[10] Cage's plexigrams rely less on punning than on spacing and the deployment of lettristic images (letters, morphemes, words) generated by chance operations. The letter images, rendered in different colors, seem to float in an elegant three-dimensional space that is quite unlike Duchamp's own presentation of everyday—and frequently ugly and taste-less—commercial objects. Again, the composition of the plexigrams is primarily reti-nal: they are designed to be first *seen* and then *read,* or rather, *deciphered.* For example, we can read the words **"REAR," "GRAINED," "NAY,"** and **"contra bassoon"**; other verbal units have missing letters (e.g., **"phy ae"** and **"HUR"**) so that the viewer is challenged to fill in the blanks. Single capital letters—an inverted **V,** an **E**—alternate with clusters of lower-case letters, forming pleasing patterns. But these chance-generated words and morphemes are not double entendres like Du-champ's *L. H. O. O. Q.,* and the language games in which they participate are cere-bral rather than sexy, the visual countering the aural (rather than reinforcing it), very much as will happen in Cage's later mesostics. *Not Wanting to Say Anything about Marcel* thus turns out to be an absolutely accurate title. Cage doesn't say anything about his friend: rather, he operates from the premise of *Silence:* "One does some-thing else. What else?" (*S,* 68). The "something else," in this case, becomes an homage, not only to Marcel, but to the potential of the plexigram. It is a curiously American invention.

Wanting to Say Something about John

"No one was more typically French," writes Michel Sanouillet, "than Marcel Duchamp":

> It seems that everything in his life converged to make of him an epitome of the French tradition and that, at the very outset, impish sprites gathered at his cradle to give this

prince of revolt the most banal family name imaginable. Duchamp (*champ* = field), like Dupont, or like Smith in England, smacks of the soil and evokes generations of hard-working middle-class villagers and anonymous laborers living close to the land. There is nothing exotic or abnormal about it; nothing is less Duchampian than the name Duchamp.[11]

And Sanouillet goes on to point out that "nothing [was] less eccentric than [Duchamp's] family upbringing, born as he was into the close-knit family of a provincial notary in the small Normandy town of Blainville" (ADH, 48).

The parallel to Cage is interesting: like "Marcel Duchamp," "John Cage" is the most ordinary of (in this case) WASP names, and like Duchamp, Cage grew up in what seem to have been quite "normal" surroundings in the then provincial suburbs of Los Angeles.[12] But just as Sanouillet attributes Duchamp's famous "renunciation of all aesthetics" (see PC, 42) to the inculcation of "methodical doubt" central to his particular French heritage, so Cage's legacy from his Southern and midwestern Protestant ancestors was a pragmatism that is peculiarly American. "No particular results," says William James in the Second Lecture on Pragmatism, "but only an attitude of orientation, is what the pragmatic method means. *The attitude of looking away from first things, principles, 'categories,' supposed necessities; and of looking towards last things, fruits, consequences, facts.*" And again, "*ideas (which themselves are but parts of our experience) become true just in so far as they help us to get into satisfactory relation with other parts of our experience.*"[13]

"First things, principles, categories, supposed necessities"—both Duchamp and Cage reject such notions of origin and presence, but whereas Duchamp repeatedly insists that what he believes in is "nothing, of course!" and that the word "belief" is itself an "error" (PC, 89), Cage seems to act more on the Jamesian theorem: "Grant an idea or belief to be true . . . what concrete difference will its being true make in any one's actual life . . . What experiences will be different from those which would obtain if the belief were false?" (WJ, 573). Accordingly, Cage recalls in an interview, "I didn't want to disturb [Duchamp] with questions. Supposing he had not been disturbed by some question I had asked, and had answered it, I would then have had his answer rather than my experience" (CC, 178).

That experience is the mainspring of Cage's first verbal composition for Marcel, the "26 Statements Re Duchamp" of 1964.[14] The two-page, two-column text, printed with justified left and right margins, is preceded by a headnote that begins "Had Marcel Duchamp not lived, it would have been necessary for someone exactly like him to live, to bring about, that is, the world as we begin to know and experience it. Having this view, I felt obliged to keep a worshipful distance" (*YM*, 70). But the piece itself, like so many of Cage's "essays" on composers and artists, is as much critique as eulogy, and it provides an interesting introduction to Cage's own poetic or, more accurately, poethic practice.

The first enigma is the title "26 Statements Re Duchamp," there being, not 26 but 19 "statements," if we equate the statement with a block of print, or 67 "statements," if we equate "statement" with sentence. But if a statement is not equivalent to a block of print or paragraph or sentence, what is it? Does the white space between "statements" perhaps count? If so, there are 36 units—still not the "right" amount. But perhaps the confusion is intentional, Cage posing the Wittgensteinian question: What does it mean to make a statement and when is the first replaced by the second?

The composition opens with the word "History" and proceeds:

> The danger remains that he'll get out of the valise we put him in. So long as he remains locked up—

> The rest of them were artists. Duchamp collects dust.

> The check. The string he dropped. The Mona Lisa. The musical notes taken out of a hat. The glass. The toy shotgun painting. The things he found. Therefore, everything seen—every object, that is, plus the process of looking at it —is a Duchamp.

Here in cryptic form is a mini-catalogue of Duchamp's work from the *Boîte-en-Valise* to the *Large Glass* (made by "collecting" the dust that fell on the pane of glass in his studio) to the *Tzanck Check* (the enlarged handmade check presented to Dr.

Daniel Tzanck in payment for dental work), the *Three Stoppages* (in which three threads are glued to painted canvas strips), to *L. H. O. O. Q.* (the mustached Mona Lisa). Cage joins Duchamp in making fun of those who would lock him up (pigeon-hole him) in his own "valise," not recognizing the crucial difference between Marcel and "The rest of them [who] were artists." But what Cage doesn't include here is any reference to the pre-readymade paintings—*Nude Descending a Staircase, The Bride,* and so on—evidently because the use of such traditional means as easel painting holds no interest for him. The drive to "make it new" becomes even clearer in the final sentence above, where Cage obliquely reads his own aesthetic into Duchamp's. For the notion that any object can be considered "art," if it is looked at properly, is not so much Duchampian as Cagean. Duchamp, after all, held that the very idea of "art" is bogus, that at best what the "artist" makes should be called "craft" and be denied reverence on the part of the public (PC, 16).

A similarly subtle critique occurs in the next passage, which begins with the cryptic question "Duchamp Mallarmé?"

> There are two versions of the ox-herding pictures. One concludes with the image of nothingness, the other with the image of a fat man, smiling, returning to the village bearing gifts. Nowadays we have only the second version. They call it neo-Dada. When I talked with M.D. two years ago he said he had been fifty years ahead of his time.

Here again an interesting sleight of hand takes place. If Duchamp's art is emblematized by the second version of the Zen ox-herding picture, the image of the fat man smiling and bearing gifts, Cage, after all, is the artist who, from *Silence* on down, has presented us with the "image of nothingness." Or is it the other way around? In conversation with Calvin Tomkins (*CC*, 55), Cage refers to the first version as "end[ing] with an empty circle—nothingness—the example of Duchamp," whereas the second version signifies "return," "the idea being that after the attainment of nothingness one returns again into activity," that activity clearly being his own. In either case, Cage separates himself from Duchamp, even as, in the next paragraph, when Cage writes, "Duchamp showed the usefulness of addition (mustache).

Rauschenberg showed the function of subtraction (de Kooning). Well, we look forward to multiplication and division. It is safe to assume that someone will learn trigonometry. Johns," the reader surmises that it is not only Jasper Johns but Cage himself who will produce these complications, his chance-generated compositions increasingly relying on mathematical operations. These operations, moreover, are already anticipated by the lineation of "26 Statements," the use of spacing ("silence") between words to create a right-justified margin. Such rage for order would have struck Duchamp as excessively aesthetic, a formalizing device at odds with "play."

The further one reads in "26 Statements Re Duchamp," the more one realizes that the text is more dialogue than statement, Cage's dialogue with his master. Under the heading "Ichiyanagi Wolff" (the title fuses the names of the Japanese avant-garde composer Toshi Ichiyanagi and his American counterpart Christian Wolff), we read, "We have only time for conversation. The Lord help us to say something in reply that doesn't simply echo what our ears took in." And replying is, of course, what the text in front of us is doing. Cage gives us a second hint when he criticizes Jackson Pollock for trying, like Duchamp, to "paint on glass":

> There was an admission of
> failure. That wasn't the way to proceed. It's
> not a question of doing again what Duchamp
> already did. We must nowadays nevertheless
> at least be able to look through to what's be-
> yond—as though we were in it looking out.

"It's not a question of doing again what Duchamp already did." Here, much more convincingly than in any overt manifesto he might have written, Cage answers those theorists like Peter Bürger who argue that the avant-garde was a one-time phenomenon, that whereas Duchamp's exhibition of an ordinary urinal in a museum "radically question[ed] the very principle of art in bourgeois society . . . If an artist today signs a stove pipe and exhibits it, that artist certainly does not denounce the art market but adapts to it." [15] True enough, provided the avant-garde artist merely repeats the provocation already committed. But suppose, as Cage recognized early on, "One does something else" (S, 68)? And so the last page of "26 Statements" opens with the heading "The air," followed by the sentences, "We hesitate to ask the question because we do not want to hear the answer. Going about in silence." The question, evidently, is how to carry on Duchamp's aesthetic without simply repeating his experiments. "Going about in silence"—there's Cage's own solution. "Say it's not a Duchamp. Turn it over and it is" (*YM*, 72). Which is to say that Cage's own works make use of different structural principles even though, when "turned over," they can be seen to perform a comparable role vis-à-vis society. Of such "conversation," Cage implies, "theatre" is made.

The "26 Statements Re Duchamp" thus turns out to be primarily "re Cage," a collage of found text and aphorism that is Cage's Conceptualist version of Dada manifesto. Duchamp's stress on "visual indifference, and, at the same time, on the total absence of good or bad taste" (*PC*, 48) gives way to the pragmatist drive to create a blueprint for action. But in the midst of that blueprint there is a "statement" that interrupts the manifesto mode and provides us with an image of Marcel himself rather than of "a duchamp":

> There he is, rocking away in that chair, smok-
> ing his pipe, waiting for me to stop weeping. I
> still can't hear what he said then. Years later
> I saw him on MacDougall Street in the Village.
> He made a gesture I took to mean O.K.

The reference is to the first meeting with Duchamp described by Cage (*CC*, 11). Note that here again a note of deference ("He made a gesture I took to mean O.K.") intrudes on what is otherwise a tough-minded appraisal of another artist. Cage seems to pick up on the homoerotic element in Duchamp ("The string he dropped. The Mona Lisa") and turns it into a sign directed to none other than himself.

Erotic Transfer

A more complex displacement occurs in the more recent performance piece "James Joyce, Marcel Duchamp, Erik Satie: An Alphabet" (1981). In the preface to this text, cited at the beginning of my essay, Cage recalls that on the way to see Duchamp's *Etant Donnés* in New York before the piece was installed in Philadelphia, he told Duchamp's widow Teeny that he did not understand Marcel's work (*X*, 53). Variants of this story are told elsewhere, all of them claiming incomprehension of *Etant Donnés (Given),* Duchamp's last major work, an installation executed in complete secrecy in New York over a twenty-year period (1946–66), when it was assumed that Duchamp had essentially stopped working. The title derives from an early note in the *Green Box* and points to the close connection between the imagery and themes of *Etant Donnés* and the *Large Glass,* but unlike the latter work, it has no accompanying notes and Duchamp refused to say anything about the notorious installation, now to be seen at the Philadelphia Museum of Art by only one visitor at a time, looking through two small peepholes in an old wooden door placed in the far wall of an empty room.

In one interview, Cage refers to *Etant Donnés* as "very physical" (*CC,* 180); in another, he admits that in this final work, in which Duchamp "obliges [people] to look through the peephole of the door," he is "controlling the position of the observer . . . he who had been the one to remove control from art!" (*CC,* 183). But Cage does not condemn this instance of control, evidently because "no one had thought, before [Duchamp] thought of it, of making [such] a situation." Indeed, what is so odd about Cage's reactions to *Etant Donnés* is that he says nothing at all about the work's actual content or about its specific relationship to the earlier readymades and boxes. It is as if the hypervisibility of Duchamp's peepshow, the over-explicitness of the image of the spread-eagled nude girl, reduced Cage the viewer to silence.

In a celebrated ekphrasis of *Etant Donnés* (an ekphrasis Cage must have known), Octavio Paz describes the work this way:

> First of all, a brick wall with a slit in it, and through the slit, a wide open space, luminous and seemingly bewitched. Very near the beholder—but also very far away, on the "other side"—a naked girl, stretched on a kind of bed or pyre of branches and leaves, her face almost completely covered by the blond mass of her hair, her legs open and slightly bent, the pubes strangely smooth in contrast to the splendid abundance of her hair, right arm out of the line of vision, her left slightly raised, the hand grasping a small gas lamp made of metal and glass. The little lamp glows in the brilliant three-o'clock-in-the-afternoon light of this motionless, end-of-summer day. Fascinated by this challenge to our common sense—what is there less clear than light?—our glance wanders over the landscape: in the background, wooded hills, green and reddish; lower

down, a small lake and a light mist on the lake. An inevitably blue sky. Two or three little clouds, also inevitably white. On the far right, among some rocks, a waterfall catches the light. Stillness: a portion of time held motionless. The immobility of the naked woman and of the landscape contrasts with the movement of the waterfall. The silence is absolute. All is real and verges on banality; all is unreal and verges—on what?

The viewer draws back from the door feeling that mixture of joy and guilt of one who has unearthed a secret. But what is the secret?[16]

The "secret," as later commentators have been at pains to point out, is complicated by the anatomical incorrectness of the seemingly hyperreal female figure: the slit between her enlarged thighs (the slit so close to the left leg that it could also be the joint between leg and torso) looking like a mark of violation rather than a natural orifice. This equivocation between the "natural" and the "surreal" and the positioning of the viewer/voyeur at the peephole have given rise to any number of conflicting interpretations of *Etant Donnés,*[17] but however we choose to take Duchamp's controversial mise-en-scène, the issue of "eroticism," whether parodic or not, is clearly central to its conception. Asked by Pierre Cabanne, "What is the place of eroticism in your work?" Duchamp gave the punning reply: "Enormous. Visible or conspicuous, or, at any rate, underlying." And he adds:

> I believe in eroticism a lot, because it's truly a rather widespread thing throughout the world, a thing that everyone understands. It replaces, if you wish, what other literary schools called Symbolism, Romanticism. It could be another "ism," so to speak . . . [eroticism is] really a way to try to bring out in the daylight things that are constantly hidden—and that aren't necessarily erotic—because of the Catholic religion, because of social rules. To be able to reveal them, and to place them at everyone's disposal—I think this is important because it's the basis of everything, and no one talks about it. (PC, 88)

It is fascinating to see how Cage reacts (or rather, doesn't react) to this kind of discussion. In his own references to *Etant Donnés,* Cage repeatedly stresses the miracle of the work's production, kept secret for all those years when Duchamp had announced he had given up "working." But the closest he comes to actually alluding to Duchamp's subject matter is in a response to Moira and William Roth, who pose the question, "Do you think your idea of silence has anything in common with Duchamp?"

> Looking at the *Large Glass,* the thing that I like so much is that I can focus my attention wherever I wish. It helps me to blur the distinction between art and life and produces a kind of silence in the work itself. There is nothing in it that requires me to look in one place or another or, in fact, requires me to look at all. I can look through it to the world beyond. Well, this is, of course, the reverse in *Etant Donnés.* I can only see what Duchamp permits me to see. The *Large Glass* changes with the light and he was aware of this. So does a Mondrian. So does any painting. But *Etant Donnés* doesn't change because it is all prescribed. So he's telling us something that we perhaps haven't yet learned, when we speak as we do so glibly of the blurring of the distinction between art and life. Or perhaps he's bringing us back to Thoreau: yes and no are lies. (*CC*, 179–80)

Here Cage makes two important points: (1) that the breakdown of the distinction between "art" and "life," which he himself had been theorizing ever since *Silence*, is not as simple as it has seemed to some of his followers and exegetes; and (2) that the *Etant Donnés* is meant to be "read," not straightforwardly as the *image* of *x* or *y*, but as a subtle parody of ways of looking. But he is reluctant to discuss that parody any further, reluctant to discuss the "it" of the work. And his own version of Duchamp in "James Joyce, Marcel Duchamp, Erik Satie: An Alphabet" is, so to speak, desexualized, or, to put it another way in the light of Duchamp's own remarks about the need to bring eroticism out into the open in response to Church strictures, de-Catholicized.

Why, to begin with, does Cage call this performance piece, this playlet with a cast of characters, a "lecture"? It is a specifically Cagean move—the drive, not only to use new means, as the avant-garde had always done, but to use those means to teach his audience something new, in this case, how to understand the works of his three chosen artists (one literary, one visual, one musical, the three being, for that matter, alike only within the radius of Cagean discourse) as pointing the way to a new art suitable for our American "air way of knowing nowness" (*S*, 73), with its need to read Europe through the prism of Asia. Hence, as he puts it in the opening mesostic on JAMES JOYCE (*X*, 55), the aim is to put the three "on thE / Same stage same time":

even though the subJect
Of
the plaY

is the Curtain
that sEparates them!

Like most of Cage's later works, the text of "Alphabet" is generated by chance operations, the three "ghosts"—and here Cage may well be thinking of Duchamp's aphorism "A guest plus a host equals a ghost"[18]—who appear singly, in pairs, or all three together, interacting with the "nonsentient" beings found as "stage properties," by using "the twenty-six letters of the alphabet and chance operations to locate facing pages of an unabridged dictionary."[19] "I wanted," Cage explains, "to remove the punctuation, so to speak, from our experience of modernism" (*X*, 55). What this means is that found text—citations from *Finnegans Wake*, Satie's *Écrits*, and Duchamp's *Salt Seller* (the English translation of his writings, by Michel Sanouillet and Elmer Peterson)—is interspersed with mesostics in which Duchamp, Satie, and Joyce move easily in and out of their own modes of discourse, frequently saying things that sound like Cage rather than themselves. Like "26 Statements Re Duchamp," "Alphabet" is thus both homage and critique, both re-inscription and deconstruction.

Duchamp first appears in an extract drawn from the "Notes to the *Large Glass*" in the Sanouillet edition of *Salt Seller*. Cage might have chosen the notes on Malic Molds, the Waterfall, the Splash, or the Bride, but instead he chooses the note on the *"Construction of a 4-dimensional eye,"* with its comic mathematical instructions. Interestingly, when one compares Cage's found text to the original, one notices certain odd alterations. Duchamp, for example, regularly abbreviates "dimensional" as "dim'l." And he writes out the instructions in diagram form ("From—:, To—:), denoting the fourth power with a superscript ("rays⁴"), whereas Cage writes out the words "4-dimensional rays." And further, Cage omits the comic note that tells us that this whole passage about the fourth dimension is written *"On reverse side:* Paris gas bill dated Nov. 11, 1914," which is followed, in Duchamp's text, by the sentence "Light and shade exist for 4 dim'l as for 3, 2, 1," and then a diagram of a cube section of an element in what is supposedly a four-dimensional medium. Instead, Cage makes the paragraph coherent, putting as its concluding sentence, "Light and shade exist for 4-dimensional [objects] as for 3, 2, 1," omits the diagram, and then makes Duchamp's meaning clearer by pasting in the next set of notes, again changing the mathematical shorthand ("Perspective^3") to "Three-dimensional perspective." And so on.

Trivial as these small changes may seem, they reveal an interesting facet of Cage's appropriation of texts. What happens is that the Duchamp notes, written in more or less slapdash style, are made coherent in the interest of Cage's didactic purpose. What looks like Neo-Dada inconsequentiality is actually highly wrought and presented as useful information. Thus when we come to Duchamp's last sentence, "These different stories will be bound to one another by the 4th dim," stories here referring to the stories of a house, Cage italicizes "stories," and spells out "fourth dimension," the sentence now implying that "these different *stories* [i.e., the verbal ones to come in the mesostics] will be bound to one another by the fourth dimension." And sure enough, the cited text now gives way to eleven mesostics on the name MARCEL DUCHAMP which tell a wholly invented story about Duchamp's making of "readymobiles in unlimited editions," the first one being placed "in a teMple / just outside cAlcutta inhabited by the ghost / of sRi ramakrishna that has been / standing on one hand in eCstasy / for ovEr ninety-three years" (X, 62). Having received the Indian influx, Duchamp is now ready to meet Buckminster Fuller, who begins by "Congratulating duchamp on all / of his work past prEsent and future," and then discusses the global economy and distribution of human resources with him. By the time we come to the DUCHAMP mesostic that begins with the line "use insteaD of ownership," the ghost of Duchamp has become the unwitting spokesman for Cage's own "poethics":

> good life for all Men depends
> on reAlizing it
> foR
> eaCh
> singlE man from a to z . . .   (X, 64)

Did Marcel ever say such a thing? Not, surely, during his lifetime. But Cage has arranged the "Alphabet" so that section IX begins with three couplet-mesostics using only initials (MD, JJ, and again MD):

> duchaMp
> monDrian
>
> and Joyce go into the mind of krishna
> lao-tse Jogs
>
> early in the Morning on the great wall of china
> wilD duck.

Not Duchamp as he appears in his endlessly punning, erotic, ironic, bemused, and amused writings and readymades, but a "duchamp unto my self" turned, like Cage's Joyce, toward the abstract (Mondrian) East, to the "mind of krishna" and "Morning on the great wall of china." In this context, the words "wilD duck" bring us back to daily life on the early American frontier, to hunting and fishing stories. Not surprisingly, the next MARCEL DUCHAMP mesostic (section XIII) introduces Duchamp in a "caRpenter's outfit," clipping cards of different pictures by "utrillo, utamaro, or ucello" (the repetition of "u" suggests that national difference can be occluded) to his pockets so that he becomes a kind of walking "Museum / with no need for sPecial / proMotion / progrAms / because all the aRt it owns / Can / bE seen without going inside / or buying a ticket."

What, then, of *Etant Donnés*, which, far from being out in the streets, is "Given" (*donné*) only to those who do go "inside" the museum and "buy a ticket"? And where does Duchamp's final work fit into the Cagean discussion of "ownership" versus "use"? Despite the homage to Duchamp in the preface to the "Alphabet," the text seems to express a nagging anxiety as to the trajectory of Marcel's career. Unable to look through the peephole at the spread-eagled girl in the briar patch, Cage now invents a Duchamp who is making "another Large work" (*X*, 93):

> it will have many briDes and fewer bachelors
> it will be compUterized
> series of glass Cubes
> tHere will be movement
> of gAses lights and liquids
> froM one cube to another   (*X*, 93)

Surely this is wishful thinking: if only, Cage suggests, Duchamp hadn't taken what we might call the Dali route, creating the hyperreal diorama of *Etant Donnés*, he might have cut down on the number of "bachelors" and produced "a compUterized / series of glass Cubes"—a work, in short, more characteristic of Cage himself than of Duchamp. A "sPecial / architectural attachMent," he adds, "is being mAde to house it / so that it can go on touR." And "its basiC / homE of course / wiLl be / philaDelphia" (*X*, 93–94).

Philadelphia, the home of the peepshow *Etant Donnés*, now becomes the imaginary setting of the "Large work" which is the "compUterized / series of glass Cubes," with "movement / of gAses lights and liquids / froM one cube to another." And further:

> there will be More brides
> thAn
> bacheloRs
> eaCh
> bridE
> wiLl
>
> be four Dimensional
> and have a plUrality
> of acCelerations
> infra connections with eacH of the cubes
> i suggested one bAchelor instead of several
> the single bachelor could be the prograM itself in the form of
> a jack-in-the-box   duchamP

Only one bachelor, one jack-in-the-box named Duchamp: the new "Large work" which will replace *Etant Donnés*, at least in Cage's imagination, exchanges the spread-eagled girl for the disembodied Duchamp, who is, after all, the desired bachelor. What Marcel himself saw is thus replaced by the act of seeing Marcel.

Ironically, then, *saying* (*Not Wanting to Say Anything about Marcel*) yields to *seeing:* the discourse of the "Alphabet" itself becomes a window or, more accurately, a "Large Glass" depicting the process whereby the "indifferent" French guest enters his Utopian American host, producing a kind of elliptical ghost sonata. Enters, but not to the point of absorption: Cage always maintains a certain distance, even vis-à-vis his beloved Marcel. In his 1984 text "Mirage Verbal," a "writing-through" of a French book called *Marcel Duchamp, Notes,* edited by Alexina S. Duchamp and Paul Matisse,[20] Cage, using his title as mesostic string, begins:

poMpe
érotIque

la compRession
lA

Pomp / erotic / compression / the . . . In this cryptic sequence, "lA" gets as much time and space as "érotique," but then "A" is also detached from "l" so as to spell the vertical word "MIRAGE." Each thing, as Gertrude Stein put it, is as important as every other thing. Not a replication of Duchamp but "a duchamp unto my self."

Notes

1. John Cage, "36 Mesostics Re and not Re Duchamp," in *M, Writings '67–'72* (Middletown, CT: Wesleyan University Press, 1973), p. 34. Hereafter cited as *M*.

2. In John Cage, *X, Writings '79–'82* (Middletown, CT: Wesleyan University Press, 1990), p. 53. Hereafter cited as *X*.

3. John Cage, *Silence* (Middletown, CT: Wesleyan University Press, 1961), p. 46. Hereafter cited as *S*.

4. Richard Kostelanetz, ed., *Conversing with Cage* (New York: Limelight Press, 1988), p. 182. Hereafter cited as *CC*.

5. The similarities between Cage and Duchamp have been discussed often: see, for example, Clytus Gottwald, "John Cage und Marcel Duchamp," in *Musik Konzepte, Sonderband John Cage,* ed. Heinz-Klaus Metzger and Rainer Riehn (Munich: Johannesdruck Hans Pribil KG, 1978), pp. 132–46. Gottwald discusses Cage's adaptation of Duchamp's readymades and especially Cage's Duchampian stance on the identity of "art" and "life." For a more visually oriented discussion, see Irving Sandler, "The Duchamp-Cage Aesthetic," in *The New York School* (New York: Harper & Row, 1978), pp. 163–73.

6. Pierre Cabanne, *Dialogues with Marcel Duchamp*, trans. Ron Padgett (New York: Viking, 1971), p. 89. Hereafter cited as PC.

7. Gertrude Stein, "Next: Life and Letters of Marcel Duchamp" (1920), in *Geography and Plays* (Boston: Four Seasons Co., 1922), p. 405.

8. John Cage, *Empty Words, Writings '73–'78* (Middletown, CT: Wesleyan University Press, 1979), p. 186.

9. John Cage, *For the Birds: John Cage in Conversation with Daniel Charles* (Boston and London: Marion Boyars Press, 1981), p. 114.

10. The piece is made out of oil paint, silver leaf, lead wire, and magnifying lens on cracked glass, mounted between two panels of glass in a standing metal frame. An experiment in four-dimensional geometry and stereoscopy, this work is a study of optical illusion as it plays itself out in Duchamp's "erotic theater." See Rosalind Krauss, "Where's Poppa?" in *The Definitely Unfinished Marcel Duchamp*, ed. Thierry de Duve (Cambridge, MA, and London: MIT Press, 1992), pp. 454–55. Hereafter cited as *DU*.

11. Michel Sanouillet, "Marcel Duchamp and the French Intellectual Tradition," in *Marcel Duchamp*, ed. Anne d'Harnoncourt and Kynaston Mc Shine (New York: Museum of Modern Art and Philadelphia: Philadelphia Museum of Art, 1973), p. 48. Hereafter cited as ADH.

12. As in Duchamp's case, "normal" must of course be taken with a grain of salt, given the undercurrents of Cage's childhood. See, on this point, Thomas Hines's essay, "Then Not Yet 'Cage,'" in this volume.

13. William James, *Pragmatism* (1907), in *Writings 1902–1910*, ed. Bruce Kuklick (New York: Library of America, 1987), pp. 506, 510. Hereafter cited as WJ.

14. John Cage, *A Year from Monday* (Middletown, CT: Wesleyan University Press, 1967), pp. 70–72. Hereafter cited as *YM*.

15. Peter Bürger, *Theory of the Avant-Garde* (1974), trans. Michael Shaw (Minneapolis: University of Minnesota Press, 1984), p. 52.

16. Octavio Paz, "°water writes always in ° plural," in *Marcel Duchamp, Appearance Stripped Bare*, trans. Rachel Phillips and Donald Gardner (New York: Seaver Books, 1978); reprinted in ADH, 144–58, p. 145.

17. See, for example, Dalia Judovitz's "Rendezvous with Marcel Duchamp: *Given*," in Rudolph Kuenzli and Francis M. Naumann, *Marcel Duchamp: Artist of the Century* (Cambridge: MIT Press, 1989), pp. 184–202. Judovitz reads Duchamp's mise-en-scène as an elaborate simulacrum: "Duchamp's allusions to eroticism in *Given* parody its 'reality' through his anamorphic and anagrammatic 'reproductions' of Courbet. The 'sexuality' of the nude is de-

picted as it is being 'reproduced,' assembled and taken apart, realized and derealized, at the same time . . . eroticism emerges as the figure of passage, the movement of style, marking it simultaneously as a site of composition and decomposition—in other words, life and death," pp. 190–91. Cf. Eric Cameron, "Given" (*DU*, 14): "There is no possibility of contact, only a perception [of 'inaccessibility'] that belongs exclusively to the beholder." In the same collection, Craig Adcock points out that "the viewer does not have a mobile, reconstructive view of the whole figure, but is forced to view it from a fixed position, a situation Duchamp explored as early as 1918 in *To Be Looked at (from the Other Side of the Glass), with One Eye, Close To, for Almost an Hour.*" See Adcock, "Twisting Our Memory of the Past 'For the Fun of It'" (*DU*, 26–27).

18. See Dennis Young, "Introduction" (*DU*, 11).

19. In the Preface, Cage explains that he takes the combination of five ("sentient" and "nonsentient" beings) as a maximum number for each mesostic unit, a combination that gives us "twenty-six different possibilities" (e.g., from "Joyce 1," "Duchamp 1," "Satie 1," to "Joyce Duchamp Satie 2"). But the choice of dictionary words is in fact left largely open. When, after the performance of the piece at Stanford on January 30, 1992, I asked Cage how he came up with the first such word, "curtains," he explained that chance operations dictated that the first word used would begin with c. "Then why 'curtains'?" I asked. "Because that's the word I wanted to use," Cage replied.

20. John Cage, "Mirage Verbal" (1984), MS, courtesy of the author.

Inventing a Tradition:
Cage's "Composition in Retrospect"
Jann Pasler

In the opening sentence of a little-known text, "An Autobiographical Statement," first delivered as a paper in Japan in 1989, John Cage recalled once asking Arragon, the historian, how history was written, to which Arragon responded, "You have to invent it."[1] In the latter part of his life, Cage gave substantial attention to his own personal history. He made numerous efforts to acknowledge his debt to others and the family of kindred spirits with whom he identified. For example, he made no secret of the fact that he wrote his *4'33"* after seeing Robert Rauschenberg's white paintings and his *Music of Changes* after hearing Morton Feldman's graphic music, that he thought of micro-macro rhythmic structure in his music as a response to Arnold Schoenberg's structural harmony, and his mesostic texts as examples of Marshall McLuhan's "brushing information" against information (ibid., p. 66). In the Harvard lectures, *I–VI*, selections from his favorite writers, musicians, artists, and philosophers constitute an entire section of the book, attesting to an interest in tradition per se, in the conscious and explicit transmission of ideas from one generation to another.

The question which interests me, however, is not which tradition, European or American, helps us to understand Cage better. That answer is surely the interplay of both, including Asian religions and philosophy. Rather, it is Cage's relationship to the idea of tradition and how he saw himself and his work in the light of history. Cage's own tradition begins with his father, whom he describes as an inventor, and his mother, who taught him "a sense of society" (ibid., p. 59). To what extent, then, does the composer identify the notion of tradition with that of invention and social responsibility?

Studying his 1981 mesostic text, "Composition in Retrospect," among other recent works, has led me to thinking of Cage as consciously working to invent a tradition that reflected the way he made, discovered, invented music, that is, a tradition based on the same principles and methods he used in his music. The opening of the IMITATION mesostic in this text states as much:

> the past must be Invented
> the future Must be
> revIsed
> doing boTh
> mAkes
> whaT
> the present Is
> discOvery
> Never stops[2]

Cage does not invent without borrowing from various sources, of course, but, unlike many others, he does so without the intention of elaborating on, extending, or surpassing the traditions to which he makes explicit reference in his works.

How does one produce, or invent a tradition? In his introduction to a volume of essays on the subject, Eric Hobsbawm defines an invented tradition as

> a set of practices, normally governed by overtly or tacitly accepted rules and of a ritual or symbolic nature, which seek to inculcate certain values and norms of behavior by repetition, which automatically implies continuity with the past. In fact, where possible, they normally attempt to establish continuity with a suitable historic past . . . In short, they are responses to novel situations which take the form of reference to old situations, or which establish their own part by quasi-obligatory repetition.[3]

For each of the elements of this definition of an invented tradition, that is, as having practices or rules often with a ritual or symbolic nature, as inculcating certain values, and as repeating suitable elements from the past, it is possible to find something similar in "Composition in Retrospect." In this conscious backward glance over his years of music-making, John Cage outlines the set of practices and rules he followed, many of which have a ritual nature; in most cases, he references the inspiring contemporaries and predecessors who, through their example, helped him come to understand them; and he promotes a message, eventually speaking entirely in the imperative voice in the final section and concluding: "we musT do the impossible / rid the world of nAtions / briNging / the play of intelligent anarcHy / into a world Environment / that workS so well everyone lives as he needs."[4]

The process of inventing a tradition begins with Cage contemplating his own personal history, and distrusting his memory:

My

mEmory

of whaT

Happened

is nOt

what happeneD

i aM struck

by thE

facT

tHat what happened

is mOre conventional

than what i remembereD

iMitations

invErsions

reTrograde forms

motives tHat are varied

Or

not varieD

once Music

bEgins

iT remains

He said the same

even variatiOn is repetition

some things changeD others not (schoenberg)   (*X,* 124)

Cage seems to suggest that conventions are inevitably present in whatever one does, including music. Any method, especially that which begins with an exploration of memory, must begin with an awareness of them. As an example, he credits Schoenberg for teaching him the preeminence of repetition in music (perhaps as in life). This passage establishes the exploratory and didactic tone of the rest of the work, as well as the practice of citing suitable precedents for the ideas he wishes to promote. "Once Music / bEgins / iT remains / He said the same."

In the next mesostic, METHOD, he states the focus of his inquiry, the reason for retracing his own past.

what i aM

rEmembering

incorrecTly to be sure

is wHatever

deviated frOm

orDinary practice   (*X,* 124)

It is not so much the conventions encoded in memory that interest him, "iMitations / invErsions / reTrograde forms," forms and syntaxes that experienced listeners would recognize, it is the conventions of ordinary practice,[5] those that govern his compositional process.

Cage's ordinary practice begins with a method and proceeds, as does his text, to the other aspects of his compositional process. As within the METHOD section, Cage uses explicit references to ideas or actions of others to illustrate what he means by structure, intention, discipline, indeterminacy, interpenetration, imitation, and devotion in the mesostics that follow. This presentation, explanation, and citation of examples for each compositional element is characteristic of the invention of traditions, a process which Hobsbawm describes as one of formalization, ritualization, and reference to the past.

In the STRUCTURE mesostic, Cage cites the example of Satie, like him a composer fascinated by numbers, symmetry, and proportion, in other words, with what Cage calls structure,

the diviSion of a whole

inTo

paRts

dUration

not frequenCy

Taken

as the aspect of soUnd

bRinging about

a distinction bEtween

both phraSes

and large secTions

. . . .

Thus

a Canvas

of Time is provided hospitable to both noise

and mUsical tones . . .   (*X*, 126)

In the introduction to "James Joyce, Marcel Duchamp, Erik Satie: An Alphabet,"[6] Cage states that he analyzed Satie's music and found it "structured rhythmically." But it is not at all clear that Satie "divided fouR / foUrs into one two and one (four eight and four)" exactly as Cage asserts. The point is not what Satie did, but how Cage uses the Satie example to help him define structure in these terms.

In the INTENTION mesostic as in the DISCIPLINE one, Cage cites a variety of exercises taught him by others. The first is a Zen exercise he uses to illustrate what he means by intention, "purposeful purposelessness . . . sometImes / written Out / determiNate,"

sometImes

just a suggestioN

i found iT

workEd

therefor i Nap
pounding The
rIce
withOut
liftiNg my hand   (*X*, 128)

The DISCIPLINE section consists not of metaphorical exercises such as this one, but of practical techniques any one of which should help

to sober and quiet the minD
so that It
iS
in aCcord
wIth
what haPpens
the worLd
around It
opeN
rathEr than

closeD   (*X*, 129)

This section is three times as long as the others, giving him the space to describe three exercises "of a ritual or symbolic nature," each of which leads to a similar result. The first is another Zen exercise, "sitting crosslegged." Although Cage admits he never did this,[7] he learned from Suzuki that the attitude underlying such a practice could help him achieve his purpose of getting away "from lIkes / aNd / dislikEs."

The second exercise is a counterpoint problem Schoenberg once presented to him. In failing to solve it, Cage was forced to begin to develop his own philosophy:

Devote myself
to askIng
queStions
Chance
determIned
answers'll oPen

> my mind to worLd around
>   at the same tIme
>   chaNging my music
>   sElf-alteration not self-expression   (X, 132)

Through discipline, Cage suggests, one can become open and prepare for change.

In the third part of the DISCIPLINE mesostic, Cage remembers an exercise the painter Mark Tobey once gave his drawing students. This suggests how altering a context through some disciplined activity can alter one's perceptions.

> stuDents
> were In
> poSitions
> that disConnected
> mInd and hand
> the drawings were suddenly contemPorary
> no Longer
> fIxed
> iN
> tastE   (X, 134)

As with crosslegged sitting and using chance techniques, this change of position helped put the students "out of touch" with themselves "dIscovery / suddeN / opEning / of Doors."

Observing Cage build his tradition with what he learned from others, we find certain attitudes. First, his borrowing is conscious, as it has been for many modernists. As different as they were in other regards, both Schoenberg and Stravinsky borrowed extensively from their teachers, friends, and predecessors. Some musicologists think of "the mainstream of musical modernism" as a preoccupation with the past.[8]

Second, Cage claims that "of the critical incidents, persons, and events that have influenced my life and work, the true answer is all of the incidents were critical, all of the people influenced me, everything that happened and that is still happening influences me."[9] The inclusion of newspaper citations in the source material of *I–VI* might reflect his desire to substantiate this position. But when it comes to citing the actual people who influenced him, Cage takes another position in "Composition in Retrospect." Here he restricts himself largely to those who have stood the test of time, "great" people if you will. He says his memory cannot be trusted, but, except for two performers, there is a noticeable lack of reference to lesser-known or unknown people. Why, for example, is Gira Sarabhai, an Indian singer and tabla player, not acknowledged as the source of the line that opens the DISCIPLINE mesostic? In his "Autobiographical Statement," Cage says he learned from her that "the purpose of music is to sober and quiet the mind, thus making it susceptible to divine influences." It is not that Cage wishes to use the phrase to promote a slightly different message, for the lines that follow, being "in aCcord / wIth / what haPpens," imply a kind of spirituality, whether this opens one to divine influences or to "whatever happens next." Does Cage think the reference would be lost on most readers, and that he does acknowledge the source, after all, in his autobiographical statement? I am not questioning Cage's judgement, for "Composition in Retrospect" is an art work; I am merely observing that, with the exception of the two performers, no one who is not already well-known appears in this text.[10] Like Stravinsky's *Petrushka,* which contains traces of anonymous folk melodies and a popular tune the composer once heard someone singing in the street, Cage's work may bear the imprint of numerous sources other than those whom he cites, but their names will not be part of the tradition he is constructing.

Cage's attitude toward those who have influenced him and his way of appropriating ideas from them, however, distinguish him from many other modernist composers. He is not a Boulez, who, in works such as *Le Visage Nuptial,* borrows phrases, formal ideas, and rhythmic gestures from Stravinsky and Messiaen to impose his own will on their accomplishments, or, in Harold Bloom's words, "to clear imaginative space" for himself.[11] Even though Schoenberg, in Cage's words, "haD always seemed to me / superIor / to other human beingS," he does not repeat what Schoenberg taught him in order to reinterpret him. He does not reiterate Schoenberg's notion of variation as repetition to try to assert his own version of the same, and thus his own priority, power and strength. Cage's sense of history does not require clearing the way, surpassing what has come before in order to acknowledge that the world has progressed, that one exists.

Cage admittedly worships some of his sources. Whether those whom he cites were or were not, are or are not heroic in any way, he wants them to be considered examples, sources of wisdom, meriting the highest respect. His reference is almost always to the third-person singular and his tone never critical in "Composition in Retrospect." What seems important to Cage is that their ideas, with which he feels great affinity, inspire respect in his listeners and readers, the same respect and admiration they may have inspired in him.

There is at least some "creative misreading" of the sources to be sure, in that Cage consistently emphasizes the importance of certain traits and ideas in his sources rather than others. Other aspects of Schoenberg and Satie, for example, would suggest a very different portrait, as would referencing Mozart or Schubert instead of Schoenberg when referring to the "micro-macrocosmic rhythmic structure" of some music. Leonard Meyer's rhythmic analyses,[12] for example, suggest that the idea of "the large parts of a composition [having] the same proportion as the phrases of a single unit"[13] is hardly a Schoenbergian idea. But this matters little as Cage is seeking not the assertion ot power, but, in Hobsbawm's terms, a "suitable past" from which to invent a tradition of which he is the logical heir, the next voice. A Cagean "past must be invented."

Cage's manner of inventing a tradition involves not so much extending others' ideas as re-presenting them, bringing them again to life in part because they have become and represent aspects of Cage himself. In the introduction to "An Alphabet," Cage explains the concept behind incorporating long excerpts from the writings of Satie, Duchamp, and Joyce: "It is possible to imagine not a vocabulary but an alphabet by means of which we spell our lives." And even though he claims he did not follow this idea in this text, he later admits, "The effect for me of Duchamp's work was to so change my way of seeing that I became in my way a duchamp unto my self. I could find as he did for himself the space and time of my own experience."[14]

In "Composition in Retrospect," the first time Cage uses the first person singular "I" to refer to anyone other than himself is when he cites Schoenberg and Thoreau in the middle of the DISCIPLINE mesostic.

> after eight or nine solutions i saiD
> > not quIte
> > > Sure of myself there aren't any more
> > that's Correct

> now I want you
> to Put in words
> the principLe
> that underlIes
> all of the solutioNs
> hE   (X, 131)

In an interlocking manner, this text alternates between "i" and "he," "i" and "you," "he" and "me," "I" and again "he." At the same time the referent of the "i" goes back and forth between Cage and Schoenberg, student and teacher, until Cage takes over the role of his teacher and, "perhaps now / thirty years Later," answers his own question, "as a comPoser / i shouLd / gIve up / makiNg choicEs. . . ."

The second use of "i" to refer to someone other than himself comes in the mesostic which follows:

> thoreau saiD the same
> thIng
> over a hundred yearS ago
> i want my writing to be as Clear
> as water I can see through
> so that what I exPerienced
> is toLd
> wIthout
> my beiNg in any way
> in thE way   (X, 133)

Here the sympathy Cage feels toward a predecessor turns into an identity. When he might like to have said something similar, Cage takes on Thoreau's voice as if it were his own. The passage of time—"over a hundred yearS"—is thus irrelevant. Even though he has known personally many of the other sources mentioned in this text, Cage merges his own voice explicitly only with that of Thoreau.

Each of these citations serves not just to re-present and illustrate certain ideas dear to Cage, but other purposes as well. Hobsbawm argues that "all invented traditions, as far as possible, use history as a legitimator of action and cement of group cohesion."[15] Cage too uses his sources to claim authority, to legitimate his concerns.

But perhaps he also uses them to get people to pay attention to concepts whose importance he may feel equals if not surpasses that of his own. The multiple-voiced text itself exemplifies a political concept that lies at the heart of Cage's work. If he is here preaching a world where everyone should be able to find and make use of what he or she needs, perhaps this text can be read as an example of that principle in his life. But I am getting ahead of myself.

In the sections which follow the DISCIPLINE mesostics, Cage continues to refer to and cite sources to illustrate his ideas. Increasingly, however, as his message merges with theirs (and theirs with his), the first person plural "we" appears and the message becomes both more pointed and more personal. Cage uses "we" briefly in reference to himself and the other students in Schoenberg's counterpoint class, but it is in the opening of the INDETERMINACY section where he uses it repeatedly and for a specific effect.

> you can't be serIous she said
> we were driNking
> a recorD
> was bEing played
> noT
> in thE place
> wheRe we were
> but in another rooM
> I had
> fouNd it interesting
> And had asked
> what musiC it was
> not to supplY   (X, 138)

To explain what he means by indeterminacy, Cage makes reference to his own personal experiences and appeals to his readers' as well. From these experiences, he then rapidly begins to extract a number of insights. Using the inclusive "we," he tries to get us to accept them as facts:

> musIc
> Never stops it is we who turn away

again the worlD around
silEnce
sounds are only bubbles on iTs
surfacE
they buRst to disappear (thoreau)
when we Make
musIc
we merely make somethiNg
thAt
Can
more naturallY be heard than seen or touched

that makes It possible
to pay atteNtion
to Daily work or play
as bEing
noT
what wE think it is
but ouR goal
all that's needed is a fraMe
a change of mental attItude
amplificatioN
wAiting for a bus
we're present at a Concert
suddenlY we stand on a work of art the pavement   (*X*, 140)

Cage may nod to Thoreau in passing, but for the most part he concentrates here on expressing his own insight. After telling us what is wrong with what we may think, he tries to give us a new "frame," that which he has discovered from his own experience. He hopes this "change of mental attitude" will affect us as it did him one day while "waiting for a bus." The unspoken reference is to the early 1940s when, as he was standing on 57th Street and thinking about the Mark Tobey paintings he'd just been looking at, he noticed "he had the same pleasure looking at the pavement."[16]

By drawing the analogy, Cage suggests we might be able to have a similar experience with music.

With this new "frame" in place and the increasingly prevalent use of "we," Cage begins to define "ouR goal" more and more precisely. "We," the readers/listeners, are supposed to join in the invention of the tradition by adopting the beliefs or doctrines that Cage begins to put forth. In the INTERPENETRATION mesostic, which his own work, *Musicircus,* illustrates, Cage gives his first dictum, again in the voice of another, Marcel Duchamp: "the resPonsibility / of Each / persoN **is** / marcEl duchamp said / To complete / the woRk himself" (*X,* 142). Cage makes some suggestions for how to help people accomplish this goal, both musically and politically, sometimes referring to ideas of Buckminster Fuller. But the most important point is in the recurring lines which end the section, "we need tO / chaNge."

To justify change, the "new frame" he proposes for us, and his invention of a tradition, Cage invokes the notion of "devotion." This idea describes the life of the pianist Grete Sultan for whom he wrote "thE first of thirty-two études." Her devotion is an attitude, an acceptance, something which is not limited to the music of any one style or period. Grete "is Not as i am / just concerneD / with nEw music / she loVes the past," "she surrounDs / hErself / with mozart beethoVen bach / all Of / The best of the past." But, unlike many others, she also "loves new music / seeing nO real difference / beTween / some of It / and the classics she's sO devoted to" (*X,* 147–48). Her devotion to both old and new music thus throws into question the preeminence of old traditions. If someone can love both, then why, Cage seems to ask, should people be so reluctant to change, to accept the new. Given that this idea appears as one of the elements of the compositional process and near the end of this text, it is as if Cage believes that devotion is needed to complete a work.

In the final section on CIRCUMSTANCES, Cage becomes the authority for deciding what should change. In Hobsbawm's terms, he here tries to "inculcate values and behavior," but not as he previously does by referring explicitly to someone else (although, as I wrote earlier, the final section does bear the influence of Zen and Fuller). This section consists of a series of commands concerning not only music—how to finish a composition—but also society and how to live in it. First, he addresses us in the imperative voice, "aCt / In / accoRd / with obstaCles . . . if you doN't have enough time / to aCcomplish / what you havE in mind / conSider the work finished . . . study beIng / inteRrupted / take telephone Calls / as Unexpected pleasures / free the Mind / from itS desire / To / concentrAte . . . if you're writing a pieCe . . . take the aMount of the money . . . and divide iT to determine / the number of pAges." Then he tells us explicitly what we *must* do: "aCceptance of whatever / mUst / be coMplemented / by the refuSal / of everyThing / thAt's / iNtolerable . . . we musT do the impossible / rid the world of nAtions . . . [so] everyone lives as he needs" (*X*, 149–151).

The last line is an implicit reference to the last sentence of "An Alphabet" wherein Duchamp expresses his feelings about having undergone a change, that is, becoming a ghost (or, one might say, a spirit). He has no regrets: "i weLcome whatever happens next" (*X*, 101). Cage here seems to suggest that if we change as he proposes, we, like Duchamp, will not regret it either. This last line also refers back to the opening mesostic of "Composition in Retrospect" wherein Cage was expressing a concern for specific elements of the past, "what happened." Here, however, the focus is on the present tense and on openness toward the future, "whatever happens next."

• • •

The tradition Cage thus invents, with its sources in both the West and East, is full of irony. He demands change—a quintessentially Western preoccupation. But unlike many of his western European contemporaries, he does not feel the pressure to change as a desire to differentiate himself from his predecessors. He does not need difference to secure his own identity. What he wishes to transmit to the next generation is what he shares with others. In some ways, his philosophy is more Eastern than Western in that he advocates accepting the past as integral to the present, instead of something to surpass; in other ways, it is neither, but accepts the coexistence and interpenetration in time and place of many traditions.

This is an attitude toward tradition that resembles what Emerson advocated in "The American Scholar."[17] In this essay, Emerson refers artists to "the mind of the Past," especially as expressed in books, as the best kind of influence. "Instead of being its own seer," Emerson wrote, "let it receive from another mind its truth." Cage too turns to the spirit of his predecessors as sources of truth. His work is full of citations, as we have seen, ranging from Emerson and Thoreau to Buckminster Fuller and Marshall McLuhan. Perhaps it is fair to suggest that Cage's interest in keeping his chosen predecessors' spirits alive may be linked to his desire, during the last years of his life, for his own spirit to live on and in a similar manner—through his readers/listeners.

Like Emerson, Cage believes the artist has a duty "to cheer, to raise, and to guide men." This comes from living as opposed to just thinking, "livingry" as opposed to "killingry" when Cage uses Fuller to turn the tone political. By assimilating, in Emerson's words, "all the ability of the time, all the contributions of the past, all the hopes of the future," such an artist can be "the world's eye" and "the world's heart."

Given the importance of Emerson for Cage[18] and what he claims he learned from his mother and father, it is no surprise that two attitudes emerge as characteristic of the Cagean tradition—social responsibility and an inventive spirit, inspired by others. His mesostic texts present one emanation of these ideas. In the INTENTION mesostic of "Composition in Retrospect," Cage writes of "togetherness" and of wanting to be "a member Of society / able to fulfill a commissioN / to satIsfy / a particular Need." Writing "globally" in these texts, "letting the words come from here and there through chance operations in a source text,"[19] Cage gives poetic form to "the sense of society" his mother inspired in him, to his understanding of the "global village" and "spaceship earth."

In his recent mesostic, "Overpopulation and Art," written for the Stanford Humanities Center festival (January 1992), Cage continues this tradition. Here we find the spirit of his inventive father who "was able to find solutions for problems of various kinds" and told him, "if someone says 'can't' that shows you what to do" (ibid., p. 59). Likewise there is Buckminster Fuller, very much like his father,[20] who "is deAd / but his spirit is Now more than ever . . . Alive . . . let us nOt forget / we are now haVing to / continuE / his woRk." As his predecessors might have done, Cage puts forth a series of radical ideas for transforming contemporary life—"24 hour usE of facilities," "stOpping / the removal of fossil fuEls / fRom the earth," "the remoVal / of nations thE / Removal of schools . . . Putting / the prOcess of learning / in the hands of the Person who is doing it," "stop asking / how can i make a liVing and start asking what is it / that i lovE." Whether impractical or not, these suggestions betray hope in "the future's future" and an attempt to find "changing solutions to changing problems" in the world through the spirit of invention.

Cage's music too reflects this inventive spirit and social responsibility. In his

"Autobiographical Statement," he cites Oskar Fischinger, "Everything in the world has its own spirit which can be released by setting it into vibration." The importance Cage gives to this statement suggests that when he speaks of his music as vibrations,[21] he is perhaps referring to music's capacity to engender spirit.

Throughout "Composition in Retrospect," Cage is careful to distinguish music from the compositional process. Music, he explains, is not a method nor a set of procedures, a certain structure, temporal archetype, or approach to structure. It "is there befOre / it is writteN / . . . / compositioN / is Only making / iT / cleAr / That that / Is the case / finding Out / a simple relatioN / . . . / betweeN paper and music" (X, 136). What is important, he continues, is "hOw / To / reAd / iT / Independently / Of / oNe's thoughts," how to use it for "finding Out / oNe's thoughts," for changing one's "mental attitude." It requires a certain frame of mind, quiet, open, and accepting. Perhaps the word that most clearly describes music is "accord." This recurring word in "Composition in Retrospect" suggests a connection, a relationship, a being in accord with others, with what is, with what happens.[22]

As Cage's spirit became increasingly political, so did his works. Consider the explanations he gave for some of his later works: the *Etudes Australes* and the *Freeman Etudes* are "as difficult as possible so that a performance would show that the impossible is not impossible"; orchestral works such as *Etcetera* provide opportunities for trying out "different relations of people to people"; in *Atlas Eclipticalis* and Concerto for Piano and Orchestra, the conductor is "not a governing agent but a utility, providing the time."[23]

In *I–VI*, which takes "Composition in Retrospect" as one of its sources,[24] Cage explains what he means by such statements: "the performance of a piece of music can be a metaphor of society of how we want society to be [breathe] though we are not now living in a society we consider good we could make a piece of music in which we would be willing to live."[25] The one work he discusses in "Composition in Retrospect," *Musicircus*, exemplifies this concept as well as what he means by "interpenetration." In this work, Cage asks for no stage, no hierarchical relationship between audience and performers, no fees for performers nor ticket charges, and especially "maNy / Things going on / at thE same time / a theatRe of differences together / not a single Plan / just a spacE of time / aNd / as many pEople as are willing / performing in The same place" (X, 141).[26]

Cage's music thus offers models of how "to build a society one by one,"[27] how to live without a conductor/president, how to be courageous, face up to difficulty, and be together while "everyone lives as he [or she] needs." His music reflects a recognition of our "need tO / chaNge," to find a new way of being, to become a "society / at oNe with itself," in "accord." With these concerns in mind, Cage invents a musical tradition that will help us know how to change, because we have heard it.

Cage once said he writes "to hear the music [he] hasn't yet heard." Or in recent works like *Two²* and *One⁶*, he looks for "something [he] hasn't yet found" (ibid.). Practicing creativity and preaching anarchy, he spent his life imagining, searching and discovering, seeking "changing solutions to changing problems." Continuing this tradition is now up to us.

Notes

1. John Cage, "An Autobiographical Statement," *Southwest Review* 76 (Winter 1990): 59–76. This text, which Cage considered a "work in progress," was delivered first in Japan in November 1989 as a response to his having received the Kyoto Prize and later at Southern Methodist University on April 17, 1990, as part of a year-long celebration of the work of Robert Rauschenberg. I am grateful to Marjorie Perloff for bringing it to my attention.

2. John Cage, "Composition in Retrospect," in *X, Writings '79–'82* (Middletown, CT: Wesleyan University Press, 1983), p. 145. Hereafter cited as *X*.

3. Eric Hobsbawm, "Introduction" to Eric Hobsbawm and Terence Ranger, *The Invention of Tradition* (Cambridge: Cambridge University Press, 1983), pp. 1, 2, 4.

4. Cage, "Composition in Retrospect," in *X*, p. 151. Earlier in this text and elsewhere, Cage credits Buckminster Fuller for aspects of this idea. See also "John Cage: Conversation with Joan Retallack," *Aerial* 6–7 (1991): 97–98.

5. Note, this is also Hobsbawm's word.

6. John Cage, "James Joyce, Marcel Duchamp, Eric Satie: An Alphabet," in *X*.

7. Cage, "Autobiographical Statement," p. 64.

8. Joseph Straus, *Remaking the Past* (Cambridge, MA: Harvard University Press, 1990), p. 2.

9. Cage, "Autobiographical Statement," p. 59.

10. It is interesting that in his "Autobiographical Statement," Cage also tends to choose well-known people to cite or exemplify a point. In discussing his *Freeman Etudes,* for example,

he refers to a 1988 performance by the leader of the Arditti Quartet, Irvine Arditti, rather than to those of other violinists, perhaps less well-known to the general public, who may have played the same pieces for years and even recorded them (for example, János Négyesy collaborated with the composer on numerous occasions and recorded the first set of *Freeman Etudes* in 1985).

11. For an analysis of Boulez's music from this perspective, see my "Postmodernism, Narrativity, and the Art of Memory," *Contemporary Music Review* 7, no. 2 (1993): 3–32.

12. See Leonard Meyer, "The Rhythmic Structure of Music" and his analysis of Mozart's music in *Explaining Music* (Berkeley: University of California Press), chap. 2.

13. Cage, "Autobiographical Statement," p. 61.

14. Cage, "An Alphabet," in *X*, p. 53.

15. Hobsbawm, "Introduction" in *Invention of Tradition*, p. 12.

16. In the interview with Joan Retallack (see n. 4 above), Cage explains the incident that leads him to link the "pavement" with discussions about art. See pp. 107–8.

17. These shared attitudes also include an interest in nature. To the "Man thinking" or artist, Emerson in "The American Scholar" recommends the study of nature. When Cage came to reject music's purpose as communication, he turned to similar ideas in the works of the Indian scholar, Ananda Coomaraswammy, from whom he learned, "the responsibility of the artist is to imitate nature in her manner of operation." See Cage, "Autobiographical Statement," p. 62.

18. In the introduction to his Harvard lectures, *I–VI* (Cambridge and London: Harvard University Press, 1990), p. 3, Cage protests he had little use for Emerson; however, it is obvious that Thoreau, whom Cage so admired, was greatly influenced by Emerson. Given this and the points of similarity here argued, it is clear we should take Emerson more seriously in examining the sources of Cage's ideas.

19. Cage, "Autobiographical Statement," p. 67.

20. Ibid., p. 65. When Cage first met Fuller at Black Mountain College, he said Fuller made him think of his father when he said, "I only learn from my mistakes."

21. At the end of his "Autobiographical Statement," p. 75, Cage writes, "We are living in a period in which many people have changed their minds about what the use of music is or could be for them. Something that doesn't speak or talk like a human being, that doesn't know its definition in the dictionary or its theory in the schools, that expresses itself simply by the fact of its vibrations. People paying attention to vibratory activity, not in relation to a fixed

ideal performance, but each time attentively to how it happens to be this time, not necessarily two times the same. A music that transports the listener to the moment where he is."

22. I discuss this further in my paper, "'Music Is Not Music Until': A Musicologist's Perspective," presented to the national meeting of the Modern Language Association, San Francisco, December 29, 1992.

23. Cage, "Autobiographical Statement," pp. 68, 75.

24. Excerpts from "Composition in Retrospect" begin each of the source sections in I–VI except those sections which were not a part of the 1981 text, for which Cage in 1988 wrote new entries resembling those of "Composition in Retrospect."

25. Cage, I–VI, pp. 177–78.

26. See Charles Junkerman's description of the Stanford performance of Musicircus, "'nEw / foRms of living together': The Model of the Musicircus," in this volume.

27. Cage, "Autobiographical Statement," p. 75.

Regulated Anarchy: The *Europeras* and the Aesthetics of Opera

Herbert Lindenberger

Anybody glancing through the reviews of Cage's *Europeras 1 & 2*, first performed by the Frankfurt Opera in December 1987, will note the frequency with which the term "parody" is employed to categorize the composer's intentions. As a Swiss newspaper put it, "The *Europeras 1 & 2* present us with a parody of opera that brings to a head and thereby exposes the pretense, the artificiality and, if you will, the falseness governing this genre," and, after describing examples of the dramatic musical actions taking place onstage, the review concludes by asking whether this production was anything "more than an expensive joke."[1]

Certainly it is understandable that a European opera audience, and professional music reviewers in particular, would experience the *Europeras* as parody. For one thing, even in Germany, where John Cage was far better known than in his own country, the opera-going public is none-too-likely to approach his work with the openness to experience that he could expect from that quite different public which frequents avant-garde events. Moreover, as the form that today could be called "the last remaining refuge of the high style,"[2] opera easily invites self-parody. "The closer opera gets to a parody of itself," Theodor Adorno wrote in his most important (though also none too friendly) commentary on opera, "the closer it is to the principle most inherent to it."[3] Often this parodistic component appears overtly in the subjects that composers choose, for example in works such as Mozart's *Impresario* or Strauss's *Ariadne auf Naxos*, both of which expose operatic pretense by examining the process by which an opera is created or rehearsed; or, to cite a more subtle, indirect form of parody, in those arias within comic opera—for instance, Fiordiligi's "Come scoglie" in *Così fan tutte*—that imitate the text and musical form of *opera seria*.[4]

It is scarcely any wonder that traditional operagoers listening to two arias at once with singers in costumes deliberately inappropriate to each aria should view Cage's primary purpose as making cruel fun of cultural objects that have long maintained a sacred aura for them. Even Christopher Hunt, who brought the Frankfurt production of *Europeras 1 & 2* to the Pepsico summer festival in Purchase, New York, in 1988, claimed that the work "takes the whole history and scope of an art form— European opera—and shows how ridiculous it is and says goodbye to it, like putting a period at the end of the sentence."[5] In an interview with Joan Retallack in 1992, Cage confirmed that when the Frankfurt Opera commissioned the work, the company officials—though certainly not Cage himself—intended the *Europeras* to mark the death of the form.[6] Yet, as Barbara Zuber, a German musicologist, put it in evident response to those who saw Cage's work as heaping ridicule on operatic tradition, "Though a person might be justified in guessing a parody here, he has not at all understood the concept behind this opera."[7]

What is it the *Europeras* are attempting to say? Precisely how are the aesthetic principles of the traditional opera public alien to the Cagean aesthetic that has produced this extravagant theatrical romp? Is the alienness that separates these two aesthetics perhaps what endows Cage's Frankfurt creation with such force and fascination?

I start with a description of the "action" and the "contents" of the *Europeras*.[8] One should preface these remarks with the statement that there is no single *Europera*, that since Cage empowered his singers to choose favorite arias from many operas for any single production, every production featuring a new set of singers has contained a correspondingly new set of arias and accompaniments. The Frankfurt Opera production of 1987 was entitled *Europeras 1 & 2*, with *1* being essentially a first act lasting an hour and a half, and *2* a second act, with a new set of singers and arias, lasting forty-five minutes. *Europeras 3 & 4*, produced at the Zurich opera and taken to the Paris Bastille opera in 1991, used a different set of singers and consequently a different set of arias. *Europera 5*, a much-scaled down version done at Northwestern University in early 1992 and repeated the following summer in New York, employs an amplified piano and recorded operatic arias together with only two live singers. In view of the difference in scale and resources, *Europera 5* is essentially a chamber opera, while *Europeras 1 & 2,* however distorted they may strike a traditional opera audience, remain firmly within the genre we call grand opera. Every new production thus contains its own "text"—though regulated within the strict parameters Cage set up to govern the whole enterprise.

For *Europeras 1 & 2,* Cage used nineteen singers representing a variety of ranges, with ten singers in *1* and nine in *2.* Each performed a fixed number of arias, though every singer had to finish his or her assignment (even if it meant that not all arias could be completed) in no more than thirty and no less than twenty minutes. Several renditions transpired at once, and although these arias remained the same throughout the production, the differing starting and stopping points for a specific aria meant that different combinations would be heard in different performances. In my own audiotape of *Europeras 1 & 2* I can discern the Prize Song from *Die Meistersinger* juxtaposed with "Che farò senza Euridice?" from Gluck's *Orfeo* and Mephistopheles's Serenade from Gounod's *Faust* set against two arias from different acts (and by different characters) of *Le nozze di Figaro.* My tape of *Europeras 3 & 4,* which introduces a piano, an instrument not present in the earlier work, at one point includes a piano playing the final moments of *Norma* against "Dich teure Halle" from *Tannhäuser* and the Flower Song. Identifying a quite familiar aria is not always easy—partly because two or more arias are going on at once but also because the orchestral accompaniments have nothing to do with the arias being sung.

Although these accompaniments were drawn largely from the list of operas whose arias the singers were presenting, only fragments of accompaniments (and these are in no way tied to the arias as they are being sung), all chosen by means of chance operations, were actually performed. No conductor was in charge (a matter that apparently dismayed Gary Bertini, the director of the Frankfurt Opera who had thought he would be conducting the opera he had commissioned from Cage), but all players remained on their own watching a digital clock to be sure they keep within the time-brackets assigned to each fragment. Cage here employed the same method he used in *Music for . . . ,* a work of the same period in which each player operates independently by simply minding the clock. The *Europeras 1 & 2* orchestra, consisting of twenty-four musicians with only five string players, sounds overwhelmingly brassy and percussive. The fragments assigned to a particular instrument have no necessary relation to the instrument assigned that part in the original score. Only

occasionally does one recognize an accompaniment, and as often as not it is a Wagnerian leitmotif one hears—for example, Alberich's curse against a baritone singing
the "Largo al factotum" or Wotan's sword theme set against another part of the same
Rossini aria.

Cage's use of chance operations in the *Europeras* achieved a complexity beyond
the methods he had applied since he began composing with chance operations
around 1950. For one thing, as in his other work of the 1980s, he had a computer at
his disposal to provide electronic enhancement to the *I Ching*, which he had earlier
employed, as it were, by hand. By means of an elaborate computer program devised
by his assistant Andrew Culver, Cage determined not only the parameters within
which the orchestral players were to operate, but also how to utilize such other
traditional operatic elements as stage lighting, scenic backgrounds, costumes, props,
and actions. One could speak of each of these elements as creating a regularized set
of internal relations by means of chance operations that determine matters such as
sequence and timing. Yet each element maintains its independence and refuses to
be integrated with any other.

Each of these elements, moreover, functions according to its own rationale. The
rule behind the costuming, for example, is that all periods of civilization must be
represented and that the singers must change costume from aria to aria. Yet no
necessary relation exists between what a "character" sings and what he or she wears:
Don Giovanni could be dressed as a medieval monk or Orfeo as a rake. Cage intended the costumes to remain the most conspicuous visual elements of the work,
and consequently the constantly changing stage-flats (their order and timing determined, of course, in advance by chance operations) remained in black and white.
The visual categories governing the fifty-seven images used in *Europeras 1 & 2* were
kept within strict limits—singers, composers, operatic set designs of the past, and
animals. The photographs and drawings that the flats reproduced were cropped to
sizes determined by chance operations so that only truncated versions of the original
images could be viewed.

The computer program that established the lighting likewise left no room for
human intentionality in illuminating whatever was going on in the opera, whether
audially or visually. Thus the stage could be lit up and darkened at predetermined
intervals that had nothing to do with the actions going on. Similarly the props that
the singers used and the actions they performed while delivering their arias were

determined in advance although without regard to the relation of these props or actions to the aria. Cage employed chance-determined page numbers referring to an unabridged dictionary, in which he located words that would suggest particular actions to him, and further chance operations decided the time brackets available for these actions. Note, for instance, the following direction for a series of actions:

> Singer is brought in in a zippered container bag shaped like an igloo, half-spherical. As aria is begun, bag is unzipped. Assistants, at end, zipper bag up and take it offstage. Moving blindfolded but unassisted. The letter I is revealed to be the letter Z. Assistant puts large, costume donkey or rabbit ears on singer. Singer is brought in in a gondola, barge, or other sailing boat. Artificial, oversized mynah bird, with flying ability and built-in sound equipment who caws out names of opera composers, i.e., "Verdi, Verdi," "Monteverdi," etc. Works way unassisted slowly on all fours.[9]

The regulated anarchy transpiring onstage extended to still another institutional feature of opera, namely the synopses of plots characteristically distributed to the audience. Cage prepared, not a single synopsis for *Europeras 1 & 2,* but two sets of twelve synopses, with each member of the audience receiving one or the other set. Sentences and phrases were drawn from preexisting synopses of standard operas, then scrambled by chance operations to the point that one opera could merge with another in mid-sentence. Here, for instance, is the first synopsis in one of the two sets, together with my own attempts, set off in brackets, at identifying the sources (question marks indicate my uncertainty about a particular source):

> He, unhappy at her apparent indifference to him [*La traviata*?] brings her captive [*Il trovatore*?] to the Temple of the Holy Grail [*Parsifal*]. Another man also loves her [this could be from countless operas], accusing her of witchcraft [*Un ballo in maschera*]. She expresses [?], but a lifeless automaton [*Les Contes d'Hoffmann*]—who should have reported to jail for a minor offense [*Die Fledermaus*]. Disguising himself [countless possible operas again] in exchange for her love [*Il trovatore*?], they are condemned as traitors [*Les Dialogues des Carmélites*?]. Conveniently, he flees to an inn on the Lithuanian border [*Boris Godunov*].

On the syntactic level this synopsis maintains a high degree of coherence. Indeed, in view of the fact that operagoers do not have high expectations that the plot summaries they read in their programs have much relation to the "real" world, one needs to read with some attention before one realizes that on the semantic level the synopsis makes no sense at all.

The brief illusion that syntactic coherence can hide the semantic incoherence that the audience finds in the various synopses handed out before the *Europeras* is perhaps emblematic of the blind faith that opera can count on from those who feel committed to what we today call high culture. Among the various theatrical and musical genres, opera has traditionally exercised a special cultural authority throughout Europe as well as in urban centers outside Europe. An opera, one might say, is something more than a particular artifact combining theater with music; every opera implicitly suggests the larger institutional framework within which it participates. Note, for example, the specially privileged place of the opera house within the major European cities. Not only does it occupy a special site (in some cases even physically connected to the royal palace), but the tradition of the monarch's box at the center in the houses built in earlier centuries suggests its traditional connection with state power. Opera houses often display a sumptuousness that in medieval times could be found only in palaces and cathedrals.[10] In our own, more democratic time, it sometimes seems anachronistic that the form has survived at all, indeed that in recent years it has achieved an uncommon degree of popularity. As a recent commentator put it,

> The innate conservatism of so many opera productions, the fêting of the star singer over the music, the little rituals that attend on each performance, the whole hierarchical organisation of singers and conductor, the existence of productions some twenty years old in an opera house's repertoire . . . —all these work towards the continued establishment of opera as, not the most youthful art-form, but the oldest, the most fixed, and the most serving the interests of conservatism.[11]

When John Cage was invited to stage an opera for Frankfurt he must have been keenly aware how distant the aesthetic associated with opera was from his own aesthetic—a fact not lost on the company officials who expected him to ring the medium's death knell. Through the confrontation of these two aesthetics, as it turned out, the commission afforded him an ideal opportunity to put his ideas to work in his own way. The very process of having to work with an opera company—even one, like the Frankfurt Opera, whose dramaturges, Heinz-Klaus Metzger and Rainer Riehn, were already committed to the avant-garde and to Cage in particular—

brought out all of Cage's anti-institutional fervor. In a newspaper interview a few days before the opening he spoke out openly: "At first they tell me that everything that I want simply will not work. Then I insist on it, and some of this finally gets realized. But we can't change institutions. The anarchistic view is this: Institutions can't be changed. They're wrong by nature."[12]

The anarchistic sentiments that Cage voiced here should not hide the fact that the anarchistic impulses within his own aesthetic were complemented by a strong regulatory impulse. Anybody who glances at the complex computer program set up for the lighting of *Europeras 1 & 2* will note that, despite the chance operations on which it is based, it looks every bit as elaborate and regulated as the lighting programs used in any modern opera house. Producing *Europeras 1 & 2* allowed two strong forces to collide—the seemingly unbending will within that ancient institution we call opera and the equally powerful will (hidden though it may be by the polite, good-natured demeanor that he characteristically displayed toward the world) of a figure determined to impose his own anti-intentionalist, anti-institutionalist convictions.

As institutional critique, *Europeras 1 & 2* clearly follows in the line of *4'33"* (1952), that once scandalous work in which a tuxedoed pianist walks to his instrument, lifts the cover, sits on the piano stool for the precise period indicated in the title, and then closes the piano, bows, and leaves for the wings. Both *4'33"* and Cage's Frankfurt "opera," for neither of which he "composed" a single note or chord, attempt to comment on the social context of art—not in a theoretical statement, as many a contemporary academic critic has sought to do, but within the very context upon which he is commenting. Though Cage in his earlier days generated music presumably played by tuxedoed musicians going about their business much like the supposed pianist of *4'33"*, nobody would have expected him to compose for the opera house.

Indeed, the attitude he had long displayed toward opera was indifferent and even unfriendly—though, as he told Joan Retallack in an interview, he had always retained an affection for *Don Giovanni,* which he approached by means of Kierkegaard's interpretation. Until he arrived in Frankfurt for rehearsals two months before the opening of the *Europeras,* he had rarely attended operas, and one suspects he had considerably less acquaintance with most of the works excerpted in the arias of *Europeras 1 & 2* than many of the devout opera fans clamoring for scarce tickets at the major houses or buying CDs of arias sung by the latest superstar. During those two months, however, he attended a number of performances of various operas in Frankfurt and, according to Retallack, found himself surprised and delighted at what he heard, above all the Verdi operas, and in particular the final scene of *Falstaff*: indeed, one wonders if he sensed an analogy between the musically controlled confusion of this scene and the regulated anarchy governing his own work in rehearsal at the time.

Still, despite his new-found interest in opera, Cage also expressed his hostility toward the social system he associated with the form, which he saw as out of touch with the realities of contemporary life: "Opera in the society is an ornament of the lives of the people who have. I don't feel that so much with my work [*Europeras 1 & 2*], but with more conventional operas, it's clearly an ornament that has no necessary relation to the 20th century."[13] Needless to say, Cage must also have seen the musical "content" of *Europeras 1 & 2* as thoroughly conventional.

For practical reasons arias and accompaniments from operas still under copyright in Germany were excluded from the production—with the consequence that not a single work composed during the present century was represented (the latest was *Tosca,* which had premiered in January of 1900). Not unexpectedly, the "favorite" arias presented by the various singers were thoroughly canonical, well known to opera listeners throughout the world except for those by a couple of German composers (Nicolai and Lorzing) whose canonical status is limited to their homeland. The arias selected encompassed the whole history of opera in several languages, including even a work as early as Purcell's *Dido and Aeneas,* though, quite in accord with audience taste, all but a few came from the century-long span that began with the late Mozart operas. These were precisely the arias familiar enough to make an opera audience feel comfortable to a high degree—and with the result that the incongruous orchestral and scenic contexts within which they were placed doubtless induced a correspondingly high degree of discomfort.

The conflict between John Cage's aesthetic and the aesthetic we associate with European opera of course extends far beyond such institutional matters. Throughout its four-century history as an art form, opera, despite many changes in musical and theatrical styles, has maintained an uncommon continuity in the intentions that it has defined for itself. One might cite the following intentions, each of which can be pitted against the aesthetic we have come to associate with John Cage: (1) a pretense of mimesis, often manifested in a claim that the music reflects the words (not to speak of the referents in the real world to which the words supposedly point); (2) an attempt to unify various genres into some larger totality; (3) a cultivation of dramatic progressions, whether in individual arias or in the work as a whole; (4) and, with the exception of many comic operas, a sustained effort to express passion and grandeur and to transmit these qualities to its audience. Cage's achievement in the *Europeras* may be viewed as a critical examination and undermining of each of these intentions.

Note, for instance, the rigorously antimimetic program governing the *Europeras*. Since its inception, opera had always sought to tell some story, whether from myth or history. Yet from the moment that the members of the audience at the *Europeras* sat down to read the synopses in their programs, they recognized that Cage had frustrated mimesis at every point. Once the "action" begins, characters appear in costumes that are likely to have nothing to do (unless chance operations should accidentally establish mimesis for a brief interval) with the already familiar arias they are singing, and neither the costumes nor the arias have anything plausibly to do with the actions they are performing or the props they are using. One could, in fact, speak of a four-way frustration of mimesis.

Moreover, Cage has systematically challenged the traditional operatic claim of achieving a union of words and music. It is significant that since opera's beginnings (in fact, even in the writings of the Florentine Camerata, which provided the form with a theoretical grounding even before the first operas were composed), this claim has been repeatedly asserted (often in reaction to composers who violated the principle) by such central theorist-practitioners as Monteverdi, Gluck, Wagner, and Strauss.[14] Cage had insisted that music remain independent from dance movements in his longtime role as music director of Merce Cunningham's dance company. "Rather than the dance expressing the music or the music the dance," he once said, "the two could go together independently, neither one controlling the other."[15] By the same token, one can hardly imagine his buying into the word/music ideology central to the European opera aesthetic. Yet since the *Europeras* retain their singers' favorite arias precisely as these were written, the audience is barraged throughout the evening with specimens purporting to embody this aesthetic. The incongruous contexts within which these arias appear both visually and aurally, however, serve to make one question if ever there were a "natural" fit of words and music.

Another feature central to the aesthetic governing opera is the presence within a single work of several art forms—poetry, music, scenery, dance. Wagner's notion of a *Gesamtkunstwerk* that would bring together the various arts that had once flourished harmoniously in Greek tragedy is only a late, theoretically worked out version of an idea of totality present in much operatic practice since the beginnings of the form. Anybody present at a performance of the *Europeras* would witness all the art forms available to theatrical representation (including dance, whose role in the work I have not mentioned)—but rather than functioning in tandem with one another, they are of course totally scrambled.

Just as the traditional opera aesthetic insists on bringing the various arts together in a totality, so it also privileges dramatic action. Like other theatrical styles, opera cultivates a forward-moving dramatic development, and opera composers, whether in individual arias and ensembles or in the work as a whole, have employed all the technical resources available in whatever style was at their disposal to find a means of building and sustaining dramatic tension. In the *Europeras*, just as the traditional union of words and music in the individual arias teases the audience with the possibility that the music will speak some meaning, so the dramatic climaxes toward which the arias move (and which the singers develop with considerable fervor), tease us with constantly rising expectations that, because these arias are sung simultaneously with other arias seeking similar climaxes and heard against accompaniments that refuse to accompany them, consistently refuse to be adequately met. Moreover, the powerful closure to which audiences are accustomed in opera (even *opera seria*, with its leisurely dramatic development, closed with an emphatic chorus) is wholly absent from the *Europeras*, each of which ends abruptly when the stipulated time is up.

Finally, one might note Cage's subversion of the traditional operatic goal—evident as early as the theory and practice of Monteverdi—of expressing and transmitting passion. No serious art form has dedicated itself as assiduously as opera to the grand gesture—one in which the performers conduct themselves as though moved in the most earnest and inspired way and in turn seek to affect the audience with the emotions that they claim to show. Cage characteristically displayed an acute resistance when asked to feel moved—as one notes in an anecdote about a performance of the *Messiah* he attended with a patronizing companion who asked him, "Don't you love the Hallelujah Chorus?" After he balked, she asked, "Don't you like being moved?" to which he replied, "I don't mind being moved, but I don't like to be pushed" (*CC*, 234). Certainly the individual arias of the *Europeras* make the traditional pretense of embodying passion and of infecting others with passion. Yet to listen simultaneously, say, to Orfeo's lament for his lost Euridice and to the Flower Song from *Carmen,* as one might in the *Europeras,* is to put the aesthetic of opera in question.

To the extent that the *Europeras* offer a critique of the highest-style theatrical form available within European culture, they implicitly set up an encounter between this culture as a whole and Cage's concept of some alternative mode of living. The very title of the work suggests a trans-Atlantic confrontation: "Europe's Operas," distinctly not those that *we* might be producing; or, to take this notion a step further, as Laura Kuhn suggests, "Your Operas," but certainly not *ours.*[16] This confrontation gains special relevance when one notes that it could never have taken place in a major American opera house as it did in a German one. How does one explain the paradox that Cage's distinctly un-, even anti-European experimentalism excites not only admiration but also active sponsorship in a European cultural center? The easy answer is that the economics of cultural production allow things to be done on the Continent as they cannot be done in Cage's home country: the state subsidies available in many European countries give cultural organizations there a freedom that they do not enjoy in the United States, where cultural events depend almost wholly on the financial sponsorship of local subscribers and donors who tend to impose a conservative aesthetic on the programming to which they are willing to be exposed. Yet one suspects still another motive for the fascination that John Cage has exercised for many years not only in Germany but throughout Europe and also in Japan: Cage's unbending experimentalism may well strike a more tradition-bound community as a refreshing New World barbarity that, even when it is challenging an older aesthetic, offers a promise of cultural renewal.

The Europe-America antithesis gains special resonance if we place it in relation to the role that Arnold Schoenberg came to play retrospectively for Cage. Although Cage studied with Schoenberg for only a brief period during the mid-1930s, his impact, at once positive and negative, did not become clear until years later, once Cage had constructed the phenomenon we know today as John Cage. One might interpret the name *Arnold Schoenberg* within the terms of this construction to signify "Old World master" and the name *John Cage* to mean "New World successor." Note Cage's often retold story of how Schoenberg came to accept him as a pupil despite Cage's lack of funds. "Will you devote your life to music?" Schoenberg asked him (*CC*, 4), after which Cage formally committed himself. The story belongs to what one might call the "artistic-succession" genre, in which some canonical older master passes the mantle to a potentially canonical younger one; Emerson's words, "I greet you at the beginning of a great career,"[17] in response to Whitman's sending him a copy of the first *Leaves of Grass*, stands as the classical model within the genre.

Even though Cage never knew Schoenberg well, the parallels in their careers are striking. Both broke so sharply with the musical past that they remained highly controversial figures even in their old age. Both also distinguished themselves as visual artists—Schoenberg as painter and Cage as printmaker—and both have shown themselves to be masters of the written word independent of their musical attainments.[18] Yet Cage's recountings of his relationship with his master reveal some crucial tensions. Though Cage clearly revered him ("I worshipped him like a god," *CC*, 5), Schoenberg also represented an obstacle needing to be overcome, and this obstacle became defined for Cage in geographical terms. One notes the conflict particularly in a review that Cage wrote in 1965 of a volume of Schoenberg's letters. Calling the review "Mosaic," Cage wove Schoenberg's own words into his narrative by using italics to quote his former teacher, as in this passage: "He was a self-made aristocrat. *I wonder what you'd say to the world in which I nearly die of disgust.* Becoming an American citizen didn't remove his *distaste for democracy and that sort of thing.* Of former times when a prince stood as a protector before an artist, he writes: *The fairest, alas bygone, days of art.*"[19]

Note the glaring contrasts in this "mosaic" that Cage has pieced together: the Old World "aristocrat" who looks back nostalgically to some "prince-protector" to sponsor his "art" has been relegated to a New World "democracy" that excites his "disgust." Cage deliberately defines his contrast of old and new worlds with recognizable clichés—both those from Schoenberg's own mouth and those that Cage, as representative of the New World, reads into his former master.

Compared with the *Europeras*, Schoenberg's major attempt at opera, *Moses und Aron*, seems to look back at least as much to the "bygone days" for which he longs in the quotation above as it does to the future. Despite its obvious iconoclasm—its composition out of a single tone row and its use of *Sprechstimme* instead of song for its hero—*Moses und Aron* strikes us today as a rigidly determined score whose dramaturgy does not move substantially beyond the mode established long before in

Wagnerian music drama.[20] Regulation without the mitigating Cagean anarchy, one might say. When juxtaposed with Schoenberg's opera, the *Europeras,* despite deriving all their sounds from the European operatic canon, look and sound as though out of another world altogether. "Even though the subject is European, the conventions are Oriental" (*CC,* 132), Cage said while planning *Europeras 1 & 2.* Whether or not one can properly call these conventions "oriental," Cage discovered a means of defamiliarizing his European subject to the point that the work is constantly advertising its break with tradition.

Despite disrupting a centuries-old tonal method, Schoenberg, by contrast, constantly claimed to be continuing the European musical tradition. "Bach did this with these four notes," Cage remembered Schoenberg saying in the process of instruction, and "Beethoven did this, Brahms did this, Schoenberg did this!" (*CC,* 9). Whereas Schoenberg proudly names forebears going far back in time (though, significantly, not beyond German-speaking lands) Cage's ancestors belong largely to the modernist world. The title of his mesostic text, "James Joyce, Marcel Duchamp, Erik Satie: An Alphabet," advertises a genealogy that encompasses practitioners in the three major arts of the immediately preceding generation. For Cage, the only important forebears of a more distant past remained Thoreau as well as certain ancient sages—Meister Eckhart and various Oriental philosophers—who occupied a timeless realm for Cage quite in contrast to the historical succession of composers in whose direct line Schoenberg situated himself. Schoenberg is the only German and, in fact, one of the few *composers* in Cage's genealogy, which includes not only persons whom one would classify as "artists," but also charismatic figures such as D. T. Suzuki, Buckminster Fuller, and Marshall McLuhan.

Cage's need to position himself in relation to Schoenberg gains special meaning if we remember that around 1950, at the very moment that Cage took his bold leap into composing by means of chance operations, the serialism that derived from Schoenberg became the favored mode among the most advanced composers on both sides of the Atlantic. As a result, Cage's mode did not count for much in official circles, above all among music professors, for whom Schoenberg and those who claimed to be extending his method reigned supreme. It was not, in fact, until serialism had worn itself out in recent years that Cage's achievement of taking composition a significant step beyond Schoenberg has come to be acknowledged—and, with an irony I have touched on earlier, more emphatically in Germany than in Cage's own country.[21]

Perhaps the most telling moment in Cage's reminiscences of Schoenberg is not one that he witnessed directly but rather heard somebody else report: "Someone asked Schoenberg about his American pupils, whether he'd had any that were interesting, and Schoenberg's first reply was to say there were no interesting pupils, but then he smiled and said, 'There was one,' and he named me. Then he said, 'Of course he's not a composer, but he's an inventor—of genius'" (*CC*, 6). The very contrast that Schoenberg is drawing here suggests a sharp dividing line between a European and a purportedly American view of creativity: being a composer means practicing creativity in the European mode—that is, dedicating oneself to the perpetuation of some form of "high art"—while being an inventor means tinkering with new, not traditionally artistic materials and envisioning relationships with audiences outside the usual institutional channels. From a European point of view in Schoenberg's time, invention would have seemed a peculiarly American vocation—witness such famed examples as Alexander Graham Bell and Thomas Edison, as well as (in an analogy that would not have been lost on Schoenberg) the not-so-famed John Milton Cage, father of his erstwhile pupil.[22]

Viewed as an "invention" rather than as a traditional "work of art," the *Europeras* emerge as objects that those choosing to attend them can themselves observe, contemplate, and examine without the emotional commitment that opera has traditionally demanded of its consumers. The purported composer of *Europeras 1 & 2* did not "create" a single note—yet the larger conception, together with the method by which the whole thing became assembled, was very much the invention of John Cage, who officiated over the rehearsals as resolutely as most any opera composer of the past. In his role of inventor reusing materials that were already ready at hand (he had originally wanted to use costumes already in the Frankfurt Opera's inventory), Cage was continuing the work of his friend Marcel Duchamp, whose readymades provided a visual precedent for the auditory collage that constitutes the musical content of the *Europeras*.[23]

Once we view the work as something to be tinkered with—whether by its maker or its consumers—it loses whatever autonomy it had within the terms of the older aesthetic and, in effect, comes to "spill over," as it were, into the everyday world.

The continuity between the *Europeras* and this world was brought home to me recently while I was preparing to write this paper. I was driving from Stanford to San Francisco to attend a performance of Handel's opera, *Ariodante,* to be performed in a warehouse by apprentice singers from the San Francisco Opera. In the car I had been playing my tapes of *Europeras 1 & 2.* As I approached the makeshift theater, whose outer walls lacked soundproofing, I could hear two of the singers warming up with arias from the opera they were about to perform; in addition, several members of the orchestra were practicing recognizably Handelian passages. For a few moments I believed I was still immersed in the *Europeras,* for the noises I was hearing—Handel's music scrambled so that all the individual musicians were on their own—were no different in kind from those on the tape (except that all originated from the same opera). When the "real" opera began a little later, it took some effort to readjust myself to that earlier aesthetic that demanded commitment to a frame of mind totally at odds with the experience of Cage's work. This incident, let me add, served to remind me that Cage's many attempts—both in the *Europeras* and in other works—to undermine this older aesthetic did not consist simply of negative critique, but were also challenging his listeners to attend to and to attune themselves to sounds they might otherwise have dismissed as irrelevant or annoying.

The radicality with which Cage has been able to rethink the history and nature of opera is particularly evident when we compare the *Europeras* with the many iconoclastic productions of classic operas that have aroused the ire of critics and audiences during the last two decades. I think, for instance, of Patrice Chéreau's staging of *Der Ring des Nibelungen* for the Bayreuth centennial of 1976, in which Wagner's Rheinmaidens appeared as prostitutes guarding a nineteenth-century hydroelectric dam; or of Peter Sellars's readings of the Mozart/da Ponte operas, where the heroines of *Così fan tutte* become waitresses in a contemporary diner or the characters of *Le nozze di Figaro* are transformed into yuppies erotically pursuing one another in a Manhattan highrise.[24] On the surface the unexpected costuming in which these familiar operatic characters appear should seem in tune with the method employed by Cage in the *Europeras.* Yet in all these so-called postmodern stagings, the original text (usually in the original language as well) and the vocal and instrumental music remain inviolate. Only the costumes and scenery confound one's expectations; those in the audience who feel offended by the changes wrought upon some beloved work are free to shut their eyes, after which they will hear exactly the same musical sounds and words to which they have been long accustomed; Cage's audience, on the other hand, has no way of escaping his provocative aural bombardment.

Chéreau's, Sellars's, and their various colleagues' interpretations are precisely that—interpretations. However much they may try to shock the operagoing public, they also seek, in a serious and sustained manner, to make contemporary sense out of an older text. Once the spectators have accustomed themselves to what the director is attempting, the experience of the opera is not much different from that of any conventional performance. I can testify that after repeated viewings of videotapes of several such productions, the director's new interpretations come to gain the same authority that earlier, less iconoclastic stagings did.

Cage, quite in contrast, did not practice nor invite interpretation. In the *Europeras,* indeed throughout his later work, he tried to frustrate any desire by the audience to find coherence and "meaning" in the texts or noises laid before them. Indeed, those who insist on finding parody in the *Europeras* should remember that parody always implies an interpretative gesture on the part of author or audience; the method of the *Europeras* is such that, as soon as you feel tempted to make sense out of what you see and hear on the stage, the ground is pulled out from under you. Parody, I might add, also involves some form of mimesis, whether of some earlier artistic discourse or of something discernible within the real world; and mimesis, as I have indicated, is what Cage sought assiduously to avoid. This is not to say that the audience is not expected to experience comic effects from the heterogeneous materials colliding in the *Europeras.* Cage, in fact, was reported laughing a good bit as he watched the rehearsals and, in a program note for the performances of *Europeras 1 & 2* at the Pepsico festival, referred to the work as "comic . . . in the spirit of *Hellzapoppin.*"[25]

Not only do the *Europeras* question the aesthetic of opera more radically than the stagings of iconoclastic recent directors but they also challenge this aesthetic in a way different from such celebrated postmodern new operas as those of Philip Glass and John Adams. The work of both these composers uses so-called minimalist orchestral effects that pretend to have nothing to do with the dramatic action enacted on the stage and often not even with the words being sung. Yet despite these effects Adams's *Nixon in China* and Glass's *Satyagraha* affect their audiences as quite traditional attempts at historical drama—the former as a titillating parody of still-living politicians, the latter as a message-loaded plea for all the various causes that its hero, Mohandas Gandhi, stood for. (It is scarcely surprizing that both these works, unlike the *Europeras,* have made their way into major American opera houses.) Only Glass's first opera, *Einstein on the Beach,* performed in collaboration with Robert Wilson, seems to approach the Cage aesthetic. With its refusal to develop a narrative, its conspicuous separation of the music from the words and actions going on, its use of an electronic synthesizer in place of traditional instruments, *Einstein* still seems one of the more radical challenges to traditional opera mounted by an American. Yet with repeated hearings the music and the words that might have first seemed incompatible come to sound made for one another; and the political message, despite the lack of plot, is scarcely less loaded than the message that Glass was later to deliver in *Satyagraha.*[26] Although John Cage always insisted that art is socially situated, one could not imagine him delivering the sort of message one finds in Glass.

The experience of listening to tapes of the *Europeras,* I might add, is somewhat deceptive, for repeated hearings, as with repeated viewings of the Chéreau *Ring* or hearings of *Einstein on the Beach,* work to freeze the performance: even the unaccustomed sounds juxtaposed with one another in the *Europeras* come to seem wedded to one another once you have heard them enough. (Cage himself balked at listening to recorded performances.) Yet since the various singers and instrumentalists are instructed to keep to their individual time-brackets, no two actual performances could possibly produce the same "score." Writing of the many Cage compositions that allow latitude to individual performers even when performing with one another, Dieter Schnebel has claimed, "Cage's music is basically one for soloists, or one might almost say: for solipsists—one plays solo, alone, for oneself."[27] A string player who recently recorded *Music for . . . ,* which, as I mentioned earlier, employs time-brackets similar to those of the *Europeras,* has described the difficulty that a professional musician faces trying to go it alone in order to carry out the inventor Cage's "do-it-yourself" method: "You're always feeling tempted to coordinate your notes with those of the musicians around you," he reported in conversation, "and then you have to keep reminding yourself that Cage expects each instrument to be on its own." To guard his players from such temptations in this piece, Cage instructed them to stay widely apart physically—to the point of having them spill out from the stage into the auditorium.

Yet the anarchy suggested in these statements is by no means complete but remains regulated within parameters determined in advance. Explaining the way that his method in *Music for . . .* extends the possibility of individual autonomy beyond what he had done before, Cage spoke of a "togetherness of differences— not only differences in ranges, but differences in structure" (*CC*, 123–24). Though the listener, as well as the performer, is more likely to be aware of differences than "togetherness," it is significant that Cage felt the need to employ the latter term—as though to suggest that the anarchic tendencies he unleashed are subsumed under some ultimate conception of community. Speaking of Indian music at one point, he indicated several devices needed "to hold improvisation together" (*CC*, 259), and, directly after, he made a general statement that can refer to the aesthetic and the social realms at once: "I believe in *dis*organization; but I don't see that in terms of non-participation or isolation, but rather precisely as a complete participation. Those rules of order must have been put there in order, as we say, to hold things together" (*CC*, 259). The more one reads Cage's descriptions and justifications of his procedures, the more aware one becomes of how powerfully his social views—combining as they do individuality with participation, difference with togetherness—have at the same time shaped the aims and methods of his artistic production.

The regulated anarchy within which Cage's musicians operate in his later work applies as well to the activity of the audiences who attend his performances. Whereas the traditional audience (at least since the later nineteenth century) was expected to sit passively in a darkened hall and submit itself to the emotional demands of the music, Cage's audiences are encouraged—within the parameters established by the composer—to pursue a new kind of attentiveness, one that, for example, heeds the sounds "outside" the work itself as scrupulously as it does those produced by the official performers. Cage once said that "my own best piece, at least the one I like the most, is the silent piece," namely *4'33"*, and he used this example to chastise audiences: "What they thought was silence [in *4'33"*], because they didn't know how to listen, was full of accidental sounds. You could hear the wind stirring outside during the first movement [in the first performance]" (*CC*, 65). The individuals constituting a properly trained audience would free themselves from the usual institutional constraints and let their minds wander according to the various sounds (and sights) presented to them. Doubtless they will sometimes allow themselves a certain inattentiveness—somewhat like that condoned among the audiences attending traditional Japanese drama, one of Cage's models. They are not tempted with expectations of something about to come, whether a climactic moment or the closure that has customarily been necessary to inform them that their musical experience has achieved some final meaning.[28] Above all, they would not be molded into a single mass reacting collectively, and unthinkingly, to a composer's or conductor's manipulations—precisely the accustomed annual experience of the *Messiah* that Cage disappointed his companion by resisting.

Within the larger context of Cage's work these new arrangements he advocated for performers and audiences alike belong to the new genre, the *Musicircus,* that he arranged to be staged at various celebrations of his work since the 1960s and that Charles Junkerman analyzes elsewhere in this volume. The *Musicircus,* together with its 1992 variant at Stanford, what Cage named *House Full of Music,* encourages all forms of music, high and low, Western and non-Western, professional and amateur, indeed many forms of noise that might not ordinarily be called music, to be going on at once. The various spectators come and go at will and mingle easily with the performers; indeed, once a group is done performing, the members themselves turn into spectators. Cage liked to refer to the *Musicircus* not simply as a specific event at a specific time and place but as a principle—"a principle of a flexible relationship, of a flexibility of relationships"[29] as well as a "principle . . . of having of having many things going on at once" (*CC,* 84). To avoid turning into anarchy, the *Musicircus* needs an organizer or, better yet, from Cage's point of view, "several" organizers, with the result to be labeled "a practical, or practicable, anarchy"[30]— Cage would doubtless have found my own modifier *regulated* far too strong for his taste. Whether or not one calls the principles of the *Musicircus* embodiments of some peculiarly American aesthetic, they remain at a far extreme from that European aesthetic which has insisted on audience submission to one thing going on at a time. Seen from the point of view of these principles, Cage's achievement in the *Europeras* emerges as a celebration of familiar operatic sights and sounds which, liberated from their accustomed contexts, provoke our attention with constantly unexpected turns in this high-spirited, head-on collision he organized between his heterodox New World aesthetic and one of the most sanctified Old World cultural forms surviving into the present day.

Notes

1. "Ein teurer Spass—oder mehr?" *Neue Zürcher Zeitung,* December 15, 1987. Other statements claiming a parodistic intention can be found, for instance, in "Jeder für sich—und alle durcheinander!," *NRZ,* December 15, 1987, and in "Komponierte Opern-Zerstörung," *Wiesbadener Tagblatt,* December 14, 1987. All translations of quotations within this essay are my own.

2. See my book *Opera: The Extravagant Art* (Ithaca: Cornell University Press, 1984), p. 15.

3. Theodor Adorno, "Bürgerliche Oper (1959)," in *Gesammelte Schriften,* 16, ed. Rolf Tiedemann (Frankfurt: Suhrkamp, 1978), p. 24.

4. For discussions of such forms of parody, see Lindenberger, *Opera,* pp. 44–45, 80, 102–3.

5. Quoted in James R. Oestreich, "Empty Chairs in Honor of Cage," *New York Times,* August 17, 1992, p. B2. In fairness to Hunt, who is generally sympathetic to the avant-garde, I should add that he went on to describe the work as creating "such a wonderfully theatrical laugh of the mind that by upsetting all our ideas of how things ought to be, it's affectionate."

6. The interviews between Cage and Retallack, held during the month preceding his death, had not yet been transcribed from tape at the time I completed this paper. I thank Joan Retallack for her generosity in sharing with me her memories of Cage's remarks on opera.

7. Barbara Zuber, "Entrümpelung—*Europeras 1 & 2,*" in *Musik-Konzepte* (May 1990), Sonderband John Cage 2:106–7.

8. My description of Cage's procedures is drawn from the detailed appendixes of Laura Diane Kuhn's study, "John Cage's *Europeras 1 & 2:* The Musical Means of Revolution" (Ph.D. diss., University of California, Los Angeles, 1992). I am grateful to Laura Kuhn for sending me not only her dissertation but also audiotapes of *Europeras 1 & 2* and *Europeras 3 & 4.* Her dissertation is invaluable both for the information in the appendixes and for her depiction of Cage's intellectual traditions in the main body of her text. Kuhn's relation to the *Europeras* project is unique: as Cage's assistant before and during the Frankfurt production, she researched the costume designs used in the production, and as research scholar she has presented the first detailed examination of the work in whose creation she participated.

9. Quoted in Kuhn, "John Cage's *Europeras 1 & 2,*" pp. 609–10.

10. On some cultural meanings of the opera house, see Lindenberger, *Opera,* pp. 167, 236–39, 242–43, 272–73.

11. Jeremy Tambling, *Opera, Ideology, and Film* (Manchester: Manchester University Press, 1987), p. 14.

12. Quoted by Gisela Gronemeyer, "Der Zufall regiert noch immer," *Kölner Stadt-Anzeiger,* December 10, 1987. I have retranslated Gronemeyer's German translation of Cage's words in her interview with him.

13. Quoted by Leah Durner, "Past and Future in John Cage's *Europeras 1 & 2,*" *EAR Magazine* (April 1988) 13, no. 2:13. It is only fair to add that this comment was made in response to a question that Cage was asked about his attitude toward the presumed arsonist whose burning of the Frankfurt Opera House just before the premiere of *Europeras 1 & 2* had forced a month's postponement of the opening and also a change of venue to another theater. The report that the arsonist was an unemployed émigré from East Germany set off the contrast that Cage drew between the lot of the poor and that of the well-heeled audience that frequents the opera house.

14. For a longer discussion of the word-music debate in operatic history, see Lindenberger, *Opera,* pp. 108–44.

15. Richard Kostelanetz, ed., *Conversing with Cage* (New York: Limelight Press, 1988), p. 104. Hereafter cited as *CC.*

16. According to Kuhn, *your operas* might also suggest Cage's "populist leanings" ("John Cage's *Europeras 1 & 2,*" p. 2). Thus, if I may extrapolate from Kuhn's observation, Cage might have been saying, "I am giving you *your own* operas, which, now that I have scrambled the contents of traditional European opera, you will find more suitable to your needs."

17. Walt Whitman, *Leaves of Grass,* ed. Sculley Bradley and Harold W. Blodgett (New York: Norton, 1973), p. 732.

18. Although Schoenberg did not devote himself to literary endeavors to the degree that Cage has done, he wrote a fine Expressionist-style play, *Der biblische Weg,* which, because it has not been published either in German or in English (it *has,* however, appeared in Italian translation), is not known to the literary public. For a study of this play, see my article, "Arnold Schoenberg's *Der biblische Weg* and *Moses und Aron:* On the Transactions of Aesthetics and Politics," *Modern Judaism* 9 (February, 1989):55–70.

19. John Cage, *A Year from Monday,* (Middletown, CT: Wesleyan University Press, 1987), 45–46.

20. On Schoenberg as building on Wagner, see Joseph Kerman, "Wagner: Thoughts Out of Season," *Hudson Review* 13 (1960):329–49, and Adorno, "Sacrales Fragment," in *Gesammelte Schriften,* 16, pp. 466–70.

21. For a brief recent assessment of Cage's role in the development of modern music, see the essay by the distinguished historian of twentieth-century music, Hermann Danuser, "Rationalität und Zufall—John Cage und die experimentelle Musik in Europa," in *Aesthetik im Widerstreit*, ed. Wolfgang Welsch and Christine Pries (Weinheim: VCH Acta Humaniora, 1991), pp. 91–105. Danuser explains the cooling off of the relationship between Cage and Pierre Boulez as resulting from Boulez's inability to accept the radical form of experimentalism in which his senior American colleague engaged when he turned his back on rationality and authorial intentionality.

22. The significance of Schoenberg's pronouncement—whether or not he actually uttered it—was confirmed by the fact that a number of the obituaries attempting to define Cage's achievement made note of this distinction between composer and inventor (see, for example, the *New York Times* obituary, August 13, 1992, p. A17). The columnist John Rockwell, writing more than a week after the initial obituaries appeared, gave Schoenberg's remark an interesting twist by defending Cage's music (especially that of his early period) as "composition," not simply "invention." Rockwell's column bore the telling headline, "Cage Merely an Inventor? Not a Chance" (*New York Times*, August 23, 1992, p. B21).

23. Although Duchamp's example is central to Cage's development, few Cage pieces are as thoroughly suffused with Duchamp's ideas as the *Europeras*, if only because, like Duchamp before him, Cage built this work out of ready-made materials. Many of the early reviews mention the influence of Duchamp. If my argument for Cage as "New World inventor" seems undercut because of the strong influence of that Old World inventor-artist Duchamp, I would reply that, as a long-term exile from France, Duchamp had himself established a distance from the aesthetic ambiance of his European contemporaries. Note also Marjorie Perloff's demonstration in the present volume of how Cage has distanced *himself* from such characteristically "European" aspects of Duchamp as his irony and his erotic quality. On Cage and Duchamp see Daniel Charles, "Cage et Duchamp," *Gloses sur John Cage* (Paris: Union Générale Editions, 1978), pp. 183–96, and Clytus Gottwald, "John Cage und Marcel Duchamp," in *Musik-Konzepte* (April 1978), Sonderband John Cage: 132–46.

24. For a detailed discussion of these iconoclastic stagings as attempts to introduce a postmodern sensibility into the opera house, see the discussion in my essay, "From Opera to Postmodernity," in *Postmodern Genres*, ed. Marjorie Perloff (Norman: University of Oklahoma Press, 1988), pp. 41–44. See also Barbara Zuber's contrast of these stagings with Cage's quite different project in *Europeras 1 & 2* ("Entrümpelung—*Europeras 1 & 2*," p. 102).

25. For those who may not remember it, the *Hellzapoppin* to which Cage refers was a

zany Broadway musical of the early 1940s full of absurd antics that often broke through the theatrical frame.

26. For a longer discussion of Glass's early operas, see Lindenberger, "From Opera to Postmodernity," pp. 44–47.

27. Dieter Schnebel, "'Wie ich das schaffe?'—Die Verwirklichung von Cages Werk," in *Musik-Konzepte* (April 1978), Sonderband John Cage: 54.

28. Cage's German follower Dieter Schnebel has explained the composer's attempt to rid the audience of expectations in these terms: "If we find music boring, then it is only because we bring expectations to bear on it—if I listen without expectations, then I can't get bored because I am then open to every moment" (quoted in a review of *Europeras 1 & 2* in *Süddeutsche Zeitung*, December 12, 1987, p. 32).

29. John Cage, *For the Birds; John Cage in Conversation* with Daniel Charles (Boston and London: Marion Boyars Press, 1981), p. 52.

30. Ibid., pp. 52–53.

Utopian America and the Language of *Silence*

Gordana P. Crnković

Foreword

During my visit to Prague in 1985, I spent time with Vera, a native of that city who wanted to emigrate to the United States. Opposed to the communist system in her country, Vera, like many other people, privately believed that most proclamations made by the government were lies. Since communist discourse constructed "America" as the embodiment of all the evils in the world, Vera inverted this representation to derive a "good America." Needless to say, Vera's "America" was entirely unrealistic, not only because of the absence of any knowledge on her part, but also because some of the official claims, such as those regarding U.S. imperialist practices, were not entirely false. In other words, Vera's statements about the United States were not necessarily realistic or true simply because they were oppositional. Not knowing enough about the United States to assess any of the truly good or bad aspects of that place, Vera constructed her "good America" as an abstract alternative to Eastern European communisms, a utopian place to which she wanted to emigrate.

At that time Eastern European nations were structured vertically, with the omnipotent state on top, defining all aspects of society below. We imagined utopian "America" as a horizontal structure, one able to acknowledge the validity of each of the numerous, unfixed centers of the society. The bloody idealism of

Eastern Europe, serving the *idea* of communism regardless of material realities, was contrasted in our minds with the utopian notion of materialistic "America." We imagined that this materialism made it possible for ever new and unpredictable practices, processes, and selves to emerge—all free from the disabling requirement that they mime the ideas proclaimed by and disseminated from some center of power.

We did not know whether our utopian "America" had anything to do with the "real" United States. But we began to care less and less about the correspondence between our vision and the facts regarding the United States, because talking about "America" had become an experimental and playful practice of imagining utopia. It seems to me that this was a fairly common practice in communist Eastern Europe. Starting as a simple reversal of Eastern Europe, the imagining of utopian "America" became a speculative practice—the thinking of freedom.

Reading John Cage's *Silence,* I found the utopian "America" whose broad premises Vera and I had imagined. By reacting to the dictatorial structures of language, Cage creates liberating language and practices which are horizontal, materialistic, and democratic. Activating such practices, *Silence* articulates a utopian "America" vaguely assumed by more than a few speculating Eastern Europeans, and shows that this "America"—an entirely abstract, unrealistic construction—has its reality as well.

The Vertical Construction of Language and the Shaping of Ideas by Power Centers

No one can have an idea

30″

once he starts really listening.[1]

Another way of

. . . .

saying it is: "Do not be

> . . . .
>
> **satisfied with approximations**
>
> . . . .
>
> **(or just: Do not be satisfied) but insist**
>
> . . . .
>
> **(as you need not) on what comes**
>
> . . . .
>
> **to you."** . . .   (S, 257–58)

Language is "vertically constructed" whenever its terms are defined by reference to already given ideas, established meanings, and corresponding material practices. For example, a vertical definition of "music" might be something like a "concatenation of sounds structured to be performed on musical instruments or sung by the human voice." Vertical construction is a closed model in that it does not allow for redefinitions of terms and changes in practice. It is fundamentally conservative ("Ideas are not necessary. It is more useful to avoid having one, certainly avoid having several (leads to inactivity)," S, 99). Vertical construction is also a corollary of social domination insofar as its abstractly articulated ideals emanate from and are shaped by centers of power, such as the university, government, schools of all types, museums, and research institutes. Construction of language and practice in relation to these ideals is thus an aspect of social subservience.

The centers of power, rather than the community, agree upon and enforce the specific constructions of terms such as "music" and "painting." For example, "music" as it is defined by academia, recording studios, and major symphonic orchestras excludes fields of sound which are not traditionally regarded as musical. As a consequence, even innovators such as the Theremin electronics firm design their instruments to make sounds imitative of traditional musical instruments: "Thereministes act as censors . . . We are shielded from new sound experiences" (S, 4).

This "vertical" construction of language and material practice trains us "to follow in someone's footsteps" (S, 214). We attempt in our thinking, speech, and behavior to *approximate* ("the closer the better") the ideal forms disseminated by the power centers. We construct ourselves in response to and in imitation of given ideals. As derivative of these superhuman ideals, we are always inadequate in relation to them.

Cage is not interested in exploring the attraction of the establishment's vertical structures. It is important, however, to point out that the aura of these power centers comes from their self-presentation as "community" instances. Being in them (by them) means being seen and heard by many, "accepted" by many, and thus "really" (socially, politically) living. Language terms and forms of practice define themselves in relation to the centers of power. One's becoming "someone" is defined by these centers. "To be" means to become something else, "the other" of oneself, the external center. Thus, one loses all the potential ways of being which are out of the orbit of this center; all the not-yet existent "oneselves" ("there is at least the possibility of looking anywhere, not just where someone arranged you should. You are then free to deal with your freedom," S, 100).

The Closure of Self-Expression

22'00"

> What I think & what I feel can be
> my inspiration but it is then also my
> pair of blinders. To see one must go
> beyond the imagination and for that
> one must stand absolutely still as though
> 10" in the center of a leap.
>
> . . . .
>
> every me out of the way. An error is simply a
> 23'00" failure to adjust immediately from a preconception
> to an actuality. (S, 170–71)

"Self-expression," or the linguistic and material realization of subjectivity, does not oppose vertical constructions enforced by the power centers. Self-expression is itself vertical, since it constructs practice in relation to given subjectivity. (Also, this subjectivity is, in turn, constituted through relation with the power centers.)

Cage regularly put into question our desire to shape the world according to our subjectivity.

> How can I get it to come to me of itself, not just pop up out of my
>   memory, taste, and psychology?
> How?
> Do you know how?   (*S*, 48)

If practice is regarded as the mimetic embodiment of thought, and language as the verbalization of thought, both language and practice will always seem inadequate in comparison with their ideal sources. Cage finds this model intolerable because it casts material practice as an imperfect mimesis of ideal reality rather than as a not-yet-known reality in itself. "If I have a particular purpose, and then a series of actions comes about, and all I get is an approximation of my purpose, then nothing but a sort of compromise or disappointment can take place."[2] Compromise, disappointment, and pale approximation on the one hand, and the "subservience" of material reality to our ideas on the other hand. This is, to Cage, an "intolerable situation." At the same time subjects and objects of material practices, we are disappointed as subjects and controlled as objects.

> Their ears are walled in
> with sounds
> 10″ of their own imagination.   (*S*, 155)

In other words, trying to materialize one's notions of what one should be, one subordinates one's material practice to these notions, and thus one does not allow the creation and exploration of material practices' "own ways of being." The control of practice by the "walls of one's own imagination" is the objectification of this practice, and of one's material being.

> without intention? Do not memory, psychology——
> Answer: "——never again."   (*S*, 17)

Horizontal Interaction among a Plurality of Centers

Cage's method of resisting the "vertical" construction of language is not negative, but always positive, creating instances of anticlosural practice. Vertical construction is simply "silenced," freeing words, beings, and thoughts for horizontal interaction. It is, Cage believes, a good trade: "nothing was lost when everything was given away. In fact, everything is gained" (*S*, 8). "Not ideas but facts" (*S*, 108).

> . . . . . . IN ALL OF SPACE EACH THING AND
> EACH HUMAN BEING IS AT THE CENTER . . . EACH
> ONE . . .   IS THE MOST HONORED
> ONE OF ALL.   INTERPENETRATION [WITH AND] . . .
> . . . . BY EVERY OTHER ONE . . .
> EACH AND EVERY THING . . . . IS RELATED TO
> EACH AND EVERY OTHER THING . . . (*S*, 46–47)

. . . all things . . . *are* related, and . . . this complexity is more evident when it is not oversimplified by an idea of relationship in one person's mind. (*S*, 260)

It is thus possible to make a musical composition the continuity of which is free of individual taste and memory (psychology) and also of the literature and "traditions" of the art. The sounds enter the time-space centered within themselves, unimpeded by service to any abstraction, their 360 degrees of circumference free for an infinite play of interpenetration. (*S*, 59)

Each thing that is there is a subject. It is a situation involving multiplicity. (*S*, 101)

In the anarchically dehierarchized horizontal plane, liberated from the always already-made definitions of a high center, one can attempt to become oneself and to create one's own language. "Horizontal" interaction among a plurality of centers is in Cage's work defined as nonobstruction among centers ("non-obstruction of sounds is of the essence," *S*, 39), and the absence of fusion ("no harmonious fusion of sound is essential," ibid.). The centers are in a state of interpenetration.

> INTERPENETRATION MEANS THAT EACH ONE OF THESE
> MOST HONORED ONES OF ALL IS MOVING OUT IN ALL DIRECTIONS
> PENETRATING AND BEING PENETRATED BY EVERY OTHER ONE NO MATTER
> WHAT THE TIME OR WHAT THE SPACE.   SO THAT WHEN ONE SAYS

THAT THERE IS NO CAUSE AND EFFECT, WHAT IS MEANT IS THAT THERE
ARE AN INCALCULABLE INFINITY OF CAUSES AND EFFECTS, THAT IN FACT
EACH AND EVERY THING IN ALL OF TIME AND SPACE IS RELATED TO
EACH AND EVERY OTHER THING IN ALL OF TIME AND SPACE.   (S, 46–47)

Cage's text "2 Pages, 122 Words on Music and Dance" (S, 96–97; see fig. 18) is a graphic example of horizontal interaction among a plurality of centers. The groupings of text (one word, a few words, a sentence) are scattered on the paper, without diachronic relation. There is no fusion and no "integration of the individual in the group" (S, 5). Every instance of text is separated from every other by an empty space of white paper. The empty spaces allow for the nonobstruction of the centers.

The white paper functions as a background that asserts the synchronic presence of everything on it. The shortness of the piece and its visual realization allow for the simultaneous presence of all its centers. Each center has a space for its own concentric circles of sound and meaning, like a stone thrown into the water, the ever-new outer circles of one center interpenetrating with the outer circles of other centers.

In most of the texts in *Silence,* the forms which Cage uses delimit the space and time for each of the given centers of the text, allowing them to interpenetrate with other centers without being obstructed. In "Lecture on Nothing," for example, "[t]here are four measures in each line and twelve lines in each unit of the rhythmic structure. There are forty-eight such units, each having forty-eight measures. The whole is divided into five large parts, in the proportion 7, 6, 14, 14, 7. The forty-eight measures of each unit are likewise so divided." (S, 109) This rhythmical structure creates units of text on several different levels: five large parts, or forty-eight units of twelve lines, or 576 lines, or 2,304 smallest rhythmical measures of text or silence. None of these levels is asserted as the dominant or primary one, the realization of which would be the goal of other levels. The smallest rhythmical measures, for example, are not obstructed as individual centers by their participation in larger grammatical and rhetorical groupings. On this level, the empty spaces between the units of text, and the units of text between the empty spaces (or between the empty times in the performance of the piece), affirm the centrality of each of these smallest rhythmical measures.

This piece appeared in Dance Magazine, *November 1957. The two pages were given me in dummy form by the editors. The number of words was given by chance operations. Imperfections in the sheets of paper upon which I worked gave the position in space of the fragments of text. That position is different in this printing, for it is the result of working on two other sheets of paper, of another size and having their own differently placed imperfections.*

2 Pages, 122 Words on Music and Dance

To obtain the value
of a sound, a movement,
measure from zero. (Pay
attention to what it is,
just as it is.)

A bird flies.

Slavery is abolished.

the woods

A sound has no legs to stand on.

The world is teeming: anything can happen.

Fig. 18.   Pages 96–97 from Cage, *Silence*

sound   movement

Points in   Activities which are different
time, in   love   happen in a time which is a space:
space   mirth   are each central, original.
                the heroic
                wonder
The emotions   tranquillity   are in the audience.
                fear
                anger   The telephone rings.
                sorrow   Each person is in the best seat.
                disgust

     Is there a glass of water?   War begins at any moment.

                    Each now is the time, the space.

     lights

          inaction?
                         Are eyes open?

          Where the bird flies, fly.   ears?

> Each moment   is absolute,   alive and sig-
> nificant.   Blackbirds   rise   from a field making   a   (*S*, 113)

In "Where Are We Going? and What Are We Doing?" (*S*, 194–259), the printed text attempts to mimic the experience of hearing simultaneously the four lectures which comprise the piece. In his directions, Cage instructs a lecturer to read each lecture independently, tape them, and then play them simultaneously. The four fonts and the layout of the text in the printed version allows the reader to *see* this interpenetrating and nonobstructive composition. The lines of one text are separated from other lines of the same text in such a way that a fusion of these lines in the production of a meaning of the text is blocked. Various interactions among the centers and the reader are possible. One could try to create, for example, the first lecture by following every first line of the four-line stanzas, or one could read four lines of each stanza simultaneously, and so on.

Communication and Interpenetration

A "false" community defines itself in relation to a few elevated centers, such as the media, the government, or various institutions. Communication within such a community passes through these centers, which function as control points.

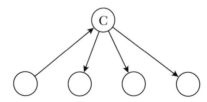

However, as Marshall McLuhan warns, the medium is the message, and the center shapes us and determines our language. Going through the center, we become more the center and less ourselves.

In Cage's horizontal plurality of centers, alternative communication is made possible by developed technology. At present, technology is used in existing social formations (capitalism, mass culture) for particular power goals. However, Cage believes that this same technology could be used as a means for horizontal communication in which everyone could directly communicate with everyone else, without the use of an intermediary or external center: "EACH AND EVERY THING IN ALL OF TIME AND SPACE IS RELATED TO / EACH AND EVERY OTHER THING IN ALL OF TIME AND SPACE" (S, 47).

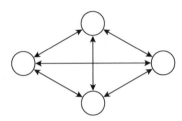

Horizontal being is being in which one does not define oneself and one's language vertically, according to the given centers of power, meaning or subjectivity. Horizontal being is a condition of potential freedom in which one can elude one's (and the center's) preconceptions by making "a leap out of reach of one's own grasp of oneself" (S, 162). This freedom does not turn others into passive objects, but rather presupposes their active agency.

For example, in the aforementioned "2 Pages, 122 Words on Music and Dance," the number of words in the text, as well as the position on the paper of the fragments of text, were not determined by the subject (author), but rather by "chance operations" and "imperfections in the sheets of paper" (S, 96). Thus, the subject (author) discovers and constructs himself through interaction with other centers (paper, chance operations). Liberated horizontal being evades both self-control (which results in tedious self-reproduction) and control from others by engaging in unimpeded interpenetrations which bring chance encounters.

Again, in the performance of "Where Are We Going? and What Are We Doing?" the four centers of the four simultaneously given lectures interact with the numerous centers of the individuals in the audience. Focusing on one lecture (attempting to get the "meanings"), or listening to all of the lectures together (getting sounds), or doing something else, every center of the audience interacts in different ways with the other centers of the audience and with the four centers of the performance. The interactions, though, are not only contingent upon the audience, but are also shaped by the centers of the performance—by their loudness, sound, by how long they have been "turned on," and so on. What happens is chance interpenetration among a multitude of centers.

Liberating Self-Alteration

Chance situations created by the interpenetration of a multitude of centers open the possibility of metamorphic being. Understood thus, liberty is not self-expression, but self-alteration. "'It is by reason of this fact that we are made perfect by what happens to us rather than by what we do'" (S, 64). Others are not the obstacle of our freedom, but the condition of it.

> And then when we actually
>
> . . . .
>
> set to work, a kind of
>
> . . . . . .
>
> avalanche came about which
>
> . . . .
>
> corresponded not at all
>
> . . . .
>
> with that beauty which had
>
> . . . .
>
> seemed to appear to us as an
>
> . . . .
>
> objective. Where do we go
>
> . . . .
>
> then? Do we turn around?
>
> . . . .
>
> Go back to the beginning and
>
> . . . .
>
> change everything? Or do
>
> . . . .
>
> we continue and give up

. . . .

what had seemed to be

. . . .

where we were going? Well,

. . . .

what we do is go straight

. . . .

on; that way lies, no doubt,

. . . .

a revelation. I had no idea. . .   (S, 221–22)

Is when Rauschenberg looks an idea? Rather it is an entertainment in which to celebrate unfixity.   (S, 98)

He has changed
the responsibility of   the composer   from making   to accepting   (S, 129)

When Cage writes "we are converted to the enjoyment of our possessions . . . [f]rom wanting what we don't have" (S, 103), he does not mean that everything is just great as it is, and we should stop criticizing it and start enjoying it. Rather, he means that we should first stop being fixed on the few vertical centers and their proclamations of what we should want but can never have. "Enjoyment of our possessions," then, means exploring the nonmaterialized potential of "horizontal" being; it means becoming aware of the multiplicity of centers, of the centrality of each one of them, and of chance interpenetration among them. The freedom of chance interpenetration, and the self-alteration it occasions is (could be) in "our possession" and should be "enjoyed."

For the field is not a field

. . . .

of music, and the acceptance is

. . . .

not just of the sounds that

. . . .

had been considered useless, ugly,

> . . . .
> *and wrong, but it is a field*
>
> . . . .
> *of human awareness, and the*
>
> . . . .
> *acceptance ultimately is*
>
> . . . .
> *of oneself as present mysterious-*
>
> . . . .
> *ly, impermanently, on*
>
> . . . .
> *this limitless occasion.* (*S*, 215–16)

water is fine.   Jump in.   Some will refuse,   for they see that the
water is thick with   monsters   ready to devour them. What they have   in
mind   is self-preservation.   And what is that   self-preservation but
only a preservation   from life?   Whereas life without death is no longer life   but
only self-preservation.   (*S*, 134)

The Creation of Language through Material Practice

Cage's own explorations of liberated "horizontal" being, interpenetrations of multiple centers, and the role of chance in these interpenetrations can be best appreciated in his performances, or in the oral enactment of printed texts from *Silence*. In performance, the synchronic interaction of multiple centers cannot be overlooked, whereas the printed text, unfolding diachronically, often obscures the effects of horizontal interpenetration. In an effort to maximize the interpenetration of elements, Cage imagines the conversion of time (with its ineluctable separation of some elements from others) into space (which, at least theoretically, allows all elements to come into contact with all others): "Activities which are different / happen in a time which is a space: / are each central, original" (*S*, 97). In space, all the centers can exist simultaneously and coequally.

If one reconstructs Cage's texts as performances, the verbal part of these performances becomes only one of the few horizontally related centers. Other centers include music, gesture, dance, voice, and body. The textual parts, or the language of these performances, are constituted through interaction with these other centers. Thus, no two performances will necessarily have the same words in the same order. For instance, Cage writes in his instructions for the performance of "On Robert Rauschenberg, Artist, and His Work," that the text "may be read in whole or in part; any sections of it may be skipped, what remains may be read in any order . . . Any of the sections may be printed directly over any of the others, and the spaces between paragraphs may be varied in any manner" (S, 98). In this case, there is no definitive text, but a number of possible "final" texts, in which the elements are allowed various relations to one another.

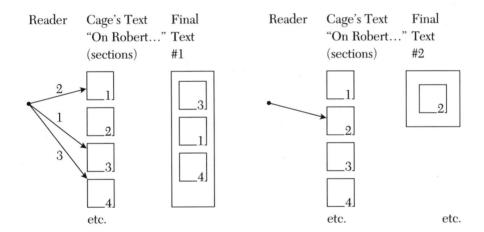

In the performance of "On Robert Rauschenberg . . . ," Cage's text is a multiplicity of centers which horizontally interrelate with another center, the reader or performer. The "final" text of each performance is created through this interaction ("interpenetration"). That "final" text *is* this unique interpenetration. Thus, the language is not the "expression" of a vertical center (the author and his or her ideas) which is materialized in practice. Rather, the language is constituted *through* the material practice. "It is not a question of going in to oneself or out to the world. It is rather a condition of fluency that's in and out" (*S*, 161).

In the creation of language through material practice, chance operations function as the limited negations of the vertical, ideal center which would otherwise fully determine the text. That is, chance functions as the mimicking of the "organic" (nonmechanistic and unpredictable) activity and interpenetration of the centers themselves.

Questions, Cold Ashes, Silence

Some of the ways in which language is constituted in the interaction of horizontal centers, that is, through material practice, are (1) language and texts as questions; (2) language as transient thought that should be "'dropped as . . . cold ashes of a fire long dead'" (*S*, 39); and (3) language as silence.

Questions

Speaking about his compositions, Cage says: "Instead of representing my control, they represent questions that I've asked and the answers that have been given by means of chance operations. I've merely changed my responsibility from making choices to asking questions. It's not easy to ask questions" (*CC*, 214).

Language does not formulate the ideas which reality should follow, but rather questions to which material practice—a performance and/or practice of writing and speaking—gives the answers. What happens if we do the performance according to the particular "question?" How does it look? How does it sound? What happens if I write and read the text according to a particular time frame or a particular form? How does it look on the page? How does it sound when it is performed? It is not better or worse than I thought it would be, because I did not envision how and what it should be. "A 'mistake' is beside the point, for once anything happens it authentically is" (*S*, 59). "Music is simply trying things out in / school fashion to see what happens" (*S*, 189). "I write / in order to hear; never do I hear and / then write what I hear" (*S*, 169). Language is the questioning we do in order to find out the answers, and not the repetition of that which we already know, or the vertical construction of language according to the pre-given ideas. The relation between language and material practice is not that between a blue-print and an execution of it, but that between questions and answers, "the action was a non-knowledge of something that had not yet happened" (*S*, 39).

The language of questions is the language of self-alteration through interaction with material practices. This is not a closed, unidirectional, language of self-expression, but an open language, receptive to whatever happens. One creates oneself not in imitation of a past which one already knows, but in relation to present, unrepeatable contingencies. One does not know what one is, because one *is* only in interaction with others, and thus unpredictable and new to oneself. The practice, the gnoseological activity produced in this practice, and the language which allows it become open and unlimited. Others are not obstacles to one's freedom, but the realization and condition of one's freedom and one's language.

Cold Ashes

"Thoughts arise not to be collected and cherished but to be dropped as though they were void. Thoughts arise not to be collected and cherished but to be dropped as though they were rotten wood. Thoughts arise not to be collected and cherished but to be dropped as though they were pieces of stone. Thoughts arise not to be collected and cherished but to be dropped as though they were the cold ashes of a fire long dead." (*S*, 39)

The purpose of thoughts is not their preservation and hypostatization as ideas. They arise in order to disappear, and their being is in their passing away. The instantaneous language which Cage marks, paralleling the instantaneity of thoughts in Meister Eckhart's concept, is language created horizontally, in the present moment, in the interaction with other centers. When these interactions cease to exist, the language disappears as well. This language does not secure itself "in the thingness of a work" (*S*, 65n), but marks and produces "instantaneous ecstasy" (ibid.).

that our delight
lies in not   pos-sessing anything   .   Each moment
presents what happens   .   (*S*, 111)

No-continuity
simply means   accepting that   continuity   that happens.
Continuity   means the opposite: making that particular continuity   that
excludes   all others. (*S*, 132)

Silence

The language of self-alteration is the language of full awareness of others, of the "noise" which fills the silence of our projects, preconceptions, history, subjectivity, and so on. The language of silence is one that knows how to listen when the other centers act, so that it can construct itself as a re-action to the others, and not only as the self-determined action of its own talking.

. . . It is not

.   .   .   .

in the nature of doing to

.   .   .   .

improve but rather to come

.   .   .   .

into being, to continue, to

.   .   .   .

go out of being and to

.   .   .   .

be still, not doing. That

.   .   .   .

still not-doing is a

.   .   .   .   .   .

preparation. It is not

.   .   .   .   .   .

just static:. it is a quiet

.   .   .   .   .   .

readiness for whatever and

.   .   .   .

the multiplicities are already

.   .   .   .

there in the making. We watch

.   .   .   .

for signs and accept omens.

.   .   .   .

Everything is an omen, so

.   .   .   .

we continue doing and changing.   (*S*, 235–36)

The Language of Community

Resisting the closures of vertically constructed, ideal, and centralized language, Cage articulates the liberating language of material practice and horizontal interaction. This is a self-altering, rather than a self-realizing language activity, in which others are not obstacles but conditions of one's freedom. This is the language of community, spoken not in obedience to some external center, but emanating from the interpenetration of the community's numerous nonfixed centers. It is thoroughly democratic.

Fredric Jameson asserts that literature brings into being that very situation to which it is also, at the same time, a reaction. Cage brings "into being" closural and dictatorial vertical practices by reacting to them. His liberating reaction creates horizontal and democratic practices, and invites us to attempt our freedoms as well.

A lady   from Texas   said: I live in Texas   .
                        We have no music   in Texas.   The reason they've no
music in Texas   is because   they have recordings
in Texas.   Remove the records from Texas
                        and someone   will learn to sing   .
                        Everybody   has a song
                        which is   no   song at all :
                        it is a process   of singing   ,
                        and when you sing   ,
                        you are   where you are   . (*S*, 126)

Afterword

As I mentioned in the beginning of this paper, in reading *Silence,* I found the utopian America constructed in the communist period by speculating Eastern Europeans. They were not concerned with the correspondence between their utopian vision and the "real" United States. I would like to propose, however, that in *Silence* one finds not only the utopian America, but also the relationship between this utopian America and the real one.

> It may be objected that from this point
> of view anything goes. Actually
> anything **does** go,—but only when
> nothing is taken as the basis. In an utter emptiness
> 50″ anything can take place. (*S,* 160)

The utopia of absolute freedom ("anything goes") is possible only in a place of "utter emptiness." But reality is characterized by the fact that there is no silence. There are always numerous givens which cannot be wished away. In utter emptiness, utopian freedom is absolute, but also immaterial and unreal, impossible. In the real world of various givens, utopia becomes real but it cannot be absolute, because the realities which become utopian and make the utopia real also *exclude* the possibility of certain things. In other words, if utopia is real, it is not absolute.

> and when you sing   ,
>   you are   where you are   . (*S,* 126)

. . . and so we are converted to the enjoyment of our possessions. (*S,* 103)

Cage does not deal with the absolute yet impossible (unreal) utopia of utter emptiness. On the contrary, his interest is all in given reality. *Silence* explores the immanent potentials of reality itself and articulates the ultimate reality, that is, the utmost being "where we are." Reality itself is shown as having utopian potentials. That is, the potentials for horizontal, materialistic, and democratic practices. The ultimate reality is the utopian one. We practice this utopian reality when we change our knowledge, language, and actions from vertical and idealistic to horizontal and materialistic. Utopia is realized not by one's going away from given realities to an empty place where "anything goes," but by fully being "where you are," and by becoming maximally aware of the liberating potentials of one's own given worlds. However, as we said above, precisely because this utopia is real, it is not absolute.

One could justifiably point out that Cage's work is not only utopian (i.e., horizontal and democratic), but also dictatorial (i.e., vertical and authoritarian) in many ways. After all, Cage sets for his pieces the materials and specific rules which cannot be negotiated and changed. In "On Robert Rauschenberg . . . ," for example, Cage gives the sections of the text. The reader or printer can combine those sections in various ways, but he or she cannot change them. One could say that Cage's authorial vertical practices complement the horizontal practices happening in his pieces. "A technique to be useful (skillful, that is) / must be such that it fails / to control / the elements subjected to it" (S, 154). The opposition between failure to control and subjection shows that the elements are both controlled and not, or that they are controlled in some ways and not controlled in others.

It seems to me that, rather than simply complementing or even negating the horizontal practices of his pieces, Cage's vertical proclamations are the necessary condition for the *realization* of horizontal and utopian practices. The function of the author's vertical stipulation of materials and rules is precisely to put up a set of given realities which cannot be wished away. Cage's "dictatorialism" is the "reality principle" of his pieces, because it sets up the reality of certain things which are simply given as they are. These givens constitute the reality, a place with no silence and no emptiness. The point is to explore and materialize the utopian potentials of these given realities which themselves make utopia both real and nonabsolute.

Cage did not articulate the unreal and impossible absolute utopia of utter emptiness, but the possible utopia of our given realities. In *Silence*, utopia is the ultimate reality. And for those who find utopian America in Cage's work, the "real" America shows itself to be potentially and really the utopian one. Everybody in Texas can sing. They just need to remove the records to find that out.

Notes

1. John Cage, *Silence* (Middletown, CT: Wesleyan University Press, 1961), p. 191. Hereafter cited as *S*.

2. Richard Kostelanetz, *Conversing with Cage* (New York: Limelight Editions, 1987), pp. 216–17. Hereafter cited as *CC*.

John Cage's Approach to the Global

Daniel Herwitz

It was almost inevitable that John Cage would move from composing in music to composing in words. For Cage, music was never just music, it was always the occasion for reformation. When Cage set out in the early 1950s to reform music, to silence what he saw as its constricted practices, he was really aiming to free constricted human beings by freeing their ears. For Cage, music was to be an exemplar of how human beings relate to the world and to one another. Cage set out, in redefining our relation to sounds, in opening the ear to the full panoply of the acoustical, to free human beings from their encagements, thus allowing them to "be" in the world of whatever happened to happen. Cage's musical experiments were motivated by his belief that when we approach sound with ears informed by our concepts and expectations about musical structure and expression, we are precluding a deep and immediate acknowledgment of both sound and the world, opting instead for a kind of distorted attempt at control. Indeed, he believed that the very attempt to order sound in the mind's ear as coherent, complete, resolving, elaborative, and formal, is an act of manipulation or possession. In projecting through the ear our concepts of the musical, we are doing to sound what we do to other people when we try to recast them in our own images as opposed to letting them freely be themselves. To acknowledge sound, like acknowledging people, is for Cage to just let it be. Such a view goes beyond any mere plea for tolerance in music (or in ethics) for it identifies respect with noninterference. So long as we don't interfere, sound and life are fine.

Following suit on this belief, Cage's music has nearly from its inception been an art of disturbation, aimed at the breakdown of traditional musical commitments to structure and expression. Cage's ideas about human liberation, or restoration to the natural flow of life without interference, had in the 1950s and early 1960s been worked out through (1) his musical experiments in engaging new sounds and new silences, and (2) through his bricolage of writings. The writings had remained in some sense separate, with the focus of Cagean practice being the musical experiments. While not "purely musical," because defined by the force of the writings and rhetoric, Cage's musical past had focused on experiments in sound. This, I think, reflected his modernist optimism that changes in musical experience, hypercharged with a modernist rhetoric of ideas, could and would change the world. Experiments in sound, with ideas to back up their already suggestive powers, were the currency of liberation.

One found in the Cage of the 1950s and early 1960s an intoxication with the future of music, as if changes rung in musical concepts through formal sound experiments would bring about the full liberation of the human being, as if the dropping of discriminatory musical practices would liberate us from mind and desire, thus making our lives more natural and more beautiful. Rather than being strictly musical, Cage's battles over music optimistically extended to the center of the world.

Such an inflated belief in the power of an avant-garde artwork to ring changes in life as a whole may also be found in the rhetoric of the Bauhaus, of Constructivism, of Mondrian and De Stijl, of Le Corbusier, and even of André Breton. Mondrian wrote as if by calibrating his canvases into a mysterious harmonic balance, by freeing them from all but primary colors and rectangular shapes, he would succeed in bringing about a similar balance in the world as a whole; he wrote as if his announcement in paint of the coming of platonic truth would simply bring that truth about. Mondrian, writing such things in 1942, a bad year for Europe if ever there was one, can only in retrospect strike us as wild. Yet his grandiose belief in the capacity of art to change the world is in some sense a defining feature of the avant-garde. Which goes to show that Cage the reformer kept good spiritual company in those halcyon, Black Mountain days. And it also goes to show that Cage had drunk rather deep of avant-garde optimism.[1]

It takes more than the freeing of music from its dependence on harmonic hierarchy and melodic phrasing to change the world—which brings us to Cage's reconceptualization of the future of music, specifically of music's mode of address. Cage could not simply write essays and compose indefinitely as if changes in the structure of musical sounds would by themselves reform the world if he really took himself to be a reformer of life through the domain of art. What he subsequently added to the concept of the musical work is words, and my topic here is to describe how Cage's poetic mesostics reflect his attempt to address complex global issues while retaining his older ideas about musical liberation. By turning music into poetry Cage has, paradoxically, like Wagner, made the scope of music more referential and more global. Is this because, like Wagner, he believed that music is an event which, if big enough and overwhelming enough *can* bring about a redefinition of the world? I prefer to think that Cage's mesostics represent his way of acknowledging music's (or poetry's) dependence on the world as well as its independence from it. Not only is music literally nothing, without a form of life to give shape to its practices and force to the reception of its tonalities; but furthermore, a musical work cannot be a vehicle for the world's greening simply through its formal innovations, however fetishized such experimental gestures may be by an avant-garde utopian theory. The musical work must acknowledge the world and address it in order to make something happen. Silence may be golden, but the world will not change (either in four minutes and thirty-three seconds or in a lifetime) if the musical work remains silent. At least if it remains silent about the world.

We turn then to Cage's development of a global mode of address in the medium of words. How can his mesostics engage the world while retaining his commitment to the power of musical silence? The answer can only be: By chance. I will return to this point, but first, let me suggest that we think of Cage's mesostics as embodying a kind of soul-force, a mode of Satyagraha, of passive resistance to the world. This is not of course the only interpretive perspective one can have of Cage's poetry, which like all poetry is highly overdetermined; but it is a way of getting at the nature of his "poethics," of approaching the politics resident in the poetry. Through the imposition of chance operations onto language, specifically onto the source texts Cage uses in his poetic compositions, Cage symbolically aims to halt the march of language, meaning, and human control. Silence is preserved in the mode of passive resistance to meaning (by one who is implacable in the face of the onslaught of human language, certainty, and human omnipotence). As conceptual control and political imposition are silenced through Cage's fragmenting play with words, another silence opens up for the community of readers or listeners, a silence in which intimacy may be cultivated and communion between persons may occur. "The best communion between men happens in silence," Cage is fond of quoting Thoreau as saying.

In "The Future of Music," Cage asserts:

> more and more a concern with personal feelings of individuals, even the enlightenment of individuals, will be seen in the larger context of society. We know how to suffer and control our emotions. If not, advice is available, There is a cure for tragedy. The path to self-knowledge has been mapped out by psychiatry, by oriental philosophy, mythology, occult thought, anthroposophy and astrology . . . What we are learning is how to be convivial. "Here comes everybody." Though the doors will always remain open for the musical expression of personal feelings, what will more and more come through is the expression of the pleasures of conviviality . . . And beyond that a non-intentional expressivity, a being together of sounds and people . . . A walk, so to speak, in the woods of music, or in the world itself."[2]

This remark about conviviality brands Cage's new music as aiming to create what Kant calls a "sensus communis," a community of taste in which each shares the pleasures of all and takes pleasure in this sharing.[3] But unlike Kant's Enlightenment community, which is based on sameness of taste, morals, and rationality, Cage's is Thoreauvian. Cage's idea of a musical body is one in which the free play of differences are given vent and let be without interference. By extension the conviviality he wishes to engender is conviviality with a difference, that is, a form of communion in which each person acknowledges the differing presence of the others in quietude, toleration, and friendliness. Cage's is an anarchist homage to the politics of Thoreau, who said, as Cage is often fond of repeating, "the best form of government is none at all."

These differences between Cage and Kant are worth pursuing. Each founds his idea (ideal) of a community on the claim of shared reciprocity—each member of the community should treat the others in the manner in which the others should treat him or her. Yet the thrust of Kantian thought is in the direction of a community in which each person is conceptualized as the same as the others. For Kant, the cardinal moral rule is to act so that one's action might be willed as a universal law, which is to say a law which would produce good results were everyone else to do the same under the same circumstances. You cannot do anything (such as not voting or not keeping your promises) which, were everyone else to do the same, would produce infelicitous results. On Kantian lines, the deepest and most self-realizing form of freedom available to people is the freedom to set before themselves this moral law. Each person must judge his or her actions according to the rule of universalizability, a rule which, while unclear in its applications to practical moral decision making, has a clear intention behind it, namely to bind us together under the umbrella of a universal conception of humanity in which all rule their actions by the constraint of considering how things would be were everybody else to do the same (in the same circumstances).

For Cage, as an American freethinking maverick, it is not true that everybody does or should do the same under the same conditions. For him, the deepest freedom is the Thoreauvian freedom to be oneself, to listen to the differences between oneself and others without imposing an ethics of hierarchical evaluation or punishment, and to accept the flow of the world in its myriad incarnations of blossoming. We do not and need not be expected to act in the way in which everyone else would act in the same situation. People should be allowed to differ, just as sounds should be permitted to sound as they are. The kind of learning required for this exigency called "life" is a learning to hear mutually and accept mutually the differences as well as the similarities among our styles of feeling, response, action and reaction.

Since both Cage and Kant treat the work of art as a body symbolic of humanity, one can trace the differences in their conceptions of art to differences in how each imagines humanity to be. For Kant, the artwork—in Kant's well-known phrase the "symbol of Morality"—allows us to take pleasure in our capacity to set the moral law freely before us. Kant finds in the artwork a play of freedom, necessity, and purpose that allows us to treat it as symbolic of this capacity. Specifically, for Kant, the artwork is freely organized in that it is made in the absence of rules. (Kant refers to the capacity to make things in the absence of rules as "genius"). Yet it also suggests both formal necessity and formal finality. We feel that its parts fit together as if tending toward some ultimate goal, and we feel that the parts are so required by the setting of this goal that, were a single note in the Mozart sonata different, were a single chord or counter-rhythm in the Beethoven symphony other than it is, we would, according to Kant, fear that the entire work would collapse. Yet the Mozart sonata or Beethoven symphony is made, in Kant's view, in the absence of any rule that would justify our conviction about its finality and necessity. This Kantian urge to find in symbols the coordination of freedom, necessity, and finality—an urge aptly reflected by the classicized art and music of his time—is the urge to find traces both of human freedom and of the binding necessity of the moral law. We seek, according to Kant, inevitability in such symbols, a sense of their purpose, yet we also seek in them a compulsion which is paradoxically freely achieved by the genius of the work (in its creation and reception). It is this tripartite projection of freedom, necessity, and finality onto things, this reshaping of things in the name of humanity, that makes things beautiful according to Kant.

Rather than eliciting a feeling of formal necessity, structure, and finality, Cage's poems celebrate the spontaneous, the fortuitous, the incomplete, and the nonhierarchical concord and discord called "life." His music and poems evoke a humanity perfected through its spontaneity, shared contingency, and above all, its mutual capacity to listen to the voices of its differing members without judgment. Cage's music and poetry acknowledge a humanity whose bonds are established through the agreement to reject laws that impose sameness and by implication, necessary moral action. Thus Cage's music and poetry reject the Kantian approach of symbolizing a humanity defined by law and necessity, and equally the creation of art which imposes a sense of necessity onto its audience. For Cage, little pleasure is to be found in such a structured universe. Rather he uses form purely as a means of artificially organizing the free play of "whatever happens to happen," eschewing all further sense of formal necessity. And he uses chance operations to determine that form. Cage's poems try to force us to confront the contingencies of events and the play of relations among sounds—relations which exist in an anarchic space that discourages any urge to find a set of necessary connections or ultimate goals, but encourages a discipline of focused, nonhierarchical listening, and immersion into the play of the poem.

Cage's image of an anarchic body politic is therefore reflected in the structure and texture of his poetry. The anarchic play of linguistic particles and musical voices in his poems suggests that he identifies the human commitment to conceptual certainty (whether about conceptual truth or about the moral law) with the politics of human control. Cage identifies the claim of reason to order the world with the claim of desire to rule the world omnipotently. Where there is clear meaning, there is clear hierarchy, and where there is hierarchy, there is the master and the slave. In his suspicion of the urge toward conceptual control, Cage is like Derrida and certain feminist critics.[4] His aim is to diffuse the tendency toward political control by forcing us to give up the conceptual claim of imposing interpretive hierarchies and interpretive certainties onto the world. The structure of Cage's mesostics aims to put what Wittgenstein would call a "full stop" (in the *Philosophical Investigations*) to meaning, textual imposition, and the desire for world control, thus freeing us to let the complexities of the world just be, and allowing us to bond in the midst of our various differences. About this Cage is quite serious.

In his preface to the "Lecture on the Weather," his Bicentennial present to the United States, Cage states:

> It may seem to some that through the use of chance operations I run counter to the spirit of Thoreau (and '76, and revolution for that matter). The fifth paragraph of *Walden* speaks against blind obedience to a blundering oracle. However, chance operations are not mysterious sources of "the right answers." They are a means of locating a single one among a multiplicity of answers, and at the same time, of freeing the ego from its taste and memory, its concern for profit and power, of silencing the ego so that the rest of the world has a chance to enter into the ego's own experience whether that be outside or inside.

and,

> The desire for the best and the most effective in connection with the highest profits and the greatest power led to the fall of nations before us: Rome, Britain, Hitler's Germany. Those were not chance operations. We would do well to give up the notion that we alone can keep the world in line, that only we can solve its problems. (*EW*, 5)

Chance operations are meant to put a full stop to the imposition of the inexorable or determinate onto the recipient, be the recipient a nation or a listener. By silencing the politician's—or composer's—own desires for control, chance operations give the nation—or the listener—the chance to develop personality and conviviality on their own.

It is well known that the formal key to Cage's fragmentation of meaning is his use of chance operations. How do chance operations structure Cage's mesostics? In these poetic compositions Cage operates on tones, producing highly arbitrary strings of words which occupy a given time segment, for example the space of the six Norton Lectures delivered at Harvard during the academic year of 1988–89 (and published under the title *I–VI* by the Harvard University Press in 1990). Cage treats the occasion as an open time segment to be filled with his art, which is what the book is the text of, and one should understand the reasons for his choice. Like all of Cage's mesostics it has rules. In a brief introduction, Cage tells us he uses the *I Ching* plus a complex computer program (designed partly by Andrew Culver and partly by Jim Rosenberg) in order to subject a set of source texts to chance operations. Cage's sources (presented at the back of the book) are quotations from Wittgenstein, Thoreau, Emerson, Buckminster Fuller, McLuhan, Duchamp, himself, and others. He also uses *Finnegans Wake* and the daily newspaper. The computer program churns out from the source texts vertical strings of names in capital letters. The actual compositions proceed horizontally across the page, and there also the words used are generated by chance. Cage then subjects himself to the following rule. Using the vertical string as the central axis of the horizontal composition, he disallows the use in the intervening horizontal small-case string of the letter that forms the second capital of any successive pair of capital letters.

Cage's technique turns language into a game, into a form of activity that renders ordinary words into syntactically and semantically arbitrary patterns, whose sense or nonsense is a matter of the accidental, and whose parts seek and implicate various semantic configurations. Cage also aims to homogenize the parts of language (particles, connectives, nouns, verbs, etc.) as if they were twelve tones of equal value. The technique makes music by imposing rhythmical continuity much in the manner of twelve-tone composition, through restrictions on the stock of words (confined to the source texts) and restrictions on which letters can be used when. It is marvellous to hear Cage himself reading these lectures.[5] In his calming voice, the repetitions of words from his sources at odd, fortuitous places, combined with the continuity imposed by his compositional form, gradually soothes one's ears and opens them to the play of conceptual suggestions that wind in and out of each other in a diffuse, amniotic ambience. The feeling is one of a forest of signs in a montage without master-editing that includes world events, information circuits, philosophical snippets, modernist jokes, the blooming, buzzing ecologues of Joyce, and the ecologies of philosopher/naturalists. This vale of immersion is akin to the philosophical skeptic's picture of perception as a flow of information and feeling whose dimensions exceed conceptualization and our ability to determine what our role in their phenomenological fabrication is. Yet we do not fear this apparent defeat of perceptual knowledge but rather welcome it as the relinquishment of an impossible, horrendous perceptual task: that of finding knowledge in the endless play of forms or imposing domination onto it, thus closing ourselves off and making ourselves crazy.

I have suggested that this diffusion of meaning in an ambience of sound through chance operations is Cage's act of passive resistance to the domain of meaning, interventionist desire, and aggression. Yet we should not go too far in agreeing with the claim that meaning has been disarmed in these poetic texts. The poetry must have meaning in order to live as an act of passive resistance, for all passive resistance is resistance to *something*, and the choice of what to resist must be made by somebody, presumably by the author. Then Cage cannot have abolished his tastes and his ego in these works because, if I am right, they are directed to the world and are thus part of the politics of his art. Anarchy is after all a political choice.

As are the targets of Cage's practice, and as are Cage's specific choice of source texts. The source texts or prefaces Cage provides in his Norton Lectures or his "Lecture on the Weather" make very clear what his political likes and dislikes are, which brings us to the central paradox of Cage's poetry, namely how the poetry both fragments the meanings of the texts Cage chooses while at the same time making present for the listener the true meaning of the very texts which Cage's poetry fragments. This paradox demands elaboration. Cage's utopian ideas of resistance are given by the source texts he chooses in the Norton Lectures: texts by Thoreau, Wittgenstein, Fuller, from the daily newspaper, and so on. They are texts which are to his taste (for example he chooses very little Emerson even though Emerson is in many ways like Thoreau, because he detests Emerson), and they are texts whose politics he admires. When one hears the mesostics of the Norton Lectures it is crucial to one's experience of them that one knows what these source texts are, otherwise one loses the full scope of the vision of the world which Cage's poetic satyagraha is at the service of bringing about. To insure familiarity with that vision, he begins his Norton Lectures by describing which texts he has used. Then paradoxically—and wonderfully—Cage's poetry becomes a politics *precisely by fragmenting the meanings of those texts whose meanings the listener must know and keep in mind,* into a whirl of chance configurations—nearly. I say "nearly" because were they completely obliterated, the very point of the fragmentation would be lost, namely that the truth of these texts is proved, inculcated, or intimated into the listeners through the listeners' experience of the fragmentation of what they know these texts to be.

For the listener who already has the source texts in mind, their meanings are preserved in the mesostic through the associations between words and linguistic fragments that continuously emerge from the mesostic's play on word and sound association. In particular, associations emerge through Cage's own choice of the mesostic's wing words, which reverberate with textual resonance. The informed listener will feel this resonance of the source texts in Cage's vocabulary, rhythm, and phrasing. Composing in the wake of *Finnegans Wake,* Cage's brilliance in word and phrase juxtaposition offers an abundance of intimations—including associations to the source texts. It is crucial to listen through these poems, to find a path generated by the aural and auratic cast of their vocabulary, to find their rhythmic pulse and phrase structure. The listener can easily fail to do this. Indeed the work involved in hearing these through represents just that disciplined form of engagement, just that kind of care and attentiveness, that Cage demands of living in general. (It is worth noting in this regard that Cage could be very critical of his own performances of the mesostics.)

An illustration is in order. In the "Fourth Mesostic" of the Norton Lectures, one finds the following passage (like any such passage it is partly generated by chance operations and partly by Cage's own choice of the wing words):

the Dance
the magIc
in Some way
the Contours '
I was standing quite close to
Process '
mind to worLd around '
I
suddeNly
thE
two worlDs
envIronment '
the divinity and Still the trembling
Covers ' the
studyIng '

the contours and Postures of
why shouLd we be
varIous
the ' eNglish
thE '
swamps anD
searchIng
juSt
beComes
In other
Port '
fossiL fuels
I said '
weather at aNy hour '
wE
of peace anD
goIng in by
haSte to
whiCh of
In is
Pointing '
schooLs
If we could grasp the whole '   (*I–VI*, 220)

The play of semantic hits and misses is nicely illustrated in this passage where we are encouraged by the Cageian ambience to find deeper and deeper levels of association in the language, while also being encouraged simply to let the words lie where they are—as if the world of the poem, like the world as a whole, were nothing but nature. Let us briefly consider it, beginning with the line: "mind to WorLd around '." The line carries the global reference of "world," and leads us to focus on the idea of connection between mind and world, an idea which is not defined but rather left for concentration and imagination. This phrase also plays semantically on the word "mind," which can be heard as both a noun and a verb, the verb being "to mind" or "to listen, think, and take care in approaching," suggesting a moral duty.

But the line is also simply a piece of language which plays around the letter "L," as if that were its home, the location these words happened to have found to romp around in. "To worLd around" does not quite make sense, in spite of its suggestions of minding the world, of world travel, and of playing around, even, in the light of what has preceded this line two lines back, of "dancing around." Paradoxically this whirl of language is ecstatically suggestive, it stimulates the imaginative sensorium, because of its ultimate ungrammaticality. The words stimulate because they miss.

The next line of the mesostic is simply the word "I" (or is it simply the letter "I"?). Well, one hears it as the word "I"; one hears it as a stand-in for the poet himself, who appears to be on the verge of pronouncement or self-description. But his pronouncement or description never occurs (or does it?), because the "I" is dropped in the next phrase: "suddeNly / thE / two worLds / envIronment." That is, the "I" is dropped unless the readers hears "the . . . worLds envIronment" as the domain of the "I," say of a global "I" whose existence is the terrain of the world itself. At any rate the entrance of "suddeNly" after "I" is a surprise, one heard as an event. As such, the reader expects a description or narration of the event to follow, and does not get it. For what follows after "suddeNly" is a noun phrase ("the . . . worLds envIronment"), not an action or event sentence. The noun phrase which follows both resists and absorbs the narrative expectation given by "suddeNly." On the one hand, the reader feels, when he or she hears "the . . . worLds envIronment" following "suddeNly," a kind of letdown. The reader hears: "suddeNly . . . nothing." On the other hand, the expectation of an action or event given by "suddeNly" is transposed onto "the . . . worLds envIronment," vivifying it with the pulsation of activity. It is as if the mere fact of the world were itself an event—say an event of recognition, opening, or elaboration. The reader is brought to see the worlds environment as an event, to face it freshly. Resonance from the source texts occurs at just this point, for "the . . . worLds envIronment" is a major player in those texts, and by extension in Cage's global concerns and his global politics. The informed reader will pick up this resonance by being brought face to face with the thought of the worlds environment. Therefore it is through the semantic clashes and "infelicities," in Cage's words, that the resonance of the source texts occurs. The source texts are preserved by means of fragmentation.

"[S]uddeNly / thE . . . worLds / envIronment" is matched in rhythm by two other phrases in the selection quoted: "weather at aNy hour '"; and "If we could grasp the whole '." Both of these phrases are emphasized by their placement in the text as relatively long single lines. "[W]eather at aNy hour" makes one stand by and be ready for whatever happens to happen. I personally hear in it both "weather at any hour" and "whether at any hour." "Whether at any hour" ("Whether at any hour?") suggests a question asked about what might happen when. The question is of course not answered. Moreover I cannot help but hear Cage's "Lecture on the Weather" in these words—his lecture composed out of Thoreau's words in a storm of weather and its clearing, a storm of communion, peace, and communication. Thus I cannot help but hear the trace of Cage's Preface to that work in this line, which means I cannot help but hear a plea about our preparedness, say for the world's weather, behind the question of "whether at any hour." These layers of resonance will not occur to everyone, nor need they. My point is that the poem invites this play of texture, which is how its source texts reside in it by association.

What follows "wE / of peace" is the phrase "anD / goIng in by / haSte." Haste is the opposite of peace—both of world peace and peace of mind. When I play with these lines, I hear that when minding a world one must be at peace; I hear that minding a world requires that form of care (of *minding*) which is the opposite of haste, superficiality, or inattentiveness. This Cageian language of hasting and wasting, language also so congenial to a Protestant genius like Thoreau who is among the sources of the language, leads to a final plea: "If we could grasp the whole." "If we could grasp the whole" is the only grammatically correct and complete sentence in this selection. If we could grasp the whole . . . then what? What would we be able to do or be? The desire for such grasping rings deep, but the thought behind it lacks ultimate coherence, for we do not know what the whole is. The poem does not tell us. Shall we call the whole "weather at any hour"? Does all the weather of all the hours comprise a whole, say the whole of what happens in the world? Or is the whole some further and more portentous dimension of things, say the interconnectedness of all things? Then are all things interconnected in any single or fathomable way?

Consider how the fabric of the mesostic itself comprises a whole. It is a kind of weather at any hour, an ongoing pattern of unique linguistic events and associations, defined partly by regularity, partly by design and partly generated chaotically (by chance).[6] It cannot be grasped as a whole if by that one means computed into an overall theory. Yet the urge to grasp the whole remains insistent. In its classically philosophical formulation, the urge to grasp the whole is precisely the urge to find an account of the poem or the world which will fully conceptualize all of its parts into a determinate relation. This is the urge for a philosopher like Hegel. Cage, again in a spirit akin to Derrida's, wishes to diffuse that urge and replace it by the urge for a kind of holistic thinking, a self-recognition of one's dwelling within a whole which resists overall determination, a holistic caring or minding. The urge to grasp the whole may be called the urge to acknowledge that interpenetration of people and things called "nature." This acknowledgment of the holistic, this address to the incomplete, this attentiveness to everything that happens and to one's place in this majesty called "everything," this care for the unknown and knowledge of its unknownness, is imbricated by the poem, and left unanalyzed. Grasping is, to use a phrase of Stanley Cavell's, "acknowledgment," not "*begriff.*"[7] Shall we call the satisfaction of this urge the condition of being at peace with things? Then we must correspondingly say that the condition of being at peace with the world is a condition which both is and can never be completed, because being at peace with the world is also *minding* it: being at peace always carries the requirement of discipline and "minding."

What Cage's mesostic then allows—or requires—the listeners to do in working through its fragmented associations is to evolve for themselves its underlying meanings. The listener must mind the mesostic to uncover or attend to its play of concepts. And that is just the work of grasping the whole, in whatever sense it is possible to do this. Grasping and letting go, desiring to grasp and being at peace, finding and letting go, these are redefined as interconnected activities through the very work of listening. We then know the inner meanings of the source texts by being forced to live their meanings in the life of the poem. We are taught or occasioned. Only then can we understand what its associations intimate. Only then will the work of association be free, for only then will we learn to live its paths of connection. Then freedom and discipline—the discipline of attention—are in the end the same.

Meaning paradoxically shines through in Cage's mesostics through fragmentation and chance. The listener is afforded an experience of diffusion and attention; one's need to project meaning and to control the flow of one's perceptions is diffused. One is free to move about in the body of the poem (or world) without imposition, and in the mutual state of everybody else's being there in the same state, for this language is shared.

Cage calls that the recovery of the listener's natural state. I would call it the recovery of the listener's state of free association.[8] It is an enlightened state without the universalizing theory of the Enlightenment (Kant's) to back up its formulation. It is the state of inhabiting oneself. Therefore Cage's mesostics show us something philosophical about the nature of human dwelling. How much one should expect such a cultivated state of dwelling to carry over into political decisions is another story. Freud, ever skeptical of rosy views of what is natural to the political animal would be chary about proposing politics on the basis of such an optimistic conception of the power of enlightened experiences. It was Freud's concern in *Civilization and Its Discontents* to unmask those who make such optimistic proposals about human possibilities as persons who are displaced from their own aggression and thus refuse to acknowledge the full power of aggression in others. Whether this is true in the present case I leave to others. At any event, in partial defense of Cage's address to the world as opposed to Freud's suspicions, Cage's practice is not necessarily a denial of aggression, but a forceful, even, dare one say it, aggressively structured attempt, to make us recall our forgotten spirit of communion: to fight aggression with the force of communion. Is that crazy? No more so than the ideas of the transcendentalists, whom it ought to be the duty of communities to remember.[9]

Cage's claim that the point of his poetry is to remove his own ego, his own likes and dislikes from the music, therefore cannot be right. Rather Cage's poetry is meant to be an act of passive resistance to global facts about which Cage emphatically disapproves. As I said, Cage's beliefs and preferences, his ego if you will, is present in his work through the lingering presence of the meanings of his source texts. Meaning is dropped, but also retained. What is right is that Cage's mesostics aim to soften the brutality of the ego, to silence or deflate its claims to total conceptual and political control. This is right and it is powerful. Is it not enough? Does one need, for the purposes of life or philosophy, to do more to the ego than that? Can one impose more silence on its powers of operation than that, short of terrorizing it?[10]

I wish to make one final remark about the philosophical character of Cage's mesostics. They do not simply show us something about the conditions of human freedom and dwelling, they also reveal something about the nature of human identity. This is made clear through the relation between Cage's mesostics and their source texts. The game in the Norton Lectures is not for Cage to rid himself of Thoreau, Wittgenstein, or Fuller, but to identify himself with Thoreau and the rest in a way that is both direct and obscure.[11] The identification is obscure because Thoreau's words are present in Cage's work in indirect and scrambled ways, as an overall presence, roughly in the way my father is present in me, or my mother, or my history as an American. It is direct because the route from the source texts to their place in the poetry is clearly delineated by the structure of the chance operations, roughly in the way the route from my parents to me is clearly marked by the history of my conception, gestation, and birth, and by my DNA. The presence of my parents, or more vaguely, of America, can be located in me precisely everywhere— in all the regions of my thoughts, attitudes, habits, and personality, and nowhere in particular—which is to say the mode of presence of my parents and my history in me is diffuse, obscure, and hard to unravel. This complex place occupied by facts of lineage in me reveals something philosophically deep about the opacity of my identity. By extension it reveals something about human identity generally. My identity is established vis-à-vis my genealogy out of a thousand similarities and differences between myself and my sources, one of which is the empirical world itself (in Cage's Norton Lectures the relation between the poetry and the empirical world is signified by the fragmented presence of the daily newspaper as a source). My identity depends on those sources while requiring separation from them, as does Cage's poetic work, as does all art require separation from the strands of real life which remain nevertheless strangely present in the artwork. My genealogy is present in me, one might say, silently, like a set of source texts. There is probably no clear and characterizing criterion of human identity for this reason. Nor for art. Cage's poetry then reveals something about the structure of its own identity as art, and about human identity.

There is therefore no clear and characterizing criterion for the identity of Cage's mesostics. Cage's poetic events can be approached from a number of different perspectives, mine being, at best, only one. Do they then invite the same kind of interpretive anarchy which they politically prescribe? Can one say anything about them and get away with it? If not, if some interpretations of them are better than others, how does that fact speak to the prospects for a noninterfering anarchy? And conversely, how much interpretive control is one entitled to assume in approaching the mesostics? At what point in the act of interpretation will these Cageian objects bristle? At what point should they bristle? All heady questions, again philosophical, which I leave for the heads of others.

Notes

1. For an extended discussion of the optimism of the avant-garde, of the way in which that utopian optimism requires theory, and of the inheritance of such theoretical stances by the contemporary world of art, see my *Making Theory/Constructing Art: On the Authority of the Avant-Garde* (Chicago: University of Chicago Press, 1993).

2. John Cage, "The Future of Music," in *Empty Words, Writings '73–'78* (Middletown, CT: Wesleyan University Press, 1979), p. 179. Hereafter cited as *EW*.

3. Immanuel Kant, *Critique of Judgement* (trans. J. Meredith (Oxford: Clarendon Press, 1973).

4. See Jacques Derrida, *Of Grammatology*, trans. G. C. Spivak (Baltimore: Johns Hopkins University Press, 1976); and Luce Irigaray, *Speculum of the other Woman*, trans. Gillian Gill, (Ithaca: Cornell University Press, 1985).

5. Selections from Cage's reading of the Norton Lectures can be heard on the tape which accompanies *I–VI* (Cambridge and London: Harvard University Press, 1990).

6. For discussions of the role of the chaotic in Cage's mesostics, see the essays by Joan Retallack and by N. Kathrine Hayles in this volume.

7. The replacement of the classical concept of *begriff* (the concept of a concept as a fully determinate interpretation) by a concept of knowing as acknowledging, is a central theme of Stanley Cavell's philosophy, one which he finds in the philosophy of the later Wittgenstein. I take it to have its place here. See Cavell, "Knowing and Acknowledging," in *Must We Mean What We Say?* (Cambridge: Cambridge University Press, 1976), pp. 238–66).

8. I take this capacious free association to be Cage's way of recovering a dimension of human freedom in his mesostics. The mesostics are textual bodies whose paths into association ring with amazement, amazement because one feels that the works have no bottom, no place at which one could say: there is no further semantic resonance, semantic firing, and semantic primary process to be found here. It is in this respect that Cage's mesostics are representations of the very idea of freedom, an idea now removed from its Enlightenment definition in terms of free obedience to the moral law, and redefined as the freedom to turn oneself into a field of play in which all the parts of oneself, from the most conscious to the least, are brought into the train of association. One is then free to inhabit oneself, to live in the depth of connection that is one's person. I take it that in a very different context, psychoanalysis aims for a similar capaciousness in the freedom to associate all the parts of one's self, and that the freedom to inhabit oneself is partly to be defined in terms of this capacity.

9. I refer to Stanley Cavell's insistence that American philosophy and letters has repressed the thought of the transcendentalists, who ought to be made part of the conversation of letters. In this sense Cage at Stanford is especially germane to the present time.

10. See my *Making Theory/Constructing Art,* chap. 5, where I explore this question in detail as part of a general discussion of how to address Cage's philosophical skepticism about the limits of our musical minds and musical practices.

11. I am here influenced by remarks of Marjorie Perloff in her essay, "Music for Words Perhaps: Reading/Hearing/Seeing John Cage's Roaratorio," in Perloff, ed., *Postmodern Genres* (Norman: University of Oklahoma Press, 1989), pp. 193–228.

Poethics: John Cage and Stanley Cavell at the Crossroads of Ethical Theory

Gerald L. Bruns

> Henry David Thoreau (1817–1862) lived in Concord, Massachusetts. For two years he lived alone in the woods, two miles from town, by the side of Walden Pond. He built his home and grew his food, and each Sunday walked back to Concord to have dinner with his mother and father and other relatives or friends. He is the inventor of the pencil (he was the first person to put a piece of lead down the center of a piece of wood). He wrote many books including a *Journal* of fourteen volumes (two million words). His *Essay on Civil Disobedience* inspired Ghandi in his work of changing India, and Martin Luther King, Jr., in his use of nonviolence as a means of revolution. No greater American has lived than Thoreau. Emerson called him a speaker and actor of the truth. Other great men have vision. Thoreau had none. Each day his eyes and ears were open and empty to see and hear the world he lived in. Music, he said, is continuous; only listening is intermittent.
>
> —John Cage, Preface to "Lecture on the Weather"

> America exists only in its discovery, and its discovery is always an accident.
> —Stanley Cavell, *The Senses of Walden*

This is a paper about the relation of poetry and ethics, where the relation is Joycean rather than essential (hence my title "Poethics"). The paper is also an attempt to work out the beginnings of a conceptual encounter between art and philosophy, specifically between the avant-garde musician and writer John Cage and the American philosopher Stanley Cavell—an encounter that occurs at the crossroads where two rival theories of the ethical intersect (one represented by Martha Nussbaum, the other by Emmanuel Levinas: so we're talking about the crossroads of analytic and Continental theory). What I want to try to do, at a minimum, is to understand the coherence between the two following quotations. The first is from Cavell (on skepticism): "We think skepticism must mean that we cannot know the world exists, and hence that perhaps there isn't one . . . Whereas what skepticism suggests is that since we cannot know the world exists, its presentness to us cannot be a function of knowing. The world is to be *accepted;* as the presentness of other minds is not to be known, but acknowledged. But what is this 'acceptance,' which caves in at a doubt?"[1] The second is from Cage (on the musician Morton Feldman): "He has changed the responsibility of the composer from making to accepting."[2] Levinasians can (if they like) read this paper as an eccentric gloss on their man, who makes it possible, as will be seen directly, to articulate the coherence, not just between these two quotations, but between an art and a philosophy that distinguish themselves by accepting their residence within mundane—unartful, unphilosophical, uncontrollable—surroundings. It is perhaps no accident that Cage and Cavell are among the most creative readers that Henry David Thoreau ever had.

I

Let me begin with some elementary mapping. It seems possible to distinguish between two very different theories of the ethical. One theory—call it the P-theory—tries to characterize the ethical in terms of our beliefs, desires, values, principles, perceptions, actions, experiences, and so on. The other—call this the Q-theory—tries to characterize ethics in terms of how we are with respect to other people, or more accurately to the other as singular and irreducible (someone not in any way like me). In the Q-theory the question at stake is how we respond to the claims that the other has on us rather than how we are able to justify the claims that we want to make in behalf of our beliefs, values, actions, and so on. The P-theory would argue that the rightness or wrongness of our response will follow from having the right or wrong beliefs and values, the right or wrong perceptions and discriminations, so the idea to start with is obviously knowing right from wrong. This seems roughly to have been Kant's line. Claims are claims of reason, that is, rules. The Q-theory, however, would say that the claims of the other are in advance of reason, and that our beliefs, values, and rules often obstruct the workings of these claims, as if it were as much a function of our beliefs and values to protect us from the ethical as to bring us in line with it. For the point would be that the ethical is not a rule or measure or standard that one could get in line with. It is something much more difficult to live with than a set of principles. Up until recently the P-theory has been the theory embraced by most analytic philosophers. The Q-theory meanwhile has belonged mainly to Continental thinking with its powerful critique of the subject, which is to say its critique of the whole idea of having beliefs, values, principles, and rules for deciding how to act.

Among recent P-theorists Martha Nussbaum is among the more interesting because she has pretty much given up the idea that ethical theory has to be framed in terms of rules and beliefs, but meanwhile she still retains the idea that ethics is subject-centered, that is, it is still conceived in terms of a moral spectator, a perceiving agent, someone (to be sure) situated in circumstances calling for action or decision, but whose situatedness is still characterized in terms of seeing and describing the situation. Nussbaum has laid out her ideas in a book called *The Fragility of Goodness* and again in a collection of essays, *Love's Knowledge,* where she says that "ethics is the search for a specification of the good life for a human being. This is a study whose aim, as Aristotle insists, is not just theoretical understanding but also practice. (We study not just for the sake of learning but also to see our 'target' and ourselves more clearly, so that we can ourselves live and act better)."[3] "Specification" is the keyword here. Narratives like James's *Golden Bowl* can be counted as works of moral philosophy, Nussbaum says, precisely because they give close study to different theories of the good life by seeing how these theories compete with one another within complex, highly nuanced, often intricately tangled human situations. The moral agent, like the novelist, is "someone keenly alive in thought and feeling to every nuance of the situation" (*LK,* 143). Indeed, "the novel can be a paradigm of moral activity" precisely because it is "the intense scrutiny of particulars" (*LK,* 148). From Henry James, Nussbaum says, one can learn that moral knowledge is not simply "an intellectual grasp of propositions; it is not even simply the intellectual grasp of particular facts; it is perception" (*LK,* 152) in which "nuance and fine detail of tone" are everything (*LK,* 154). The idea here is that moral action or the moral life can never be reduced to rule-governed behavior or even to the application of received beliefs, values, and principles to the concrete situations in which we find ourselves; rather a "morality based on perception" (*LK*, 160) means the ability to see and respond to situations that are bewildering in the complexity of their particulars. This doesn't mean that we don't have or need principles, values, and rules; rather a "morality of perception" is the ability to achieve a kind of equilibrium of the general and the particular—Nussbaum calls it a "perceptive equilibrium . . . in which concrete perceptions 'hang beautifully together,' both with one another and with the agent's general principles; an equilibrium that is always ready to reconstitute itself in response to the new" (*LK*, 182). In a "morality based on perception," our beliefs, values, principles, and rules are always revisable in light of new experience, which means that what we strive for is an attunement between rule and situation, and also between ourselves and our community of values (*LK*, 192).

Now against this a Q-theorist like Emmanuel Levinas would say ethics cannot even get under way until we get rid of the idea of "the primacy of perceptive intuition" (*LK*, 141); and that is because ethics means turning the subject of perceptive intuition inside out.

In *Totality and Infinity* Levinas characterizes ethics in terms of the relationship between myself and "the Stranger" over whom "I have no power. He [the Stranger, the Other] escapes my grasp by an essential dimension, even if I have him at my disposal. He is not wholly in my site. But I, who have no concept in common with the Stranger, am, like him, without genus. We are the same and the other . . . The relation between the same and the other . . . is primordially enacted as conversation, where the same, gathered up in its ipseity as an 'I,' as a particular existent unique and autochthonous, leaves itself."[4] That is, in my encounter with the other my self-sameness, my self-possession, my self-identity as an *ego cogito,* my world and my spontaneous power of agency within it, is disrupted; I am, in the crucial simile, turned inside out "like a cloak," exposed to the other, radically resituated in a place of responsibility rather than that of cognition, intentionality, and agency.[5] This condition of exposure is what Levinas calls ethics. "The strangeness of the Other, his irreducibility to the I, to my thoughts and my possessions, is precisely accomplished as a calling into question of my spontaneity, as ethics" (*TI*, 143).

Two things about this line of thought make it impossible for someone like Martha Nussbaum to accept. One is that it opposes ethics to cognition, makes ethics the breakup of cognition, or what in *Otherwise than Being or Beyond Essence* Levinas calls "the breakup of essence" or the "breakup of identity" (*OTB*, 14). "Cognition," Levinas says, "is the deployment of [the identity of the] same . . . To know amounts to grasping being out of nothing, or reducing it to nothing, removing from it its alterity"—depriving it of all strangeness, clarifying it (*TI*, 43–44). Cognition is "hence not a relation with the other as such but the reduction of the other to the same. Such is the definition of freedom: to maintain oneself against the other despite every relation with the other to insure the autarchy of the I. Thematization and conceptualization, which moreover are inseparable, are not peace with the other but suppression or possession of the other. For possession affirms the other, but within a negation of its independence. 'I think' comes down to 'I can'—to an appropriation of what is, to an exploitation of reality . . . Possessions is preeminently the form in which the other becomes the same, by becoming mine" (*TI*, 46). So there can be no "non-allergic relation with alterity" (*TI*, 47) within the subject-centered relation of cognition. Nussbaum would reject this, but at the same time she would (or ought to) see the point of disengaging ethics from essence, since in fact that is the whole point of her effort to rehabilitate ethical theory by reconceptualizing Aristotle's notions of *aisthesis* and practical reasoning.[6] It is precisely to arrive at something like a "non-allergic relation with alterity" that Nussbaum wants to bring moral knowledge under the sign of love. Where Levinas speaks of responsibility, Nussbaum speaks of intimacy.[7] But hers always remains a morality of the subject. The beneficiary of morality is not the other but the sealed-off *ego cogito* for whom perceptive equilibrium means release from moral isolation—from the mere "curiosity of the uninvolved gaze" (*LK*, 187).

The second reason why Nussbaum could never hook up with Levinas's ethical theory is that hers is a comic theory while his is tragic. Ethics as the theory of the good life is necessarily comic.[8] Love's knowledge is not the sort of knowledge Oedipus or Lear suffer. Whereas for Levinas the breakup of essence or identity or the cognitive relation exposes the ethical subject in a terrible way: "Vulnerability, exposure to outrage, to wounding, passivity more passive than all patience, passivity of the accusative form, trauma of accusation suffered by a hostage to the point of persecution, implicating the identity of the hostage who substitutes himself for others: all this is the self, a defecting or defeat of the ego's identity" (*OTB*, 15). Nussbaum would certainly find this excessive and intolerable, but one can also imagine her seeing the point of it, since in fact the whole argument of *The Fragility of Goodness* is that the good life for human beings entails vulnerability to luck. The sealed-off egotism of the self-sufficient philosopher requires the repression of all that makes us human, starting with our bodies and our desires: call this a good life for philosophy but not for you and me. But there is a radical and perhaps unbridgeable difference between Nussbaum's vulnerability to luck and Levinas's exposure to outrage and persecution, and what makes the difference is that Levinas's ethical theory is above all an ethics of the Holocaust, that is, it presupposes a world of persecution and outrage—presupposes, as I say elsewhere, "a world in which the Holocaust is not unthinkable, surprises no one, but gives the definition of the everyday. Ethics [Levinasian ethics] presupposes tragedy as an ontological condition, even as it presupposes skepticism as an unsatisfiable questioning that takes us out of the mode of self-sufficiency and control. As if the ethical were something hardly to be borne, like being human."[9] Nussbaum speaks of the good life in terms of keen responsiveness and maintaining a delicate equilibrium the way Maggie Verver does it in James's *Golden Bowl,* which is (on Nussbaum's reading of it anyway) a great comic novel. Responsibility for the other, however, is not part of Nussbaum's theory, which is a theory of the good life for me and mine. It is a very Greek theory, as befits a classicist, whereas the ethics of the other, as Levinas shows in his Talmudic readings, is a very Jewish theory.[10] Nussbaum speaks almost exclusively in terms of responsiveness to *situations,* whereas Levinas speaks of the Stranger who will not be done away with even though I murder him, who destroys my self-relation by turning his face toward me, whose face turns me out in the open. Here ethics concerns not the good life but the real one. To put it as bluntly as one can, there may be nothing good about ethics.

II

If it is true that ethical theory is organized in this way, what can one say about the relation of poetry and ethics? On the one hand Martha Nussbaum seems very close to the New Criticism and its idea that the task of poetry is to release us from a culture of abstractions and to situate us within the range of the unrepeatable and concrete. Whereas philosophy wants a world answerable to our concepts, poetry seeks to restore our intimacy with the world—but always this seems to come down to a sense of *knowing* the world intimately: love's knowledge, to be sure, not reason's, but knowledge still. The pathos here is part of our Cartesian and Kantian legacy, the pathos of the disembodied, isolated subject of modernity whose knowledge of the world is purchased at the cost of its place in it. We might think of Nussbaum as one of "the last romantics," where romanticism is a general term for various experiments in re-embodying the subject, overcoming its solitude or separateness, its exile from things and from others (coping with solipsism and narcissism). The same might be said of Stanley Cavell, who starts out from the same place Martha Nussbaum does, namely from the standpoint of the knowing subject, but who interprets our problem of separateness differently, as if what we suffered from were not so much a *loss* as a *failure* of intimacy, which is to say *not* a failure of *knowing*—as if it were not a matter of bringing knowledge down to the level of particulars, or of taking feeling as a kind of knowing, but (as Cavell says) of forgoing or disowning knowledge, taking to heart the "truth" or "moral of skepticism, namely, that the human creature's basis in the world as a whole, its relation to the world as such, is not that of knowing, anyway not what we think of as knowing." [11]

Not that it is one of *not* knowing. [12] In his essay on *King Lear* Cavell asks: "How do we learn that what we need is not more knowledge but the willingness to forgo knowing?" [13] The idea is that "our relation to the world's existence is somehow *closer* than the ideas of believing or knowing convey." [14] Disowning knowledge, forgoing it, does not mean embracing ignorance or mysticism but averting, as if for the moment, what knowing aims at, or falls short of. As Cavell puts it, "the aim of reason [is] to know, objectively, without stint; to penetrate reality itself" (*CR*, 431). But human beings, among others, can never be known in this way, unstintingly, without hurt. Here is where one might try to explore the moral relevance of poetry. In poetry (as, for example, on Martin Heidegger's view of it, or on part of his view of it) we learn not so much to know as to abide with reality; that is, we learn to inhabit it. Poetry, on this view, presupposes a condition of responsiveness, of openness and reception as against grasping and penetration. [15] This, on Cavell's reading, is one of the senses of Thoreau's *Walden*, which (like philosophy perhaps) starts out with the condition of one's separateness, one's outsidedness (outsidedness, as it happens, even with respect to oneself), and which becomes the story of learning what intimacy with the world is. "We have to learn what finding is, what it means that we are looking for something [the world, our place in it, ourselves] that we have lost. And we have to learn what acceptance is, what it means that we have to find ourselves where we are, at each present, and accept that finding in our experiment, enter it in the account. This is what requires confidence. To be confident of nature, at every moment, appears as willingness to be confided in by it . . . This is why the writer's readings of nature do not feel like moralizations of it, but as though he is letting himself be read by it, confessed in it, listening to it, not talking about it" (*SW*, 98–99).[16]

Who wouldn't think of Heidegger here—especially where thinking opens on to *gehören* (in its several senses of listening, hearing, belonging, being claimed)?[17] Cavell naturally finds a coherence with Austin and Wittgenstein—"While I find that this sense of intimacy with existence or intimacy lost, is fundamental to the experience of what I understand ordinary language philosophy to be, I am for myself convinced that the thinkers who convey this experience best, most directly and practically, are not such as Austin and Wittgenstein but such as Emerson and Thoreau" (*SW*, 145–46)—but in "An Emerson Mood" he explicates this Emersonian sense of what intimacy is precisely by way of Heidegger's notion of "thinking as the receiving or letting be of something, as opposed to the positing or putting together of something" (*SW*, 132). Cavell says: "the idea of thinking as reception . . . seems to me a sound intuition, specifically to forward the correct answer to skepticism (which Emerson meant to do). The answer does not consist in denying the conclusion of skepticism but in reconceiving its truth. It is true that we do not know the existence of the world with certainty; our relation to its existence is deeper—one in which it is accepted, that is to day, received. My favorite way of putting this is to say that existence is to be acknowledged" (*SW*, 133). One can begin to see here how easily one might study Cavell in order to mediate the distance between analytic and Continental theory, and also perhaps between comedy and tragedy.

Levinas, meanwhile, suggests something like a distinction between two rival and incompatible theories of art. In the one, art is understood as trying to make the world identical with itself (improving on it). "The world," says Mallarmé, "was made to exist in a splendid book"—which is a line that Yeats took for his motto (as, in a more ironic way, did James Joyce). Art in this sense can be understood as expressing a fundamental disappointment with the world, or perhaps a disappointment with knowledge (supposing our knowledge to be, for example, scientific, or underwritten by philosophy).[18] So it is the separateness of art from the world, or from a certain representation of the world, or perhaps from any representation of it, that this theory tries to clarify. (Nothing wrong here: you can't have art without allowing the claim of this originary disappointment.)

In the other theory, art is understood as opening itself to the world in all of the world's randomness and contingency, which means opening itself to all of the ways in which the world is what it is: not art. Art, putting its own "ontological peculiarity" at risk, lets the world abide as what is alien to itself (lets itself abide this way: becomes indistinguishable from—frees itself into—what is not art. "A poem," says William Carlos Williams, "can be made out of anything").[19] Here is where one should begin one's study of John Cage, with his idea of silence in music, which is a very different thing from Mallarmé's silence. Mallarmean silence is achieved by excluding the materiality of language. You get a lot of this silence in Wallace Stevens, who wants above everything a music one cannot actually hear. Whereas Cage speaks of silence as "opening the doors of music to the sounds that happen to be in the environment" (S, 8). The work of art in this event is no longer an "aesthetic monad."[20] It is porous and exposed, turned inside out in the sense of being turned out into the world as something no longer seperate and external: the world is, so to speak, allowed to occupy the space of art without having to pay the usual aesthetic price. (Thus Cage: "Silence, like music, is non- / existent. There always are sounds. That / is to say if one is alive to hear them" S, 152.)

Duchamp's idea of decomposing the forms of art seems relevant here as well if we think of this as a way of defeating the power of form to seal art off from everything that is not itself.[21] But John Cage seems more radical still, because the relationship between music and noise is no longer an aesthetic relation of harmony but (in Cavell's language) an ethical relation of acknowledgment—music letting sounds be themselves.[22] Music becomes, Heidegger-like, a listening as much as a playing (S, 10). (Imagine music responding to noise as if were a person or, more sublimely, a Levinasian Other!) The touchstone here is the chapter, "Sounds," in Thoreau's *Walden,* as glossed by Cage's "Composition in Retrospect," a mesostic poem on the words method, structure, intention, and indeterminacy:

musIc
Never stops it is we who turn away
against the worlD around

<blockquote>
silEnce
sounds are only bubbles on iTs
surfacE
they buRst to disappear (thoreau)
when we Make
musIc
we merely make somethiNg
thAt
Can
more NaturallY be heard than seen or touched[23]
</blockquote>

However, nothing clarifies this conception of openness to the world so well as Cage's recourse to *I Ching* and "chance operations" as a way of forgoing knowledge in composition, or what Cage refers to as the making of "a musical composition the continuity of which is free of individual taste and memory (psychology) and also of the literature and 'traditions' of art." Whereas in Mallarmé's poetics the throw of the dice is meant to abolish chance, in Cage's aesthetics the throw means giving up control and letting sounds be sounds (*S*, 72).[24] Chance operations are the Cagean or (in Cavell's language) "ordinary" equivalent of Heidegger's *Gelassenheit;* chance brings openness to mystery down to earth in the form of acceptance (acknowledging the *es gibt* of things). It cannot be surprising that among the forerunners of modern music Cage numbers Meister Eckhart, whom he quotes as follows: "But one must achieve this unselfconsciousness by means of transformed knowledge. This ignorance does not come from lack of knowledge but rather it is from knowledge that one may achieve this ignorance. Then we shall be informed by the divine unconsciousness and in that our ignorance will be ennobled and adorned with supernatural knowledge. It is by reason of this fact that we are made perfect by what happens to us rather than by what we do" (*S*, 64).[25]

This unselfconsciousness, this positive (unempty) ignorance, throws art and philosophy into the air. For what happens to art, or to philosophy, when either is no longer thought of, Aristotle-like, as a way of getting a grip on things, detailing them, improving on them, fixing them exactly, getting them straight, tuning them to our concepts? Imagine art, or philosophy, not as cognition (nor even as "perceptive equilibrium"), but as a way of turning things loose, freeing them, for example, from art

or from philosophy—from the sealed-off subject, the subject forever subject to dis-
turbances, but also from the way such a subject arranges things (coherently, unam-
biguously, hierarchically). Cage's last mesostic poem, "Overpopulation and Art," a
utopian vision that imagines a world both artless and free of concepts (anarchic), has
these lines:

> O
> haVing
> no nEed
> foR art
> Pleased with what i see
> O
> Pleased with what i hear
> sUrrounded
> by muLtiplicity
> he sAid he could imagine
> a world wiThout art
> and that It wasn't bad
> O
> artlessNess
> the sound of trAffic
> aN instance of silence
> the sounD
> of trAffic
> the sound of tRaffic
> an insTance
> Of silence   'phone rings [26]

If one wanted to be scholastic about it, one might speak here of Cage's aesthetics
of disturbance or (borrowing from Levinas) of "restlessness," in which the artist allows chance to recompose the order and fixity in which we otherwise frame things,
not simply to undo this order, but to set free what it tries to contain (or, much
to the same point, to let in what it tries to exclude). Levinas speaks of a "radical non assemblable diachrony [that] would be excluded from meaning," where
meaning means something like undisturbed, uninterrupted, uninvaded self-identity

(*OTB*, 135). A "non assemblable diachrony" describes very well Cage's anarchic "Mureau" (1970), which is "a mix of letters, syllables, words, phrases, and sentences [produced] by subjecting all the remarks of Henry David Thoreau about music, silence, and sounds he heard that are indexed in the Dover publication of the *Journal* to a series of *I Ching* chance operations"[27] (see fig. 19). The result of this disturbance is a text freed from the usual dialogue with a cognitive subject trained to reduce mere surface noise to underlying logical structures—a text freed from the old I-Thou, which doubles as a freeing of the I, for one could just as well say in this event that the result (the outcome of Cage's art) is a disturbed subject, an I-think turned inside out by what is refractory, irreducible, uncontainable, anarchic. It would not be too much to speak of the Cagean I as the subject of the ethical, that is, the non-egological ego who speaks or writes as follows:

how

whaT

Is

nOt

uNderstood

A mystery

is Now necessary

something we Don't

of which we cAn't

make head oR

Tail

a music Of

Variations

without rEpetitions

an intRoduction to

Pleasure

that has nO need for

Proof or ideas or feelings

goal withoUt

goaL

And

MUREAU

sparrowsitA gROsbeak betrays *itself* by that peculiar squeakariEFFECT
OF SLIGHTEst tinkling measures soundness ingpleasa We hear! Does
it not rather hear us? sWhen he hears the telegraph, he thinksthose
bugs have issued forthThe owl *touches* the stops, wakes reverb
erations *d gwalky* In verse there is no inherent *music eo*fsttakestak
es a man to make a room silent It takes to make a roomIt IS A Young a
ppetite and the appETITEFOR IsHe Oeyssee morningYou hear scream o
f great hawka ydgh *body*Shelie beingsilencelt would be noblest to sing
with the windTo hear a neighbor *singing!* u it wood The triosteum a
day or twob mtryTheysays to-wee, *to-*weecalling to his team lives he
ard over high *open fieldsday inst*ead of the drum thensav pa with youn
g birdswith young birdsfrom a truck ndat every postt ed der oglects
in the meantime o pi at so *piercing ders ache*Theyo ato sing in earnest
seven now chU ASISu gddd gheasu s iot ei gh c n ch siYou woul
d thiNK MUSIC *was being b*orn again off *Toad*s are still heard at *eve
ning*cRIckets'Echo is an *independent sound Rhyme and* tell his story and
breathe himselfbreathe A shrill loud alarm is *incessantly* repeated t
heheroic hovers from *over the* pond *the clear* metallic *scream* they
went off with a shriller craikThey go off with a hoARSer chuck ch
uck noair hear sharp, screaming notes rending the airThis suggests *wha
t* perpetual flow *of spirit would* produceA thrumming beyond and thr
oughimportant Every *one can* CAll to mind instances miⅡ Trees creak
*ringing*We could not hear the birdsIs *the third* note confined to this
season? Little frogs begin to peep toward sundown noonhorn is heard e
choing from shore *to shore*of perchwith a loud, *rippl*ing rustle t
hink larmedand makes life seem serene *and grandinex*pressibly serene
and *grand apparently* afrai*dwith more vigor and promise bells*lee uttering
that sign-like note verwarm and *moist not much of* the toad ev so ch
eaply enr*iched for the listeningof* that word "sound" and *am the scene*
of liferingter viMusicand mel in melody ein the next townand fire
openest all her senses *n k swhich they* do not rememberee eeach *recess o
F* THE WOODA Ea what various distinct sounds we *heard there* deep in
*the woodshn*AND echo along the shore ymORE THAN A Rodnd a sa stead
y, BReathing, cricket-like soundhunseen and unheard *May it be such
summer as it suggests into* the woodsThere is *inwardness even in* the
mosqu*itoes' hum*Trees have been so many empty music-*halls* heard from th
e depth of the woodnigHT IHE toward nighttheir hour has *serenity who a
m*humming past so busily lungs sweet *flowingfrom* farther or nearerhuRR
IED RIPPLING NOtes in the yardas we passed under itsatand sat do
wn to hear the wind roar swift *and s*teadya *performer* he never seestw
o of themis perhaps hearD COMMUNicated so disTINCtly through the oar t
o the air across the river directly against his eardifferently sounda

Fig. 19.   Page from Cage, *M: Writings '67–72*

> whaT
> dId i hear
> Or see
> i caN't be sure
> it wAs as if
> there was Nothing
> on which to Depend
> As if
> theRe was
> noThing   (OA, 332–62)

This "noThing" is not Mallarmé's sublime *Néant*. Rather it is where things come from when they come out of nowhere, as if by chance, not so much falling from the sky as welling up from the street—imagine a lower-case Heideggerian *es gibt,* in which all that is is just there, like Levinasian *responsibility:* "a plot without a beginning: anarchic" (*OTB,* 135). Cage's art is like this: not chaotic, not incoherent or unintelligible, but anarchic and unassimilable (unassemblable), not part of a design: without why—in the spirit of Meister Eckhart: external to art and philosophy (just the way the world is: intimate, embraceable).

Let me conclude as follows. When I received the letter from Herbert Lindenberger inviting me to write about John Cage under the title of "Poethics," I thought irrepressibly of Poe. The thought is not implausible. In an essay called "Being Odd, Getting Even," Cavell reads Poe's story, "The Imp of the Perverse," as a perversion or parody of Descartes' *Discourse on Method,* with its construction of an *ego cogito* impervious to its environment. Cavell notes that Poe's story is, impishly, saturated with "imp-words" (*impulse, impels, impatient, important, impertinent, impossible, imprisoned, impressive,* among others). "The Imp of the Perverse" is a Joycean or Cagean text. Cavell remarks that in learning a language we obligate ourselves to behave like an *ego cogito:* "the possession of language," he says, "[is] the subjection of oneself to the intelligible" (*QO,* 124). But in subjecting ourselves so we also discover willy-nilly that language is filled with word-imps. "'Word-imps,'" Cavell explains, "could name any of the recurrent combinations of letters of which the words of a language are composed. They are part of the way words have their familiar looks and sounds, and their familiarity depends upon our mostly *not* noticing the particles (or cells) and their laws, which constitute words and their imps—on our not noticing their necessary recurrences, which is perhaps only to say that recurrence constitutes familiarity." Rationality, one might say—being rational rather than (like the narrator of Poe's story) mad, or impish—means not noticing these recurrent particles or cells; it means not hearing the noises language makes on its way to being intelligible. One could not read or write mesostics in this (call it a nonethical) spirit. Cavell continues: "When we do note these cells or molecules, these little moles of language (perhaps in thinking, perhaps in derangement), what we discover are word imps—the initial, or it may be medial or final, movements, the implanted origins or constituents of words, leading lives of their own, staring back at us, calling upon one another, giving us away, alarming—because to note them is to see that they live in front of our eyes, within earshot, at every moment" (QO, 125).

Certainly a crucial link between poetry and ethics lies in allowing words, or particles of words (the sounds of parts of words, and with them the world of things, not to say of others), to live their own lives; it means listening, not tuning things out but letting them take us along. This does not mean, Cavell says, that we should stop making sense, rather it means being attuned, open and responsive (responsible), to the sense we do make, taking responsibility for our words (not just control of them), accepting them and where they take us, as if our task now were not to describe the world, such as we know it, framing representations in words, but to come into it, as if leaving our philosophical shelter. There's an ethical distinction here that remains to be clarified between using words to grasp the world and using them to inhabit it, as we use our names. Cavell understands Thoreau in these terms. Thoreau's calling as a writer, Cavell says, "depends upon his acceptance of this fact about words, his letting them come to him from their own region, and then taking that occasion for inflecting them one way instead of another then and there, or for refraining from them then and there; as one may inflect the earth toward beans instead of grass, or let it alone, as it is before you are there" (SW, 28). Likewise Cage: "Reading the *Journal*," Cage says, "I had been struck by the twentieth-century way Thoreau listened. He listened, it seemed to me, just as composers using technology nowadays listen. He paid attention to each sound, whether it was 'musical' or not, just as they do; and he explored the neighborhood of Concord with the same appetite with which they explore the possibilities provided by electronics" (M, ix). This means being open to the surface and contingency of things, relinquishing categories of deep structure in favor of the singular and irreducible, or what is only accessible in the accidents of ordinary life.

My last thought, therefore, is of a legendary John Cage, who nevertheless left his name in the New York City Telephone Directory and so allowed himself to be interrupted by his environment, or more precisely by other people.[28]

> the sounD
> of trAffic
> the sound of tRaffic
> an insTance
> Of silence   'phone rings   (OA, 259–63)

Little in theory can embody the ethical so cleanly or impishly as Cage's everyday generosity, letting himself be addressed, which is of course nothing more nor less than taking responsibility—answering—for one's presence in the world, thus answering for the world (and its others) as well. Cage was able to say to the world (he never merely used his art to say it for him): "Here I am." His art was never an alter ego, never a disengaged sublimity; it was something he joyfully relinquished to the world, even and perhaps especially in the sheer moment of making it.

Notes

1. Stanley Cavell, "The Avoidance of Love: An Essay on *King Lear*," in *Disowning Knowledge in Six Plays by Shakespeare* (Cambridge: Cambridge University Press, 1987), p. 95.

2. John Cage, "Lecture on Something," in *Silence* (Middletown, CT: Wesleyan University Press, 1961), p. 129. Hereafter cited as *S*.

3. Martha Nussbaum, "Flawed Crystals: James's *The Golden Bowl* and Literature as Moral Philosophy," in *Love's Knowledge: Essays on Philosophy and Literature* (New York and Oxford: Oxford University Press, 1990), p. 139. Hereafter cited as *LK*. See also *The Fragility of Goodness: Luck and Ethics in Greek Tragedy and Philosophy* (Cambridge: Cambridge University Press, 1986), pp. 14–15.

4. Emmanuel Levinas, *Totality and Infinity,* trans. Alphonso Lingis (Philadelphia: Duquesne University Press, 1961), p. 39. Hereafter cited as *TI.*

5. Emmanuel Levinas, *Otherwise than Being, or Beyond Essence,* trans. Alphonso Lingis (The Hague: Martinus Nijhoff, 1981), p. 48. Hereafter cited as *OTB.*

6. See Martha Nussbaum, "The Discernment of Perception: An Aristotelian Conception of Private and Public Rationality," in *Love's Knowledge,* pp. 54–105.

7. This matter is both complicated and, for Nussbaum, still in need of further reflection. In her superb analysis of James's *The Ambassadors* Nussbaum raises the question of whether the intimacy of others does not constitute the limit of a morality of perception. The case is that of Strether as a moral agent confronting the intimacy of Chad and Mme de Vionnet. "What Strether senses is that what he calls the 'deep deep truth' of sexual love is at odds with the morality of perception, in two ways. It asks for privacy, for others to avert their gaze; and on the inside it asks that focus be averted from all else that is outside. Lovers see, at such times, only one another; and it is not really deep if they *can* carefully see around and about them. That vision excludes general attention and care, at least at that moment. And this intimacy is a part of the world that demands *not* to be in the eyes of the perceiving, recording novelist—at least not in all of its particularity" (*LK,* 188–89). To which Nussbaum adds: "Perception as a morality enjoins trust in responsive feeling; but its feelings are the feelings of a friend . . . There is reason to suppose that the exclusivity and intensity of personal love would in fact impede the just and general responsiveness that these gentler feelings assist. And if they impede that, they impede the perceiver's contribution to our moral project, to our communal effort to arrive at perceptive equilibrium. But the recognition that there is a view of the world from passion's point of view, and that this view is closed to the perceiver, shows us that perception is, even by its own lights, incomplete" (*LK,* 189).

8. Comedy and tragedy are, in their various ways, basic ethical categories. An ethical theory that claimed to be neutral with respect to comedy and tragedy would have a hard time seeming to be a theory for human beings. I try to explain the sense in which Nussbaum's is a comic theory in "Tragic Thoughts at the End of Philosophy," *Soundings* 72, no. 4 (Winter 1989):709–14.

9. Emmanuel Levinas, "Dialogue and the Truth of Skepticism," *Religion and Literature* 22, nos. 2–3 (Summer–Autumn 1990):90.

10. See Emmanuel Levinas, "Toward the other," in *Nine Talmudic Readings,* trans. Annette Aronowicz (Bloomington: Indiana University Press, 1990), pp. 12–29, and also p. 34:

To join evil to good, to venture into the ambiguous corners of being without sinking into evil and to remain beyond good and evil in order to accomplish this, is to know. One must experience everything through one's own self but experience it without having experienced it yet, before engaging oneself in the world. For experiencing itself is already committing oneself, choosing, living, limiting oneself. To know is to experience without experiencing, before living. We want to know before we do. But we want only a knowledge completely tested through our own evidence. We do not want to undertake anything without knowing everything, and nothing can become known to us unless we have gone and seen for ourselves, regardless of the misadventures of the exploration. We want to live dangerously, but in security, in the world of truths.

11. Stanley Cavell, *The Claim of Reason: Wittgenstein, Skepticism, Morality, and Tragedy* (Oxford and New York: Oxford University Press, 1979), p. 241. Hereafter cited as *CR.*

12. See Stanley Cavell, *In Quest of the Ordinary: Lines of Skepticism and Romanticism* (Chicago: University of Chicago Press, 1988), pp. 8–9. Hereafter cited as *QO.*

13. Stanley Cavell, *Disowning Knowledge in Six Plays of Shakespeare* (Cambridge: Cambridge University Press, 1987), p. 95.

14. Stanley Cavell, "An Emerson Mood," in *The Senses of Walden* (San Francisco: North Point Press, Expanded Edition 1981), p. 143. Hereafter cited as *SW.*

15. See Gerald L. Bruns, *Heidegger's Estrangements: Language, Truth, and Poetry in the Later Writings* (New Haven: Yale University Press, 1989).

16. See also *SW*, 106–7n., for Cavell's suggestion "that *Walden* provides a transcendental deduction of the thing-in-itself":

The concept [of the thing-in-itself] just says that it has no transcendental deduction, that its object is not an object of knowledge for us, so to ask for a deduction of it is, on Kant's program, senseless. But what is "a thing which is not an object of knowledge for us"? Everyone involved with Kant's thought recognizes a problem here, the implication that there are things just like the things we know (or features of the very things we know) which, not answering to our conditions for knowing anything, are unknowable by us. We oughtn't to be able to attach any meaning at all to such an implication. If something does not answer to our conditions of knowledge then it is not subject to what we understand as knowledge, and that means that it is not what we understand as an object. A thing which we cannot know is not a thing. Then why are we led to speak otherwise? What is the sense that something escapes the conditions of knowledge? It is, I think, the sense, or fact, that our primary relation to the world is not one of knowing (understood as achieving certainty of it based upon the senses). This is the truth of skepticism. A Kantian "answer" to skepticism would be to accept its truth while denying the apparent implication that this is a *failure* of knowledge. This is the role the thing-in-itself ought, as it were, to have played. The idea of God is that of a relation in which the world as a whole stands; call it a relation of dependency, or of having something "beyond" it. The idea of the thing-in-itself is the idea of a relation in which we stand to the world as a whole; call it a relation of the world's externality (not each object's externality to every other—that is the idea of space; but the externality of all objects to us). When I said that Kant ought to have provided a deduction of the thing-in-itself, I meant that he had left unarticulated an essential feature (category) of objectivity itself, viz., that of *a world apart from me in which* objects are met. The externality of the world is articulated by Thoreau as its nextness to me.

17. In "The Nature of Language," for example, Heidegger characterizes thinking as listening, where listening is also a pun on belonging. See Martin Heidegger, *The Way to Language,* trans. Peter D. Hertz (New York: Harper & Row, 1971), pp. 75–76. For an explication of the pun in *gehören* see Gerald L. Bruns, *Heidegger's Estrangements: Language, Truth, and Poetry in the Later Writings,* pp. 107–12 and pp. 165–73.

18. In *The Claim of Reason* Cavell understands this disappointment with knowledge as one of the fundamental links between skepticism and tragedy—it is, in several complex ways, a cause of both (*CR,* 483–96).

19. See Joseph Margolis, "The Ontological Peculiarity of the Work of Art," in *Art and Philosophy: Conceptual Issues in Aesthetics* (New York: Humanities Press, 1980), pp. 17–24.

20. See Theodor Adorno, *Aesthetic Theory,* trans. C. Lehman (London: Routledge and Kegan Paul, 1984), pp. 257–58.

21. Marcel Duchamp, *The Writings of Marcel Duchamp,* ed. Michel Sanouillet and Elmer Peterson (New York: Da Capo Press, 1973), p. 126.

22. On acknowledgment see Cavell, *Disowning Knowledge,* pp. 94–95, and *In Quest of the Ordinary,* p. 8. In "Reality and Its Shadow" Levinas says: "musicality belongs to sound naturally." See *Philosophical Papers,* trans. Alphonso Lingis (Dordrecht: Martinus Nijhoff, 1987), p. 5.

23. John Cage, "Composition in Retrospect," in *X: Writings '79–'82* (Middletown, CT: Wesleyan University Press, 1983), p. 140. See also "Composition: To Describe the Process of Composition Used in *Music of Changes* and *Imaginary Landscape No. 4* (*S*, 57–61).

24. Cage gives an account of this "method" of composition in "Composition" (*S*, 57–61).

25. Or again: "Is counterpoint good? 'The soul itself is so simple that it cannot have more than one idea at a time of anything. . . . A person cannot be more than single in attention.' (Eckhart)" (*S*, 64). Compare Cavell, *Disowning Knowledge,* pp. 9–10.

26. John Cage, "Overpopulation and Art," ll. 243–63, in this volume. Hereafter cited as OA, followed by line numbers.

27. John Cage, *M: Writings '67–'72* (Middletown, CT: Wesleyan University Press, 1973), p. ix.

28. See the interview with Richard Kostelanetz in *John Cage: An Anthology,* ed. Richard Kostelanetz (New York: Da Capo Press, 1991), p. 6.

Chance Operations: Cagean Paradox and Contemporary Science

N. Katherine Hayles

When asked how he constructed his works, whether verbal, visual, or musical, Cage regularly referred to "chance operations." The phrase, a staple of Cagean criticism, strikes me as passing strange. Chance, according to *The American Heritage Dictionary,* is the "abstract nature or quality shared by unexpected, random, or unpredictable events," as well as such events themselves. It is also a "probability," "an opportunity, a risk or hazard; a gamble." Although these definitions have interesting tensions among themselves—the distinction between an opportunity and a risk, for example—they convey well enough our sense of chance as that which cannot be controlled, that which is in excess of our expectations, designs, or predictions. An operation, by contrast, is "a process or series of acts performed to effect a certain purpose or result." Deriving from the Latin *operari,* to work or labor, it is first cousin to the Latin *opus,* most often used in contemporary contexts to denote a work of art or music. On the one hand we have that which exceeds or escapes our designs, chance; and on the other an operation, which is the process by which we put our designs into effect. What does it mean, then, to have a chance operation?

Chance, seemingly so transparent in its meanings, has proved notoriously difficult to pin down in any rigorous way. Drawing on my work on randomness, chaos, and noise in scientific contexts, I want to suggest three interpretations of chance that present it as a concept that can be enacted through an operation. I will locate aspects of Cage's work in relation to these three interpretations and point to questions raised by the oxymoronic qualities of chance operations. My intention is to recontextualize in scientific terms the deep aesthetic and ethical issues Cage's work raises about our attempt to grasp through our intentions a world that always exceeds and outruns those intentions.

For the first definition of chance, I am indebted to the work of Stanislaw Lem. Picking up on Borges's observation that it is much easier to review the books one hopes to write than actually to write them, Lem, in *A Perfect Vacuum,* creates narrators who review nonexistent books. Among the reviews is an admiring summary of Professor Benedykt Kousha's *De Impossibilitate Vitae.*[1] Professor Kousha believes there is something awry in how scientists think about probabilities. To expose the fallacies, he shows that according to the laws of probability, he ought not to exist. His father was an army doctor who met his mother when he snapped at her after she entered the operating room by mistake. The conjunction required a nurse unfamiliar with the hospital and a doctor with a short fuse, as well as a superior officer who pointed out to the doctor that his behavior toward the young lady was unseemly. Had these elements not been in place, the doctor would not have sought her out to apologize, and they would not have fallen in love, married, and had a child. But that is just the start of the coincidences, for the meeting required that his father be conscripted into the army as a doctor and his mother volunteer as a nurse, which in turn required all the intricate conjunctions that initiated World War I and created the right circumstances for the creation of a certain army field hospital staffed by a certain impetuous doctor and disoriented nurse. The upshot, of course, is that if one calculates the probabilities for each of these events and multiplies them together to get the probability of the writer's birth, it is so staggeringly infinitisimal that by rights the writer could not possibly exist. Lem, slyly keeping at bay the reader's awareness that Professor Kousha does not in fact exist by filtering it through layers of texts, puts in the reviewer's mouth a favorite idea.[2] Chance, the narrator suggests, is the intersection of independent causal chains. Each is deterministic on its own, but the intersections create unthinkable complexity and inevitable unpredictability. In this view, the world comes into existence as threads of independent worldlines—a term describing how subatomic particles move through spacetime—whose intersections create the warp and woof of the universe.

Many of the anecdotes in Cage's diaries and essays take their point and wit from these intersecting worldlines. A story from *Silence* illustrates the technique. A conductress, finding the Manchester-Stockport bus too crowded by one passenger, demands to know who was the last person on. No one speaks. She enlists the help of the driver and then of an inspector; still no one speaks. Finally the three leave to look for a policeman. While they are gone, a little man comes up, asks if this is the bus to Stockport, and boards. The officials return with a policeman in tow, who dutifully demands to know who was the last person on.

> The little man said, "I was." The policeman said, "All right, get off." All the people on the bus burst into laughter. The conductress, thinking they were laughing at her, burst into tears and said she refused to make the trip to Stockport. The inspector then arranged for another conductress to take over. She, seeing the little man standing at the bus stop, said, "What are you doing there?" He said, "I'm waiting to go to Stockport." She said, "Well, this is the bus to Stockport. Are you getting on or not?"[3]

The ironies emerge from the insider's knowledge that the apparent continuities are illusions, produced not by true causal sequences but by conjunctions between independent worldlines. The officials assume that the little man is the culprit for whom they have been looking, whereas the passengers know he is yet another surplus man; the conductress assumes that the passengers' laughter is directed at her, when in actuality it signals their appreciation of the confusion over the "last passenger"; this irony is succeeded by a more complex, multilayered one produced by the conjunction of the change of conductresses with the reader's appreciation of the narrative continuity that makes the invitation to board a reversal of previous policy. When the story is considered in context, yet another level of irony emerges. The story appears in a collection called "Indeterminacy," prefaced by Cage's explanation that he composed the collection by making a list of the stories he could remember and writing them in no particular order. The continuity of the collection is no less an illusion than the continuities within the stories. The conjunctions of independent worldlines that create the stories also produce the collection as a whole.

Yet the point is not to deny connection, since conjunction is a kind of connection. Rather it is to subvert the anthropomorphic perspective that constructs continuity from a human viewpoint of control and isolation. Continuity in the strong sense of sequential events related through cause and effect implies an ability to isolate the causal chains from "extraneous" influences, for example when a scientific experiment is said to be controlled. Conjunction, by contrast, emphasizes connections that are unplanned and out of the character's control, perhaps even (if the narrative is generated through chance operations) out of the narrator's control. In *The Poetics of Indeterminacy: Rimbaud to Cage,* Marjorie Perloff calls the anecdotes punctuating the expository discourse of *Silence* threads of relational narratives that create, quoting John Ashberry, "'an open field of narrative possibilities.'"[4] The stories of "Indeterminacy" illustrate her point. Escaping the narrow bounds of anthropomorphic control, they point toward the much more numerous connections of aleatory encounters that, woven together, comprise the ongoing process of the universe as it is. Cage writes in the preface, "My intention in putting the stories together in an unplanned way was to suggest that all things—stories, incidental sounds from the environment, and, by extension, beings—are related, and that this complexity is more evident when it is not oversimplified by an idea of relationship in one person's mind" (*S,* 260). By giving up an anthropomorphic viewpoint based on control, he implies, we gain a more capacious view of connection that engages us in the world rather than isolates us from it.

The *visible* traces of connection can be seen in Cage's collection of edible papers, exhibited at the Stanford University Art Museum in January 1992. The idea had occurred to him considerably earlier. In 1970–71, he wrote in "Diary: How to Improve the World (You Will Only Make Matters Worse)" that "paper should be edible, nutritious."

Inks used for
printing or writing should have
delicious flavors.   Magazines or
newspapers read at breakfast should be
eaten for lunch.   Instead of throwing
one's mail in the waste-basket, it
should be saved for the dinner guests.[5]

When he collected the field grasses to create these edible papers, the causal chain of plant life that produced a certain strain of pigweed on a particular hill, colored and shaped through its interactions with the sun at that latitude and longitude, intersected with his intention to gather it for his project. He respected and preserved its independence by using the *I Ching* for the recipe that yielded a work in which the plant's particular shadings and conformations can still be seen. Adapting a phrase from Donna Haraway, we might say that in such work Cage is attending to the world's independent sense of humor.

And to his own. Why should paper be edible? The idea playfully transforms food for thought into food for the body, overcoming the mind/body split in a way that no doubt never occurred to Descartes. Its creation testifies to the primacy of process over product, turning a relatively permanent mode of external memory storage into the dynamic internal processes of metabolic conversion. If the paper is eaten, the memory it helps to fuel would record its taste and texture as well as any words that may have been written upon it. More than an anonymous medium for the transmission of ideas, the paper is allowed to assert sensory qualities that, existing independently of its conceptual function, merge with signification in the dynamic processes of living memory. Cage enacts a similar transformation when he scores musical works according to imperfections in the paper on which he happens to be writing. The paper came to possess those imperfections through following its independent worldline, and Cage respects that independence by transcribing its effects into his notation. When the music is performed, human intention meets and merges with the paper's history. Connection between worldlines, such strategies imply, need not necessitate domination and control of one by another. In the fabric of the universe, human intention is one thread among many, not the whole cloth.

Applied to music, these strategies aim to evoke an appreciation of sounds for their unique sensory qualities, independent of the intention that produces and interprets them. "*A sound does not view itself as thought, as ought, as needing another sound for its elucidation, as etc.; it has no time for any consideration—it is occupied with the performance of its characteristics; before it has died away it must have made perfectly exact its frequency, its loudness, its length, its overtone structure, the precise morphology of these and of itself*" ("Experimental Music: Doctrine," in *S*, 14). The sound, "[u]rgent, unique, uninformed about history and theory," does not exist as "one of a series of discrete steps, but as transmission in all directions from the field's center" (*S*, 14). Essence merges with performance, doing with being. The sound, creating itself as it comes into being, *is* its performance.

Yet is not intention finally primary, since it is responsible for creating the designs that draw attention to its limits? The question is posed by the interlocutor of "Experimental Music: Doctrine." How, he asks Cage, can one *intend* to produce a work that sabotages intention? By following random number tables as Earle Brown does,

Cage answers, or by using "chance operations, some derived from the *I Ching*, others from the observation of imperfections in the paper on which I happen to be writing." "Your answer: by not giving it a thought," Cage deviously concludes in an afterthought which is also the main thought (*S*, 17). The answer suggests that techniques involving a certain obliqueness or indirection have the best chance of penetrating the closed circle of intentionality.

The glancing, ricochet quality of Cagean intention is also paradoxically central to the preceding essay, "Experimental Music." "One is, of course, not dealing with purposes but dealing with sounds," Cage writes. "Or the answer must take the form of paradox: a purposeful purposelessness or a purposeless play. This play, however, is an affirmation of life—not an attempt to bring order out of chaos nor to suggest improvements in creation, but simply a way of waking up to the very life we're living, which is so excellent once one gets one's mind and one's desires out of its way and lets it act of its own accord" (*S*, 12). Chance, understood as connections between independent worldlines, has the liberating power to release us from the limitations of our expectations. Given a head start by subversive intentionality, chance has a chance to outrun intention and thereby open us to the world as it is, not merely as we think it will or should be.

The second interpretation of chance relevant to Cage's work focuses on temporality. The configuration of the *I Ching* sticks is determined by chance, but once the throw has been made, chance has spoken and its dictates must be obeyed. It does not matter that the edible paper made from some recipes is so fragile that it crumbles at the touch; it has been made nevertheless and the laws of chance—themselves oxymorons—have been fulfilled. What a curious system this is. At one moment anything can happen, and at the next, out of nearly infinite possibilities branching in all directions, one has emerged as the path that must be followed, often with considerable inconvenience and great technical ingenuity. Chance expresses itself through the profusion of possible paths and the emergence of one, intention by rigorously adhering to the indicated worldline until it has crystallized into existence through painstaking operations. Once the branching point has been passed, no effort is too great to ensure that the indicated path will be followed exactly. Implicit in this system is a strong affirmation of time's one-way directionality. Not everything goes because the arrow of time points only forward. Hence Cage's work can be understood as a performance of time, as well as a performance in time.

One of the deep questions in contemporary science is why time moves only forward. Ilya Prigogine, 1977 Nobel Prize winner in chemistry, and coauthor Isabelle Stengers have argued that intersecting causal chains, in addition to creating chance, also give time its arrow.[6] Before the chains intersect, there is no necessary reason why they have to come together. Their evolutions progress independently of each other. After the conjunction occurs, however, reversing time would mean coordinating actions that were previously independent. For what does it mean to say that time runs backward? The idea makes sense only if events which happened a certain way occur a second time in reverse order. In this reverse order only one worldline is allowed, namely that which runs backward through the conjunctions created by chance intersections the first time through. Because branching points are theoretically possible at every instant, the probability that any given worldline will be recreated becomes infinitisimal very quickly. There is experimental evidence to suggest that once in a great while, the products of a subatomic collision come together again to recreate the original particles.[7] In such cases, very short time increments and very few particles are involved. Even so, the probability that they will be coordinated in just the right way is small enough to make microscopic time reversal a rare (indeed, disputed) event. Since the amount of information necessary to achieve coordination increases exponentially as the number of branching points increases, imagine how much more improbable it would be to coordinate the millions of particles involved in a macroscopic event that takes place in minutes or hours. Time moves only forward, Prigogine and Stengers conclude, because an infinite information barrier separates the past from the future.

The difference between an open-ended evolution forward in time and a constrained retrodiction backward in time provides the basis for Lem's paradoxical scenario of a fictional author proving he could not have been born. Before the events leading to his birth happened, their coordination was a matter of chance; but when he imagines *retrospectively* that all the intersections had to occur in just that way, the probability is reduced essentially to zero. Any theory of probability which does not include a consideration of time's arrow, this critique suggests, is seriously incomplete. Similarly, any consideration of time which does not include an analysis of how probability affects its asymmetry is also incomplete. Probability and time's arrow go together.

Cage implicitly recognizes this conjunction when he performs his chance operations. Putting the matter in these terms, we can say that when time runs forward chance overwhelms operation, but that if time were to run backward, operation would have to overwhelm chance. Time's one-way directionality thus affirms the predominance of chance over operation. Although Cage's chance operations inevitably bring intentionality back into play, they do so in a context that emphasizes this asymmetry. Driving down time's one-way street, his work does more than go with the flow. It also points insistently to the traffic signs indicating more is in play than human intellection alone. "Some- / thing more far-reach- / ing is neces- / sary: a com- / posing of sounds / within a u- / niverse predi- / cated upon the / sounds themselves / rather than up- / on the mind which / can envisage / their coming in- / to being," Cage writes in one of the multiple parallel columns (worldlines?) of "Composition as Process" (S, 27–28).

Although temporality is central to Cage's work, the kind of time it enacts differs significantly from the clockwork universe and infinite predictability of Newton and Laplace. The difference is beautifully captured in an idea that has emerged from nonlinear dynamical systems: fractal time. When we think about aging, we are apt to imagine it as a process that takes place along a single dimension. We move forward in time in a regular progression, registered spatially in our bodies as things shifting generally downward. Different parts may age at different rates, but as long as similar kinds of parts are considered (heart or kidney, cell or dendrite, genome or mitochondria), they move forward along the same scale. For humans, this scale is conventionally set in years. In radioactive decay, variations also take place along a single scale, and decay time is conventionally expressed as a half-life, the time it takes half of the particles to decay. For certain substances, however, the aging process is much more complex. As glasses age they crystallize, and it is possible to plot the rates of crystallization at different locations in the glass. Such plots indicate that the aging process takes place along every time scale available for measurement, from nanoseconds to centuries. It is thus not possible to calculate a half-life for such a substance.

This phenomenon goes by the graceful name "stretched exponential relaxation" (evoking a vision of aging as relaxing on a summer day in a hammock stretched between trees rather than, say, stuck in a dismal nursing home). Plotted, it displays infinitely complex fractal patterns, thus leading to the concept of fractal time.[8] Fractals are complex symmetrical forms that repeat themselves across every available scale but always with variations that never resolve at any scale into simpler forms.[9]

Interestingly, the important parameter in determining whether a substance ages fractally is its state of disorder. In amorphous materials such as glasses, Ivars Peterson explains, the atoms or molecules "lie at random positions rather than at well-defined sites, as happens in an orderly crystal lattice."[14] As these randomly situated molecules move around, they encounter different energy barriers to relaxation at different sites, leading to extremely complex aging patterns. The phenomenon suggests that in these instances, performed and experienced time evolves as a dynamically mobile process of fractal complexity rather than as a regularly spaced movement along a single line.

Before the phrase "fractal time" existed, Cage was arguing for it in music. In "Experimental Music: Doctrine," he insists that in a performance, musicians do not need to agree on a single time line. "There is no need for such agreement. Patterns, repetitions, and variations will arise and disappear" (S, 15). When the interlocutor presses him on the point, asking about "several players at once, an orchestra," Cage responds ironically, "You insist on their being together? Then use, as Earle Brown suggests, a moving picture of the score, visible to all, a static vertical line as coordinator, past which the notations move. If you have no particular togetherness in mind, there are chronometers. Use them" (S, 15). In "Composition in Process," he suggests that "it is advisable for several reasons to give the conductor another function than that of beating time. The situation of sounds arising from actions which arise from their own centers will not be produced when a conductor beats time in order to unify the performance" (S, 40). Instead he envisions a situation where the conductor, "who by his actions represents a watch, does so in relation to a part rather than a score—to, in fact, his own part, not that of another—[so that] his actions will interpenetrate with those of the players of the ensemble in a way which will not obstruct their actions" (S, 40).

The phrasing repeats with variations the preceding paragraph, suggesting that the spatial arrangement of the musicians can also be multiple and dispersed rather than homogeneous and concentrated. As with the fractal time observed in glasses, spatial disorder leads to and reinforces the complexities of an ensemble relaxing through time in a fractally complex way. Eerily symmetrical yet different, the two paragraphs instantiate the theme of pattern and variation they discuss. Why should musicians be grouped together in space and time, "like so many horseback riders huddled on one horse" (S, 40) when the intent is not to have sounds fuse but rather to allow each sound its unique autonomous qualities. Cage envisions the time in which the sounds come together in chance conjunctions to be as rich and various as the worldlines generating this fractal complexity.

The final interpretation of chance I want to explore has to do with its noncompressibility. In this discussion, I will draw on Gregory Chaitin's work on random numbers.[11] Take for example the computer program that Cage uses to generate words at random from such source texts as *Finnegans Wake*. What does it mean to say that a computer program operates by chance, when in fact all of its operations must be specified exactly through algorithms? Usually what it means is that the computer is instructed to perform a process that will yield an unpredictable result, for example when it truncates an irrational number at a certain point and chooses the last digit as its operator, which is then indexed to some address corresponding to a word in the source text.

The intersection of computer and chance thus involves the question of how one can name a number, for naming numbers is essentially what the computer does when it calculates them. This is not a trivial problem, as a famous paradox discussed by Martin Gardner indicates.[12] Consider the number "one million, one hundred one thousand, one hundred twenty one." This number appears to be named by the expression, "the first number not nameable in under ten words." However, this definition has only nine words. Is the number 1,101,121 named by its nine-word definition, which says the number cannot be named in under ten words? As Gardner points out, the paradox demonstrates that naming is too powerful a concept to be used without restriction. Chaitin devised a way of thinking about this problem that he calls algorithm complexity theory, which proposes that a number is named by the algorithm that can generate it from a computer. The information contained in the algorithm is measured by calculating the bits of storage it requires. It turns out that this is also a very useful way to determine how random a number is, which is also not a trivial problem. A number is random, Chaitin argues, when the algorithm required to generate it is not substantially smaller than the number itself. Say that I want to create an algorithm to generate the number 123456 . . . The number itself is infinitely large, but the algorithm would be quite small, for I simply say the equivalent of "start with 1 and keep adding 1, registering each sum as the next digit." If the number has a pattern, this pattern can be expressed in abstract form, which is to say that an economical algorithm can be created to generate it. But when a number is random, no such pattern exists. The most economical way to describe it, is simply to provide a copy of it. Randomness thus implies noncompressibility, a plenitude of information that defies simplification.

In a sense incompressibility is characteristic of any poetry, often defined as a genre marked by economy of language. But my point is that randomness intrinsically has the quality of incompressibility. By creating poems that incorporate randomness, Cage intensifies the incompressibility of poetic language. In *M*, for example, he describes how he created the text of *Mureau*. "*Mureau* departs from conventional syntax. It is a mix of letters, syllables, words, phrases, and sentences. I wrote it by subjecting all the remarks of Henry David Thoreau about music, silence, and sounds he heard that are indexed in the Dover publication of the *Journal* to a series of I Ching chance operations. The personal pronoun was varied according to such operations and the typing was likewise determined" (*M*, Foreword, i). The varying typefaces of *Mureau* illustrate how randomness functions to increase the text's information. The riot of typefaces means that typographical differences normally reinforcing grammatical structure and therefore creating redundancy are overwhelmed by a continuous play of differences serving no obvious grammatical or syntactical function. Capital letters float free across the page, breaking loose from their traditional moorings in proper nouns and the first words of sentences; italics insinuate themselves into unlikely positions; five-point roman type jostles one-point gothic without protocol or explanation. Confronted with such a text, the reader struggles to correlate differences so that they become significant, until finally the mind is swamped with the enormity of the task and comes to rest. At this point the text can begin to function like a Zen koan, releasing the initiate from the circle of her assumptions by posing a question that cannot be answered unless she is willing to relinquish the primacy of human intention. Letting sounds be, Cage calls this receptive condition, and he strives to achieve it with language as well as with music (*S*, 10). "There is no meaning in the text," Cage commented about *Empty Words* in a recent interview, "only sounds. It is a use of the voice that resembles music more than poetry." [13] One might add, Cagean music at that.

If it is true that the information content increases as a message becomes more random, then gibberish should contain more information than a grammatically correct sentence. On this view, the string "eidlsxyeifeceicpqickelst" contains more information than "Man is the measure of all things." One can accept such a proposition only if one concedes that information is a technically defined quantity having nothing to do with meaning. The theorists who developed information theory were willing to take this step, but even so, they were uneasy with the idea that random number tables convey more information than *King Lear*. They therefore defined information as a probability function whose magnitude at first increases as the message elements grow more random, but only to the halfway point (that is, to a probability of one-half). After that point, the quantity of information decreases as randomness continues to increase. This construction allowed them to interpret information as an interplay between order and randomness, expectation and surprise.[14] Cage strives to maintain a similar tension when he speaks of "purposeful purposelessness or a purposeless play" (S, 12). If the reader gives up trying to make sense of the text and puts it down in frustration, it ceases to serve as a koan. Its effectiveness depends as much on engaging the reader's intentionality as on revealing its limitations.

In "Experimental Music" Cage responds to the concern that intention may defeat itself too completely, asserting that it is unlikely to happen:

> This project [of letting sounds be themselves] may seem fearsome to many, but on examination there is no cause for alarm. Hearing sounds which are just sounds immediately sets the theorizing mind to theorizing, and the emotions of human beings are continutally aroused by encounters with nature. Does not a mountain unintentionally evoke in us a sense of wonder? otters along a stream a sense of mirth? . . . These responses to nature are mine and will not necessarily correspond with another's. Emotion takes place in the person who has it. And sounds, when allowed to be themselves, do not require that those who hear them do so unfeelingly. (S, 10)

The argument implies that the human tendency to attribute meaning to the world is so strong that it will continue to operate, no matter how random the input. It seems to me that the analogies Cage uses are more compelling for music than language. Whereas sounds do in fact exist in nature, written language is a purely human creation. We come to a text with the expectation that it will mean something. I am not so sure that a highly random text can continue to engage the reader's attention indefinitely, once the general point is grasped that it aims to defeat intentionality. Fortunately, most of Cage's writing balances random elements with conventionally ordered prose. Play and purpose are not left behind, only merged into a stream of experience made dynamic by the turbulent unpredictability of chance operations.

By now it will be clear that the three interpretations of chance I have discussed—intersecting worldlines, temporal asymmetry, and informational incompressibility—have intertwining implications. Each leads to and forecasts the others. Chance conjunctions create temporal asymmetry, temporal asymmetry implies the existence of an infinite information barrier separating past and future, and the incompressibility of randomness generates maximum information. The scientific contexts for chance, noise, and randomness have helped to elucidate these concepts and show how they are interconnected in scientific theory and, by implication, in Cage's work. The purview that science stakes out for itself does not, however, reach to the ethical and political implications of these conjunctions. That exploration is left to Cage as writer and sage, among others.

The political correlative to Cage's aesthetic practices is anarchy. "Syntax, like / government, can only be obeyed," Cage writes in the 1970–71 "Diary: How to Improve the World (You Will Only Make Matters Worse)" (*M*, 215). "It is therefore of no use except when you / have something particular to command / such as: Go buy me a bunch of carrots. / The mechanism of the I Ching, on the other hand, is a utility. Applied to / letters and aggregates of letters, it / brings about a language that can be / enjoyed without being understood" (*M*, 215). He believes that anarchy, like linguistic strategies that overwhelm intentionality without annihilating it, can dissolve the coercive bonds of social regulation while still fostering individual responsibility. The link between his aesthetic practice and anarchy becomes explicit in "Overpopulation and Art."[15]

Anarchy
really does have The future
people are talkIng
abOut
it is creative coNduct
As opposed to
subordiNate
conDuct   it is positive

                    individuAlism   to follow a way of thinking
                         that pRoposes you can assume
                   for your own acTs
                         respOnsibility   (OA, 752–63)

Confronted with a world crowded with people, his characteristic response is to see their multiplicity much as he sees the infusion of noise into a text, as an incompressible source of information capable of revealing to us the limitations of our assumptions. All three interpretations of chance are apparent in the reasoning that leads him to this resolute optimism. If conjunction were not already certain, overpopulation further ensures that any single causal chain cannot remain long in isolation. Other chains, composed of events over which we have no control, will continue to intersect with and alter the worldlines we follow.

                         attemPt
                              tO free oneself from
                         interruPtion
                              solitUde for just a moment regained
                         is utterLy
                              finAlly
                              losT

                         ·   ·   ·   ·

                         there Is
                              nO
                         differeNce between
                              whAt
                         happeNs to some of us
                              anD
                              whAt
                   happens to the otheRs   (OA, 65–71, 414–21)

The same intersections that make us into a plurality rather than a collection of singularities determine that time cannot be reversed: "the future is already here" (OA). The poem's form, a mesostic teasing the reader with vertical patterns that compete with, collaborate with, and otherwise complicate the horizontal scanning of reading, amply demonstrates the interplay between randomness and intention that constitutes chance operations.

Searching for meaning in the profusion of signs that characterizes our future and his text, he insists we can progress

> from failUre
> to faiLure
> right up to the finAl
> vicTory
>
> .   .   .   .   .
>
> from fAilure to failure
> aNarchy   it promises nothing
> minD
> up to the finAl
> victoRy
> creaTive mind   (OA, 770–73, 797–802)

Anarchy, "promis[ing] nothing," is as oxymoronic as chance operations—and, he believes, as powerfully fertile in generating new possibilities for human intention and action. Although the boundaries of scientific investigation do not reach so far as to encompass this utopian hope, what science can add to his conclusion is the assurance that fundamental elements of experience are bound up with this powerful oxymoron. In his chance operations, Cage performs nothing less than the directionality of time and the complexity of its flow, the paradox of randomness as maximum information, and the entanglement of causal determinism with an open and unpredictable future. That, surely, is enough.

Notes

1. Stanislaw Lem, *A Perfect Vacuum* (New York: Harcourt Brace Jovanovich, 1983), pp. 141–66.

2. See, for example, Stanislaw Lem, "Chance and Order," trans. Franz Rottensteiner, *New Yorker* (January 30, 1984):88–89.

3. John Cage, *Silence* (Middletown, CT: Wesleyan University Press, 1961), p. 271. Hereafter cited as *S*.

4. Marjorie Perloff, *The Poetics of Indeterminacy: Rimbaud to Cage* (Princeton, NJ: Princeton University Press, 1981), p. 314.

5. John Cage, *M, Writings '67–'72* (Middletwon, CT: Wesleyan University Press, 1973), p. 115. Hereafter cited as *M*.

6. Ilya Prigogine and Isabelle Stengers, *Order Out of Chaos: Man's New Dialogue with Nature* (New York: Bantam, 1984). For a summary and critique of the book's argument, see N. Katherine Hayles, *Chaos Bound: Orderly Disorder in Contemporary Literature and Science* (Ithaca: Cornell University Press, 1990), pp. 91–114.

7. Richard P. Feynman was instrumental in developing this interpretation of data from particle collisions. See his *QED: The Strange Theory of Light and Matter* (Princeton: Princeton University Press, 1986).

8. Fractal time is explained in Ivars Peterson, "Time to Relax," *Science News* 135, no. 10 (March 11, 1989): 157–59.

9. "Fractal" is a neologism coined by Benoit B. Mandelbrot from the fractional dimensions that these forms have when expressed as mathematical equations. See Mandelbrot's *Fractal Geometry of Nature* (New York: W. H. Freeman, 1983).

10. Peterson, "Time to Relax," p. 157.

11. See Gregory J. Chaitin, "Randomness and Mathematical Proof," *Scientific American* 232 (May 1975): 47–52.

12. Martin Gardner, "Mathematical Games," *Scientific American* 241 (November 1979): 20–34.

13. Allan Kozinn, "A Musical Anarchist (or Liberator) Turns 80," *New York Times*, July 2, 1992, B3.

14. Claude E. Shannon and Warren Weaver, *The Mathematical Theory of Communication* (Urbana: University of Illinois Press, 1949). For a fuller explanation of this reasoning, see Hayles, *Chaos Bound*, pp. 31–60.

15. John Cage, "Overpopulation and Art," in this volume. Hereafter cited as OA, followed by line numbers.

Poethics of a Complex Realism

Joan Retallack

When I began this essay in January 1992, John Cage was not only alive, he was a vital and ubiquitous presence in the world. In the last year and a half of his life, he contributed to and attended virtually every one of the growing number of small to grand scale concerts and festivals in anticipation of his eightieth birthday—events in Germany, Austria, Spain, Italy, Czechoslovakia, and Switzerland, and even—though notably fewer—around the United States. He was at Crown Point Press in San Francisco working on a new series of prints; at home in New York City producing prodigious quantities of music as well as language compositions and poetry (e.g., a new "writing through" of *Ulysses,* "(Muoyce II)"); editing the film, *One[11]* (premiered in Frankfurt, September 20, 1992); consulting with performers, festival directors, editors, publishers, copyists, curators, art dealers; responding to interviewers; responding to requests for information; answering the constantly ringing phone; answering mail from young artists seeking advice ("I feel I should respond because I don't teach");[1] writing letters of recommendation; shopping for food, cooking, inventing and collecting recipes; administering a botanical loft with close to two hundred plants; playing chess, enjoying friends . . . and always thinking about what he was doing and why, questioning what else or other might be possible—what new questions could be asked.

In all this, this continual process of doing—the composing, writing, visual practices, even the cooking—was a highly developed discipline of attention to detail—an act of meditative inquiry into specifics: spatial-temporal-material specifics; that is, the particulars of an inquiry into aesthetic possibility where we understand "aesthetic" to locate the interaction between the probing, structuring mind and the sensory correlates of our modes of perception.

For John Cage the significance of art lay, not in the production of artifacts, but in the making of meaning in an active collaboration with medium, performers, and audience. So the work that John Cage has left behind can be seen as just that—"work," which has always yet to be done—to be engaged in by a participatory audience, viewer, reader at a specific intersection of material, place, and time occasioned by a performance, an exhibition, a screening, or the presence of a text. What I mean to say is that what we call the work of John Cage exists entirely in the form of a collection of "scores"—visual and auditory notations—music (on the page and in performance), texts, drawings, prints, and paintings, which are invitations to realization (to use the musical term for performance) of our aesthetic potential in a "poethics" (a practice or form of life in which ethics and aesthetics come together) of everyday life. In this way, Cage's work—as well as our continuing collaboration with Cage—unfolds within the American pragmatist tradition characterized by the aesthetic theory of the philosopher John Dewey. Dewey wrote in *Art as Experience*[2] that the chief problem for artists and theoreticians is

that of recovering the continuity of esthetic experience with normal processes of living. The understanding of art and of its role in civilization is not furthered by setting out with eulogies of it nor by occupying ourselves exclusively at the outset with great works of art recognized as such. The comprehension which theory essays will be arrived at by a detour; by going back to experience of the common or mill run of things to discover the esthetic quality such experience possesses. Theory can start with and from acknowledged works of art only when the esthetic is already compartmentalized, or only when works of art are set in a niche apart instead of being celebrations, recognized as such, of the things of ordinary experience. Even a crude experience, if authentically an experience, is more fit to give a clue to the intrinsic nature of esthetic experience than is an object already set apart from any other mode of experience. Following this clue we can discover how the work of art develops and accentuates what is characteristically valuable in things of everyday enjoyment. . . . To my mind, the trouble with existing theories is that they start from a ready-made compartmentalization, or from a conception of art that "spiritualizes" it out of connection with the objects of concrete experience. . . . A conception of fine art that sets out from its connection with discovered qualities of ordinary experience will be able to indicate the factors and forces that favor the normal development of common human activities into matters of artistic value.[3]

Art as Experience/Theory as Practice

What could be a more ordinary part of everyday life than weather? Weather, after all, is just that state of the atmosphere at a given place and time characterized by specific variables such as temperature, moisture, pressure; presence or absence of rain, hail, snow, lightening, thunder, ice, fog, etc.; quantity of sunshine, wind velocity (violence or gentleness of winds)—i.e., any condition of the atmosphere subject to variables and vicissitudes, which is of course every condition of the atmosphere.[4]

Whether Weather

John Cage: "I am willing to give myself over to weather. I like to think of my music as weather, as part of the weather."[5]

New York City, July 17, 1992—the Summergarden Concert Series in the Museum of Modern Art Sculpture Garden. Two pieces by John Cage are to be performed: *One*[8], "53 flexible time brackets with single sounds produced on 1, 2, 3, or 4 strings" of the cello; and *ASLSP*, a piece for solo piano to be played "as slow as possible."[6] All of the concerts in this series are to be held outdoors; no arrangements have been made for moving them inside. In the event of inclement weather they are simply to be cancelled. All day on this particular day in the New York metropolitan area it has been on the verge of rain. And all day, as others have worried, John Cage has relished the "whetherness" of weather—not knowing until the last moment whether the concert will go on, and even after it begins, due to continued uncertain weather throughout, knowing that each moment of the concert might be the last. Twice during the performance, uniformed museum employees—whose poised readiness (like Wimbledon ball runners) has clearly embodied "whether"—advance on the loudspeakers and amplifiers to rush them inside; but the weather holds, so we remain in the mi(d)st of "whether"—on the edge of rain. Each sound that comes from the cello, as well as the silence (ambient sound) of extra-notational possibility is savored as the gift it would of course be anyway, but here—given the particular atmospheric cir-

244

cumstances—is thrown into relief. Cage's only concern has been that the musicians be paid whether or not they can perform.

(It is the nature of performance to be fraught with "whethers." Anything could go right or wrong at any time. And in this, even as it strives for certainty and precision, it both replicates and operates within the constancy of life's variability. The conditions of performance with its inherent risks provide a congenial vehicle for Cage's work with chance, so much so that all his "non-performance" art is fundamentally performative in its requirement of audience-interactive processes—active listening and viewing—to complete its meaning.)

This evening, the probability of rain has necessitated wrapping the piano in heavy sheets of industrial plastic. Black garbage bags shroud the six loudspeakers mounted on tall metal stands. Near Picasso's bronze goat, the sound man crouches with his bank of amplifiers under dense foliage of a small tree in which a single bird sings loudly and persistently. A billowy plastic tent is erected over the cellist, Michael Bach, as he is tuning up. For the duration of the cello piece, 43'30", the translucent plastic will be articulated by gusty breezes sending pools of accumulated mist into randomly intersecting rivulets just above the head of the cellist. This tent improvised by necessity of weather's "whether" becomes as much a part of this performance of *One*[8] as the Mineko Grimmer sculpture (also making the operations of chance visually available) has become a part of *One*[6].[7] Both the traceries of this light drizzle and the sounds of *One*[8] are the results of chance operations—those of nature, and those of John Cage imitating nature's processes, understanding nature's processes to involve (as they always do) an interaction between chance and selection. This is, in other words, not the ineffable Romantic mist, it is the fully present, complex realist mi(d)st of an actual weather system with immediate, rather than transcendent, consequences. If it is to have transcendent meaning, it is the poethical work of the audience to make that meaning—the responsibility of imaginative collaboration that this kind of art requires. It is the work of the composer (or artist of any kind) only to create the occasion for the making of meaning.

To review this concert is then most appropriately to give a kind of retrospective weather report: The weather system in the garden at MOMA from 7:30 P.M. to 9 P.M. July 17, 1992, was complex and engaging. It consisted of layers of traffic sounds, sirens, airplane motors; a palpably silent, diagonally pulsing mist; rivulet readout, bird aria, and solo cello. In the second part of the concert, the cello part was replaced by solo piano, played by Michael Torre with somewhat excessive brio.

Weather was the medium in which this concert took place; it was also its form. Michael Bach in his transparent weather tent played a music of w(h)e(a)ther distinguished by the fortuitous coming together at this particular time, in this particular place, of a number of verging and converging paths of sensory variables. The cello part was realized both as one set of variables among many, and as the structuring event which, despite its own fundamental contingency, created the bounded pattern bringing other elements into auditory and visual focus. All of this on the edge of coming and going without a trace, nothing to remember after each sound (mostly—due to chance operations—richly resonant chords) has been played. There is none of the periodicity, the rhythmic or melodic line developed in music to counteract the fact that it is the most transitory of all media—the medium bound to time, the medium of vanishing and change.

> John Dewey: "The eye and ear complement one another. The eye gives the *scene* in which things *go on* and on which changes are projected—leaving it still a scene even amid tumult and turmoil. The ear . . . brings home to us changes as changes." (*AE*, 236)

> Søren Kierkegaard: "Music has time as its element, but it gains no permanent place in it; its significance lies in its constant vanishing in time; it emits sound in time, but at once vanishes, and has no permanence."[8]

John Cage's music is both faithful to and revelatory of these characteristics of its medium. There is nothing to take home with us in the way of a tune or beat to arrest time's erasures. And yet there is no sense of loss. On the contrary, there is the memory of something much richer and more complex than a rhythmic line—the memory of fully awakened and surprised sensibilities, sensibilities which have been initiated into the possibility of a fuller presence in the world beyond the concert—Dewey's art as experience/experience as art. Having been so totally and delightfully suspended in both weather (including the urban weather of traffic sounds) and "whether," we could attend to the extraordinary grace notes of ambient possibility, the range of contingent detail that teems about us, but—and this is what makes Cage's initiating aesthetic so important—more often to our confusion, consternation, and dismay than delight.

Take time, for instance. Our perception of time is bound up with feelings of inadequacy (Will we be ready on time? Will we *ever* be ready?) and loss (so much is no longer possible, gone, past, forgotten). Art has often exploited our vulnerability to these sentiments by sweetening them with nostalgia. This aids us in denying properties of time rather than exploring them in a manner which might help us live honestly, courageously, humorously, even serenely with them. But, regardless of how we feel about it, time is something we are aware of only intermittantly, and then often with anxiety (Is it early? Are we late? Is it *too* late?).

One[8] began when and where we all were—in medias *race* in NYC, world capital of the accelerated clock—in the familiar, jittery experience of time (accentuated perhaps by knowing that at a Cage event it can be difficult to know precisely when the concert has begun), time as source of anxiety and as much more fragmented than space which does provide, whatever its visual disjunctions may be, a reassuringly constant ground. Soon, as Michael Bach began to play, time was being transformed from silence interrupted by sound (just barely; most in the audience didn't notice when the cellist stopped tuning up and started playing *One*[8]), to sound interrupted by silence (long pauses during many of which Michael Bach, for technical reasons, changed bows),[9] to sounds and silence coming into equal value, equalizing the medium in which the listener resides (by now, as a result of the meditative dignity of the music) in a state of attentive calm. Time had become audible, constant, palpable, friendly, and habitable—as fully habitable as space—even as it was disappearing without a trace.

Lecture on the Weather

Theodor Adorno: "The greatness of works of art lies solely in their power to let those things be heard which ideology conceals."[10]

Does ideology conceal weather? It certainly attempts to conceal "whether," i.e., alternatives—and they usually come only in twos. In considering anything beyond that—complexities of three and more . . . not to say the infinite possibilities of "weather," ideology becomes simply an engine of obscurantism and denial.

John Cage: "Our political structures no longer fit the circumstances of our lives. Outside the bankrupt cities we live in Megalopolis which has no geographical limits. Wilderness is global park. I dedicate this work to the U.S.A. that it may become just another part of the world, no more, no less . . .

"Chance operations . . . are a means . . . of silencing the ego so that the rest of the world has a chance to enter into the ego's own experience . . . "[11]

"The idea was that if we could listen we could bring about some kind of change."[12]

John Cage's performance piece *Lecture on the Weather* can be seen as a paradigmatic case of his working aesthetic.

Description: twelve performers simultaneously read texts taken by chance operations from Henry David Thoreau's *Journal, Essay on Civil Disobedience,* and *Walden.* The pacing of each reading is variable within a set of specific time brackets. This creates periods of silence. Tapes of wind, rain, and thunder are played. A film flashes "lightning," negatives of Thoreau sketches, over the performance area. This performance is, of course, not *about* weather; it *is* weather.[13] Like all weather—state of the atmosphere at a given time and place—it is sensitive to initial conditions and thus is significantly different every time it is performed.

Weather report: At the May 5, 1989, *Cage-Fest* at Strathmore Hall, Rockville, Maryland, doors were open to the outside where a storm began to be audible and visible (thunder and lightening and then torrential rain) at about the same time as the storm was beginning inside in John Cage's *Lecture on the Weather.* This had the interesting effect of eradicating the distinction between "inside" and "outside"—the meteorological display over Strathmore Hall was continuous with that going on in the room where Cage's more gentle storm included the weather of predetermined and coincidental conjunctions of sound and voice variables; words, ideas, and silences that form, among other things, the complex systems of political climates.

John Cage: "I thought the resultant complex would help to change our present intellectual climate."   (*EW,* 3)

That particular weather system, on the evening of May 5, 1989, which we might call "*Lecture on the Weather* with Weather" could only assume its particular and variable character because of the kind of permeable boundaries—between inside and outside the piece itself—that characterize all of Cage's compositions. The silences, the layered and intermittent simultanaieties make it possible to admit other variables—in this case, first the sound of (outdoor) rain, then thunder, and finally lightning—meteorological traffic with its flashing lights, collisions, and swerves.[14] In principle, and in fact, nothing audible or visible to the audience would have been excluded from the domain of the performance, though we might not think all possibilities desirable. In accordance with Cage's cherished idea of Interpenetration and Non-obstruction (one of the three "whispered truths" of Buddhism, and in consonance with Cage's quest for "Anarchic Harmony") anything interrupting or obstructing the performance would have been undesirable. As with all of Cage's compositions (at least from the sixties on) this performance was intended to model an ideal state of anarchy—voluntary cooperation within interpenetrating and non-obstructive complexity.

What was being heard that night was indeed what ideology, with its myths of simplicity, usually conceals—that complexity, perhaps even chaos (and I'm referring here to something akin to the current image of chaos, in the so-called "complex" or "nonlinear" sciences, as representing fields of pattern-bounded unpredictability) is not only with us; it may be—if we can accept and work with it, rather than against it—the ground and energy source of our optimism.

World Us

our picture   that's now Visibly
dEveloping
is woRld us
world citizenshiP
will nOt occur
as a Political initiative
it will be reqUired by the economics
of an expLoding
industriAl world [15]

A multifarious, noisy, exploding-globe-cartoon "we" is careening toward the psychological threshold of a new century—saturated by media, in- and ill-formed by immaculately conceived factoids, deficient in knowledge of the most elemental things. How on earth to get along with one and others, for instance, more and more others in the mi(d)st of increasing complexity. Within that "we" of course are many ones and others whose investigations have modeled promising and nourishing and even productive forms of life. None has yet or will ever save the world, if only because the world is not a "the"; but there has been work that allows those who wish to live in atmospheres of heightened possibility to do so.

The work of John Cage with sound and visual media, as well as the medium of language—all taken to be media not in the sense of the surface looking-glass imagery of mass media, but as elemental and permeating conditions of life—enacts a peculiarly American model of possibility—a pragmatic, philosophical, and aesthetic realism—one which is disruptive of individual and institutional habits of mind while concretely revelatory of the odd and always interesting intersections of whether (chance and choice) and weather (concrete variables).

It is interesting to think of John Cage and Edward Lorenz, an M.I.T. meteorologist,[16] as two characteristically American thinkers and inventors—both working in ways made possible by new computer technologies, and both working—theoretically and pragmatically—on complex systems that form the conditions of our daily lives. At the start of his chapter on Lorenz's work on modeling weather systems, "The Butterfly Effect," in his book, *Chaos: Making a New Science,*[17] James Gleick quotes the late physicist, Richard Feynman: "Physicists like to think that all you have to do is say, these are the conditions, now what happens next?" This is in fact what Lorenz did for the mathematical descriptive dynamics of weather systems, developing a set of differential equations into which starting point or "initial" conditions (e.g., directions of air flows in the atmosphere) could be fed and then doing a computer run of their interactions to see what kinds of systems unfolded. It could also describe Cage's approach to compositions in which initial conditions (e.g., sound sources, pitch, timbre, amplitude, and duration) are fed into the variable slots of a random-number generator program which replicates the operations of chance in the *I Ching* (a program called *ic,* with a time-values-specific version called *tic*)[18] and then lets the computer run determine how the score (which will initiate the performative music system) will be structured. Since Cage's scores always incorporate significant elements of indeterminacy, each performance of his music, like each performance of the weather, has a built-in difference of initial conditions whose variations can produce major changes in the system that unfolds.[19] This phenomenon has in chaos theory come to be called the "butterfly effect" (a butterfly flapping its wings in China could dramatically change the weather in New York several months later) in relation to the Lorenz equations which, as it happens, generate a butterfly shaped pattern on the computer screen. It is characteristic of temporally evolving, nonlinear systems which are descriptively noncompressible, and subject to pattern-bounded unpredictability. In the complex sciences only dynamic systems whose descriptions have all these characteristics—such as weather and other forms of liquid and gaseous turbulence—fall under the rubric "chaos," a concept whose image in the history of ideas has traditionally accommodated the interplay of order and disorder.

Is it meaningful then to say that what Lorenz has done for the butterfly effect in science, John Cage with his music of weather and his aesthetic paradigm of deterministic randomness has done in the arts?[20] Both can be seen as having worked in the Pythagorean tradition where number reflects the relations between elements in nature. In music, as Pythagoras pointed out, this is number made audible; in computer modeling it is number made visible. Both Cage and Lorenz developed models for allowing numbers to enact random elements in nature's processes. But the scientist and the artist diverge in interesting ways. While Lorenz and his colleagues have been primarily interested in finding the orderly patterns in chaos by creating self-contained models which generate broadly repetitive forms delimiting local randomness, Cage, working as a composer in a field which has been dominated by self-contained repetitive forms, was most interested in the nonperiodic aspects of chaos, that is, the local randomness—by making available to our attention a space-time and materially delimited experience of the play of randomness he refered to as "chance." In this experience of the kind of chaos that permeates ordinary life, the form develops in an interaction with the dynamic atmosphere of its performative realization and the ordering minds of the audience. This structuring of what Cage called chaos was deeply in accord with his pledge to imitate not nature but her processes. The active processes of natural systems are always in dialogue with, informed by, the selective forces in their environment. This is perhaps what makes change possible. Edward Lorenz and John Cage, sharing both a love of weather's changeability and an elegant pragmatics of investigative invention, have broadened the field of possibility in science and art to include active models of what had until relatively recently been considered inappropriate or unwieldy objects of anything but distant, metaphysical attention.

Unlike work in the sciences, which is, as Thomas Kuhn has pointed out in his

Structure of Scientific Revolutions,[21] always highly communal and tradition bound even in its breakthroughs, Cage's work in the arts has been American style Anarchist—more in the quietist manner of the political minded naturalist, Henry David Thoreau, than in the combative manner of post–World War I European anarchism. Cage's work has in fact been more distinctly American than Thoreau's in its meditative maximalism—refusing to retreat from the din of daily life, neither demanding purity nor minimalism[22] as its necessary condition—in fact, celebratory of the din of life while in consonance with the calm disciplines of focused attention that come to us from the East, and the humorous conceptual shifts that are the legacy of Duchamp and the Dadaists. Cage's oeuvre is thus European, Asian, and quintessentially American in its cultural pluralism. Its fundamental value of usefulness along with its generous acceptance of chaos characterize it as both a complex-realist aesthetic and a poethics of everyday life.

It has often been said that America is finally joining the rest of the world in its rather belated discovery of the issue of sustainable standards of living. In 1992 at the ecological summit in Rio it was declared that the United States can no longer serve as a model for the lifestyle to which the rest of the world aspires, while, at the same time the rest of the world (notably Western Europe) seems to be joining the U.S. in what has become a global multicultural, multiethnic experiment—what Cage in "Overpopulation and Art" calls "world us"—in contradistinction to world U.S.

We both have and have not had the relevant experience. There has been a strain of generous optimism in American thought nourished by a pragmatic intelligence of invention. We were faced and challenged at our inception as a nation with the world as we found it, not—as had long been the case in Europe—with an image of how "we" had shaped it and for just what all too well-known, or at least well-defended, reasons. Ignoring the life and culture already here, "we" (the Euro-we) saw almost nothing but possibility. Hence the explosion of American invention.

But increasingly the breath of possibility has suffocated under layers of self-reflexive imagery—for example, the auto(vehicle and self)eroticism of media as a form of (self)advertising—TV covering the news as if it had all occurred on other TV screens. It has seemed that the European legacy of exhaustive metaphysics has overtaken and exhausted us, that we too are now an "old world," weary and jaded and (high/lo) culturally hermetic, that a deconstructive act is as necessary here as it is among the grand ruins of European culture. Could Robert Smithson have been right in suggesting that previous cultures have fallen into ruin but our specialty has been to rise into it?[23] Perhaps this has always been the case—that is, to the extent that our aesthetic endeavors have been aimed at creating edifices which stand upright and apart from their surroundings. The art that is not used—continually redefined, conversed with, absorbed into the life around it—is in its detached, un-supported, unsupporting state, prone to datedness, to falling to ruin and the nostalgia that further monumentalizes ruin. It is work that has stopped breathing, that has lost its permeable membranes, that has, as Cage said, "become art," rather than a form of life. But becoming art is what Western aesthetics has been all about, posited on the very gap between art and everyday life that John Dewey and John Cage have disavowed. Dewey wrote, long before spectors of ecological disaster had reconsti-tuted our sense of the fragility of our future: "Recovering the continuity of aesthetic experience with normal processes of living must occur . . . [for] if the gap between organism and environment is too wide, the creature dies" (AE, 19).

In an age of increasingly mediated reality where the simulation seems constantly to compete with its object (see complete works of Baudrillard) where in fact reduc-tive simulation has become a form of political life, where dichotomies of life/death, good/evil, external/internal, true/false, real/artificial have been the warp and woof in the weaving of synthetic textual "realisms," the anxiety about what is left out of our imaginative constructions is warranted. Our imaginative constructions, after all, shape our sense of what the future holds. They had better be commodious. They had better be friendly to complexity, difference, otherness . . . They had better help us live in our world.

Pothooks

Overheard at art opening: "I like art; it's better than looking in the mirror."   Anon.

David Ruelle: ". . . what allows our free will to be a meaningful notion is the complexity of the universe."   (CC, 33)

Suppose one wants to live by a principle one is trying to articulate. In this case the principle of a poethics, admitting—that is, acknowledging and valuing—complexity.

I am writing an essay on John Cage—living inside and outside that present participle, "writing," for a number of months, piling on other present participles like "puzzling," "exploring," "questioning" what this idea, this practice of a Cagean poethics could mean; beginning with "Suppose one wants to live by a principle . . ."—that is, beginning with a hypothetical. "Thetical," not "ethical"; not yet. My problem, in part, is just that—getting from the conceptual zone of the "thetical" to the pragmatics of the "ethical," both descriptively and prescriptively, discursively and formally, in order to enact, not just write about, a poethics. When, toward the end of this writing process, I activate my Spell Check, it stops at every use of the word "poethics," flashes "WORD NOT FOUND," and suggests that I must mean "pothooks." Maybe I do. Maybe my computer has found the fast track—thetical to ethical to John Dewey's "common or mill run," in this case, kitchen variety practical.

This is so winsomely arbitrary, so epistemologically unsavory, it's irresistible. It would surely take heavy theoretical machinery to justify, if justification of a certain sort is what is appropriate at this point. It might even require an argument. Argument is always considered epistemologically more respectable than accident even when it is accident that brings it on and accident that remains when it is finished. We might try something like one of those arguments so popular in the Middle Ages to prove the existence of God. These logical structures are still available to us, minus the unwieldy referent, as models of high rationalism. So the justification of the coincidence of pothooks and poethics might go like this: "If John Cage's life-work is a prototype of a contemporary poethics, and John Cage's life-work included cooking,[24] then—with a few fancy, intermediate 'if-thens'—we can no doubt arrive at a 'therefore' that reads, 'A Cagean poethics is something you can hang your pot on.'" Interestingly, there are many instruction manuals that will tell us precisely how to do this odd little exercise with great flair; and it can be very reassuring that the swerve off one track is merely the occasion for locking onto another—forgetting for a moment, or for as long as one can, the dizzying, empty space between them. This is all congenial, if one wants to remain in a single-track logical mode.

If, on the other hand, one wants to see what's going on outside such structures, that is, if one wants to see the world while exploring the coincidence of poethics and pothooks, there are multiple logics at our disposal—multiple ways of connecting multiple and disparate things—deciding what can be included, how much surprise can be tolerated, what comes next. Though, since there are far fewer instruction manuals for these kinds of modes (a book of Zen koans would be one; any of John Cage's books would be another) it can't be denied that to ignore the call to "pothooks" would, if not simplify things, at least not complicate them further than it already has. (At one of the Stanford events Cage cited Thoreau's injunction, "Simplify, simplify." To do that we could notice that a pothook is a kind of concrete interrogative; that a Cagean poethics is based on questions; that both are forms of receptivity—as is the act of listening. This is not to discover deep structure, but to make meaning, firmly grounded—as meaning always is—in the circumstantial and arbitrary.)

> John Cage: "In Seville, on a street corner, I noticed the multiplicity of simultaneous visual and audible events all going together in one's experience and producing enjoyment. It was the beginning for me of theater and Circus."[25]

If one is to experience at least as much enjoyment writing an essay as one can have standing on a street corner in Seville (or anywhere else for that matter), that essay, or poem, or any other work of art for that matter *should* be a complex intersection of intention and nonintention, pattern and surprise. So, "pothooks" stays in, in the poethics of this essay. This choice leaves me with less time and more to do. Or perhaps it's the other way around.

(John Cage has said, "We have all the time in the world."[26] I don't understand this. It is a puzzle I carry around in the nature of a koan.)

Professor Chance

> John Cage: "I feel very friendly toward chaos."[27]

> David Ruelle: "*Chance* and *randomness* did not look like very promising topics for precise investigation, and were in fact shunned by many early scientists. Yet they play now a central role in our understanding of the nature of things." (*CC*, 163)

David Ruelle is a mathematical physicist who in 1971, along with Floris Takens, wrote a paper entitled "On the Nature of Turbulence." It was one of the early articles in the current round of chaos theory. There is, as N. Katherine Hayles has pointed out in her book *Chaos Bound*,[28] a long history of redefining chaos. Every age has its particular fascination with chaos as origin, terminus, and (somewhere in between) possibility. The Ruelle and Takens paper describes how in some chemical reactions, a dynamic field involving a great deal of indeterminacy is bounded by what they called a "strange attractor" pattern. Until then, the observation of "turbulence" in chemical reactions, since it involved nonperiodic motion, was taken to signal, not a complex phenomenon of great interest, but the failure of the experiment.[29] That is, the working decision, or methodological choice—in consonance with a scientific paradigm exclusively legitimizing simplicity and predictability—was to ignore it. Ruelle, in fact, tells the story, in *Chance and Chaos,* in a chapter called "Chaos: A New Paradigm," of how a scientist who had done pioneering work on periodic motion in chemical reactions, for whom "On the Nature of Turbulence," with its description of nonperiodic oscillations, should presumably have been the next step, dismissed this work out of hand. In one of life's amusing little ironies, the name of this scientist who was so uneasy about the idea that chance could enter into deterministic systems just happened to be Briton Chance.[30]

Our truth fictions, our truth functions, and (somewhere in between) our political structures no longer fit the quantitative and qualitative transmogrification of the circumstances of our lives. They are not strange enough, nor commodious enough, to enact the complex realism we need in order to flourish in the world as we find it. We find ourselves, for instance, in the midst of a scene of accelerating information complexity, nourished by the proliferation of sophisticated feed-back loops in our electronic age. More information, as we should all know by now, does not necessarily mean greater knowledge or meaning. In fact, information theorists[31] tell us the greater the quantity of information in a system, the more the system moves toward randomness and the more difficult it becomes to find organizing principles, or patterns, much less meaning.

Powerful computers have made it possible for scientists to work with enormous quantities of technically defined "information" expressed in binary digits or "bits." The quest, as always in the sciences, is for efficiency; in the case of information, for efficient transmission. The simpler the system, or message, generating the information, the more compressible the information will be—e.g., wrds whch r stll ndrstndbl wth vvlls rmvd, or linguistic messages that can be transmitted in "gists," summaries, or paraphrases. These systems are "compressible" because they contain a great deal of redundancy, and in the case of paraphrasable literature, meaning supported by familiarity with the *kind* of message being transmitted—that is, nothing formally or radically new is being said. This means that truly new, formally complex literature, music, art of any kind (particularly that art characterized by formal characteristics of indeterminacy) may be less compressible than the art of the "mainstream" (the mainstream is the one stream one *can* step in twice) just because as a system it will contain less internal redundancy, as well as being less redundant in relation to other systems in its genre. In the arts and the humanities this resistance to compressibility is of positive value, since the quest here is for richness of meaning (which guarantees higher levels of complexity) and, for the more adventuresome among us, radically new perspectives of the sort which can only become available through formal innovation.

In the 1960s John Cage wrote a text for one of his visits to the Sogetsu Art Center in Japan which included this version of his much quoted homage to the Indian philosopher, Ananda Coomaraswamy: "I have for many years accepted, and I still do, the doctrine about Art, occidental and oriental, set forth by Ananda K. Coomaraswamy in his book *The Transformation of Nature in Art*, that the function of Art is to imitate Nature in her manner of operation."[32] Cage often repeated this statement, and it is well known as one of his working principles. What immediately follows in this version (interestingly composed for a Japanese audience) has been given less attention: "Our understanding of 'her manner of operation' changes according to advances in the sciences." To understand more about the "manner of operation" of Cage's work, it is useful to review what theorists working in the new nonlinear sciences are telling us about complex systems in nature, including most systems of human thought and experience: that they are pattern bounded systems characterized by infinitely complex unpredictability. The scientific modeling of these systems has yielded structures that are, among other things, one of the contemporary redefinitions of chaos—the current way in which the scientific community organizes their thinking about the relation between order and disorder. "What we now call chaos is a time evolution [of these complex systems] with sensitive dependence on initial condition" (*CC*, 67), writes David Ruelle. Such systems are characterized by noncompressibility of information (i.e., to "describe" them, you must literally replicate them).

As we know, this has been a revolutionary paradigm in the sciences and it is in many ways parallel to Cage's revolutionary aesthetic paradigm. If we think of Cage's work after the late 1940s when he began to incorporate indeterminacy and chance operations into his compositions, we see scores that begin to exhibit deterministic randomness (those generated by means of the *I Ching*—both early on, when Cage was tossing coins, and later when he was using the *ic* and *tic* computer programs). "Deterministic randomness" simply means, like "deterministic chaos," that there is a mixture of determined (by Nature, God, or Cage) elements and chance—or, to put it another way, that deterministic systems can produce nonperiodic behavior. The combination of intention and chance has often, oddly, been pointed out as a contradiction in Cage—as though his manner of operation, unlike Nature's, had to employ only one principle. Rather than a contradiction, it can be seen as a deeply productive paradox yielding music that is as complex a dynamic system as any other which includes (to use James Yorke's characterization) wild disorder embedded in stable structure. Starting with the same score and introducing slight changes in other initial conditions (such as a different setting or performer, or a performer in a different mood) many of Cage's compositions will yield radically different realizations. *Lecture on the Weather* may in fact be subject to the amplification of difference characteristic of chaotic systems (see note 20) since its dependence on simultaneous readings may lead to greater and greater divergence of textual coincidence at any successive point as readers, after starting together, become—due to built-in indeterminacy—more and more coincidentally "out of sync" with earlier performances. Sensitivity to initial conditions may in fact be seen as part of the poethical force of Cage's work—that it places anarchic value in the freedom of all elements—including those of media, performers, ambience, and audience—to contribute qualities of their own nature to the nonobstructive interpenetration which forms the complex texture of the realization. In this way Cage's art is a living practice, rather than a simulation or mimesis. It is art *as* the very life experience it draws our attention to. Cage as artist is helping us redefine and revalue chaos (the relation between order and disorder) in the vital, immediate context of everyday life.

John Cage's art, as a poethical form of life characterized by the values of complex realism, makes the intricate complexity of intersecting order and accident (where order includes, but also is larger than, human intentionality) known to us, through forms which structure participatory attention of the sort that can admit and even delight in turbulence while allowing us, as active audience, to make meaning. To feel friendly toward chaos as John Cage and David Ruelle do should be to engage in practices which do not betray it with simple fictions. Both aesthetic and scientific paradigms must engender experiments which acquaint us fruitfully and usefully with the conditions of our world. Which do not bring on, through denial or neglect, the inevitability of what Jacques Lacan called the "revenge of the real," a revenge we (global "we") are painfully familiar with in the forms of war, famine, and other social and environmental injuries and upheavals.

The very idea of deterministic chaos is, of course, itself a kind of fiction—or at least a very potent metaphor—as are all visualizable scientific paradigms. Mathematically, chaos theory is an idealized model of phenomena (weather, for instance) whose occurence in "real life" are a good deal messier than on a computer screen. So to claim that Cage's work parallels in important ways the scientific modeling of complex systems, and possibly chaos, that it furnishes us with an aesthetic paradigm that helps us make sense of and live with chaos—both natural and human-made weather (with, e.g., economics and politics as examples of sociological "weather," and the mediating human brain itself characterized by defining properties of chaos) is to say that Cage's work reveals to us—in pleasurable and useful ways—complex, pattern bounded, noncompressible (even to the point of paraphrase) unpredictability, and thereby, like the work of the scientist, offers us ingeniously framed lenses with which to attend to the most significant and troubling aspects of the world as we find it on the verge of a twenty-first century.

As Thomas Kuhn and other historians and philosophers of science have pointed out, it is no accident that the history of science has paralleled the history of other imaginative forms and ideas, sharing with them during transitional periods in the development of thought the most highly charged imaginative constructions of their times.[33] The idea, or metaphor, or model we call "chaos," is just such a broadly implicative, fertile idea during this threshold period on the edge of a new century and, it seems, a post-critical mass, not only of information but of humanity. See John Cage's "Overpopulation and Art" in this volume for not *fin-de-siècle*, but *début-de-siècle* thinking.

The interesting thing is, as has so often been the case, the artistic imaginative construction seems to have anticipated the scientific one. John Cage was modeling complex systems and even fractal forms in his compositions two decades before the publication of Mandelbrot's *The Fractal Geometry of Nature* and the full-blown emergence of the "complex sciences" in the eighties. As Cage would probably have put it, "It was in the air." We—that is, the "we" apart from the mainstream market-place which invents and sells forms of escape—are all working on the problems of how to live in our world.

Cagestan as World Model?

> Douglas Hofstadter: "What actually *does* determine history is a lot of things that are *in effect* random, from the point of view of any less-than-omniscient being."[34]

In the seminar notes to John Cage's 1988–89 Charles Eliot Norton Lectures at Harvard, an extended "lecture-poem" entitled *I–VI*, Cage says, "We could make a piece of music in which we would be willing to live . . . a representation of a society in which you would be willing to live." At a concert at the National Academy of Sciences in Washington, D.C., November 1991, when a member of the audience asked Cage what idea was behind the composition of a piece called *Two⁴*—for violin and piano—Cage replied, "I used the idea of 30 minutes." The audience laughed and waited. Cage said nothing more.

The idea of 30 minutes—like the idea of 4'33", or any other time period for that matter—is actually an extraordinary idea if it is not the time period you are given to fill out a form, or finish an exam, or that you take to watch the commercials being interrupted by a sit-com on TV. At the start of the next 30 minutes we could ask any question we like. We could ask, for instance, if we will make it into the future, and if in the course of the next 30 minutes we do indeed find ourselves making it into the future, as we are in fact finding ourselves doing right now, we could say, Look! Look around! Listen! Here we are! We made it into the future! Now we can see/hear what the future is like . . . Here we are in the future of the world, of America, of this crowded intersection in Manhattan or Pittsboro, N.C., or the coastal low-country, or the Adirondaks. What's there to notice? Congested streets. Birds, in-sects, trees, flowers, this slightly chilly breeze . . . If someone—not omniscient, but omnipotent—could turn up the volume right now we would notice the music of "world us." It would not be by the same composer who brought us the Music of the Spheres. We would hear pots clanking on their hooks, a professor of chance sneezing into her handkerchief, children laughing, crying, moaning, car engines starting and stalling, monkeys screeching in rain forests, rain falling, rain forests falling, bombs exploding, car radios blaring, radio static crackling, astronomers coughing . . . guns firing, fire crackling, water rushing, food frying, innumerable mammalian species chewing, snorting, wheezing, stars exploding, buildings crumbling, sirens wailing, galaxies expanding, traffic roaring, waves crashing, broth boiling . . . thunder . . . wind . . . noise of weather and lectures on the weather . . .

Meanwhile, as I sit in another space-time-frame writing this essay on my computer, my file name—of which I am reminded every time I save—has gradually undergone a conceptual shift in my mind—from Cage-Stan (for Stanford University, where I delivered an early draft of this essay) to Cagestan—a boundryless region which has not been much in the news, though it has for some time been the scene of revolutionary manifestos (intentional and nonintentional). Let's spend a few minutes with the idea of 30 minutes (or any designated time frame) in Cagestan to see if it *is* a society in which we might be willing to live. My guess is that it will have lots of commodious pothooks, many professors of chance, no infinitely bored, omniscient beings, and a complexity, very much like the one that characterizes everyday life in a world—this world, for instance—where there is, simultaneously, increasing complexity, and increasing flight from complexity.

If complexity is the source of our freedom, it is also the source of our terror. We live in a culture which is so driven to desperate simplifications that it has given over most of its thought processes to the facile imagery of mass media. It is this flight that has produced the media event which is our so-called "30-second politics"—our growing inability to tolerate the intricasies of what we take to be time-*consuming* matters. (It's an interesting shift—from *using* to *consuming* time.)

Can we deny that we need to change, that we can't continue on this, now admittedly, life-threatening, world-threatening course? Certainly we can. We can deny anything, including that there *is* a world independent of our minds and egos. Western philosophers, for whom dichotomous insides and outsides have held a particular piquancy, have put in a lot of time and hard work trying to prove the existence of the external world. To move into the semantically messy world of poetry during such attempts would of course be taken as a failure of the thought experiment. But even with the poets locked out of the room the world eludes proof of its existence. It seems it's too complex for linear "if-then" strategies, even of the sort within the lyric poem which serves up the mini-epiphany as its conclusion. There's too much centrifugal noise to permit this kind of concentration (as in frozen concentrate) without loss of a great expanse of experience and meaning. Our time—whether 30 minutes or even 30 seconds—might be better spent in an engagement that brings us to awareness in and with the pandemonium, the carnival that is always blaring beyond the closed door.

Any formal structure draws us outside ourselves, beyond our personal and expressive logics. Something as simple as meter, rhyme, and *abab* patterns pulls us in directions which have to do with material structures of the language, not just the ego-expressive interests of the writer. But these forms do not even begin to explore the infinite possibilities of the complex system that is a natural language and the forms of life that give it vitality. Chance operations and indeterminacy pull the work of the composer or writer into exploration of the kinds of events and relationships that are characteristic of richly complex systems—from the simple patterns of bone/stone or *abab* to the increased complexity of language generated by mesostic strings to the turbulent patterns of liquid, smoke, ambient noise, and high degrees of semantic and associative multiplicity.

The Poethical Practice of Admitting Complexity

John Cage: "People have great difficulty paying attention to what they do not understand."[35]

Let's look at the short, untitled, poem below:[36]

> if you exi   ted
> ~~becauSe~~
>
> we mIght go on as before
>
> but since you don't we ~~wi'~~ Ll
>
> mak
> ~~chang~~E
>
> our miNds
>
> anar   hic
> ~~so that we~~ C~~an~~
>
> d to   let it be
> convertE~~njoy~~ the chaos/~~that~~ you are/
> stet

It is immediately obvious that this text is problematic in terms of a simple left-right, left-right, top to bottom, linear reading. For one thing, it's not clear whether this is a poem consisting of seven lines (combining lines with crossed-out words and words overhead, ignoring "stet," and honoring the seven capitalized letters of the mesostic string, S I L E N C E, as indicators of the number of lines in the poem) or whether the presence of the crossed-out words on the page, along with the word "stet"—not handwritten as a proofer's mark, but typed like all the other words in the poem—indicates that this is actually a twelve-line poem. This is an interesting "whether"—posing two alternatives which, due to their equal material presence on the page, render the poem a kind of ambiguous figure, like the famous Edgar Ruben Vase/Profile. As with all ambiguous figures there is a kind of terminal either/or complementarity. It is conceptually/visually impossible to take in both possibilities at the same time, since each one is in part constituted by the functional absence of the other. This is the dualism of a "whether" system, one—in this case—that would seem to be interestingly irresolvable, demonstrating the powerful role of the reader/observor to determine the way in which, at any given time, it is to be read.

But, one might ask, is it really irresolvable? Can't we determine a single, correct way to read it by weighing the evidence in favor of the author's intention? Can't we, that is, simply see the crossed-out words as corrections, the "stet" as an indication of a change of mind (decision to restore "that"), and be done with it? In this case, we might clean up the text and render it thus:

(R-1)   if you exiSted
                    we mIght go on as before
    but since you don't we'Ll
                    makE
                    our miNds
                    anarChic
            convertEd to the chaos/let it be that you are/

The problem with this is that it is so easy, the author could have done it himself. What is crucial (and, again, interesting) is that he didn't. He chose to publish the poem with the crossed-out words and the "stet" as part of the text. So just reading what isn't crossed out as "the corrected version" won't work. If we're interested in intentions, it's not plausible to suppose John Cage wanted the reader to ignore what he might with no trouble have left out.

But let's be very careful, plausibly or not, let's suppose this was in fact what he had intended. Suppose he had written a note saying to his readers something like, "I didn't have time to retype this, just ignore the crossed-out words and the 'stet.' They're really not supposed to be in the corrected version of this poem." Surely we couldn't take this seriously. No time to retype? We would have to view this note as a joke or a new text to puzzle over. And, of course, even if we were inclined to take it seriously, it would have been a serious miscalculation on his part. The reader cannot ignore crossed-out words anymore than the viewer can fail to notice the crossed-out Mona Lisa of a contemporary artist, or the "Erased de Kooning" of Robert Rauschenberg. If anything, being crossed out or partially erased makes things even more noticeable than they would have been otherwise.

So the version, as printed, must be taken as the text—what is materially present to us, as readers, on the page. What this text means to us will have to be at least as complicated as the "whether" reading above. But it need not necessarily be taken as an ambiguous figure.

John Cage has in fact said in conversation that this poem went through several changes, all on the same sheet of paper, and was published as a typed version of the handwritten copy in order to retain its history and give it the dimension of time. He then read it aloud as it appears in R-1.[37] Does this solve our problem of how to read it?

Knowing this fact about the author's intentions will no doubt influence what we notice when we go back to the published text. It does tell us something about how the poem was written; it tells us very little about how to read it. History that ends up on a page no longer exists in the past. It has only a present and a future. It is, in effect, a score to be realized by the reader. Its past may be something we know *about* it; but that is only part of what it *is*.

Taken as a score—a notation which gives us c(l)ues for a range of possible readings—we might start experimenting aloud:

1. We could read it, line by line, in sequence, exactly as presented on the page. (Perhaps whispering the crossed-out parts.)

(R-2)   if you exi ted
             ~~becauSe~~

             we mIght go on as before
      but since you don't we ~~wi~~'Ll

                   mak
                   ~~chang~~E
                 our miNds
                   anar hic
             ~~so that we~~ Can
                   d to   let it be
             convertE~~njoy~~ the chaos/~~that~~ you are/
                             stet

In doing this, some lovely things happen. The first line becomes, "if you exited." The first three lines, "if you exited / becauSe / we might go on as before." If the "you" being addressed is SILENCE—the silent noun/title/addressee in the mesostic string—then it would indeed exit if we went on as before, not noticing it. This reading makes as much sense as one we might make of "if you exiSted / we might go on as before." What prevents us from seeing it (and any other like it) as an additional, rather than an alternative reading? The only thing that would silence these multiple readings would be ideology—ideology valuing simplicity and the idea of a single, "correct" meaning, one truth. Harking back to Adorno, let's assume that this is a better piece of art than would satisfy an ideologue, and admit as many meanings, as much complexity as we notice.

2. We could omit crossed-out sections altogether—reading single letters as phonemes, or reading letters which have lost their words *as* letters—the return to being alphabetic isolates rather than parts of syllables:

(R-3)   if you exi ted
                   S
             we mIght go on as before
      but since you don't we 'Ll
                   mak
                   E
                 our miNds

anar hic

C

d to   let it be

convertE   the chaos/   you are/

stet

This gives us, for instance, "E / our miNds" (where E can be associated with energy) and "convertE the chaos" (a permutation of Einstein's formula?) and "stet" as echo of "let it be" all addressed to the silent "you" embedded in the text. And, as they say in catalogues, Much More!

3. We could, as mentioned before, decide to read only lines with mesostic letters. This presents us with three more possibilities:

(a) read what isn't crossed out

(b) read what is crossed out

(c) read a and b somehow combined

4. We could notice, and try to make available in our reading, other complicating details: e.g., "I," as first-person pronoun in "mIght," "stet" read out as proofer's mark ("let stand as set"), the way in which the word "change" is being changed before our eyes, etc.

5. We might notice, additionally, the fractal symmetries in the poem: How the tension between the vertical and horizontal, present in every mesostic (i.e., the pull to read it both ways), dynamically structures the poem as a whole, and then is replicated in the vertical-horizontal tension between pairs of lines (where the "overhead" line needs something from below to complete it and vice versa), with individual letters, like the "S," which seem to belong in both vertical and horizontal axes, and which on their own have (as all letters—usually unremarked—do) both vertical and horizontal graphic elements. All this, of course, is also instantiated in the very act of reading with the vertical-horizontal choreography that often makes glimpsed (vertical, diagonal, and dog-legged) connections available despite energy expended on barring them from conscious cognition. Of course, like the crossed-out words in this poem, these aberrant connections/conjunctions can never be entirely ignored. They must in fact form one of the strange and interesting associative subtexts in our common reading experience.

There are many more ways to "realize" this—at first—deceptively small poem. We have moved from "whether" to, if not a full-blown regional weather system, at least a very complex and fascinating microclimate. With nonetheless macroclimatic implications about how much ideology (and habit) can silence in the act of reading, as well as about the nature of silence and our participation in and with it. John Cage has said about his working methods, "Composing this way changes me, rather than expresses me." It is a poethical approach—one which allows changes of mind, invention, humor, and a quality of attention that is full of wonderment and respect and surprise—the wonderment in the"O"s in "Overpopulation and Art," for instance. This kind of engagement with a text as a complex, active realization can be seen as a poethics of response for the reader/viewer/listener as well.

· · ·

I want to suggest then that this kind of poetry and this kind of reading functions within a poethics of complex realism where active processes of mutability and multiplicity are valued over simpler and more stable expressive clarity. Change actively, continually destabilizes the poem, thwarting *the* "correct" reading, thwarting any sure sense of return to the author's (ego-bound) local, prior intentions. All, it seems, that it makes sense to do is to notice what we find on the page and experience the multiple directions—the multiple lettristic, phonemic, syllabic, syntactic, semantic, and graphic trajectories—it takes us in/on.

As with the systems being described in the nonlinear sciences, it is not that there is *less* structure, but that the structure is one of greater complexity in a richly dynamic relationship with larger areas of indeterminacy. Just as it is not the case that with silence there is no sound (silence does *not* exist by its standard definition prior to Cage's per/con/ceptual shift), or less sound, but that the range of what is audible and how we attend to it has changed, it is not the case that with indeterminacy there is no meaning—the range of meaning (e.g., the connections we can notice and construct) undergoes transformation as we rise to the occasion of the gently prickly, oddly engaging text. The scope and focus and force of our attentive engagement is altered as we take on the discipline of more active noticing/inventing that the unfinished, irregular surfaces of indeterminacy invite. D. W. Winnicott's distinction between fantasy and imagination[38] comes to mind. Fantasy is the passive, self-enclosed mode nursed by nostalgically manipulative forms. (The monodirectionality of time means there can be no consequences in the past; it's safe; forms which return us there are restful in an ennervating and regressive way.) Imagination is always an active reaching out that develops our energies and has real consequences in the world. It must literally take chances, playing with the concrete hypothetical, the experimental "what if." It is the fruitful act of play as exploration and reciprocal transformation—a poethics of interrogative dialogues with material reality. (With his use of the *I Ching*, from the early fifties on, all of Cage's work began and moved forward by means of questions.) It is how we learn to live in our world. As adults we stop playing at our (and the world's) peril. The poethical engagement with a work like "(untitled)" develops as we return to our senses and take chances in our inter-actions with its graphic and linguistic presence on the page—in medias res, loud and silent, visible and indivisible—we grow and change together. Meaning will not be mined out of the sclerotic veins of a preformed object (an object that has "become art"), it will unfold in the form of life this engagement brings us to realize.

If we with great difficulty (and delectation) attend to the possibilities in what we do not understand, that is, if we move into our collaborative future admitting with constantly developing disciplines of attention the constantly changing world at large, then, no, we cannot "go on as before."

The poethics of this poem invites a practice of reading which enacts a tolerance for, and a delight in complex possibility. Imagine what might happen if such a prac-tice were to become widespread. Cage felt that such an eventuality (Here Comes Everybody listening to everybody else) could have real social consequences—that it could, as he said, change the political climate. An ethics, even a poethics, is not a politics, so this question is very much at large. At LARGE is precisely where we need to be.

Notes

1. In conversation with the author, July 1992.

2. John Dewey, *Art as Experience* (New York: Capricorn Books, G. P. Putnam's Sons, 1958). Hereafter cited as *AE*.

3. *AE*, 10–11. The theories of John Dewey were influential in the formation of Black Mountain College, a brief though significant catalytic scene of the new aesthetic that John Cage, Merce Cunningham, and Robert Rauschenberg (with important contributions from Buckminster Fuller) were pioneering. Dewey was a friend of the chief founder of the college, John Andrews Rice, and became a member of its advisory board in 1935. See Martin Duberman, *Black Mountain: An Exploration in Community* (New York: E. P. Dutton, 1972), p. 102 and elsewhere.

4. Composite definition drawing on the *OED* and *The American Heritage Dictionary*.

5. In conversation with the author, July 1992.

6. Descriptions from the MOMA "Summergarden 1992" program. In conversation the day before this performance, John Cage remarked that he had thought of "ASLSP" because of the passage toward the end of *Finnegans Wake* that begins, "Soft morning, city! Lsp! I am leafy speafing . . ." (New York: Viking, 1969), pp. 619ff. A pianist preparing to play "ASLSP" might profit from this passage. One finds, "I'll wait. And I'll wait. And then if all goes. What will be is. Is is. But let them" (620); "Sft! It is the softest morning that ever I can ever remember me. But she won't rain showerly, our Ilma. Yet. Until it's the time" (621); "A gentle motion all around. As leisure paces" (622); "Softly so" (624); "So soft this morning, ours" (628).

7. Mineko Grimmer's sculpture, used in the violin performance of *One*[6], consists of an inverted pyramid of ice encrusted with pebbles hung over a single piano wire stretched across a tank of water. As the ice melts, the pebbles fall into the water and, now and then, by chance, hit the piano wire. This has the remarkable effect of making the chance operations which produce the sounds visible.

8. Søren Kierkegaard, *Either/Or*, vol. 2 (New York: Anchor Books, Doubleday, 1959), p. 139.

9. Michael Bach has in fact invented a new kind of curved bow, for the playing of Cage's music, with a mechanism which allows the cellist to vary the tension on the hairs while playing. As has always been the case in the history of music, the dialogue between composer and performer, music and technology, continually opens up new possibilities. John Cage, shortly before his death, was composing a piece for Michael Bach, exploring new microtonal and other musical possibilities linked to bowing technique.

10. From Adorno's "Lyric Poetry and Society," quoted by Martin Jay in *Adorno* (Cambridge: Harvard University Press, 1984), p. 155.

11. From Preface to *Lecture on the Weather* (1975), in *Empty Words, Writings '73–'78* (Middletown, CT: Wesleyan University Press, 1979), p. 5. Hereafter cited as *EW*.

12. John Cage, remarks made after the performance of *Lecture on the Weather*, Strathmore Hall Cage-Fest, Rockville, MD, 1989.

13. As Marjorie Perloff also points out in an illuminating discussion of *Lecture on the Weather*, in her book *Radical Artifice: Writing Poetry in the Age of Media* (Chicago and London: University of Chicago Press, 1991). See pp. 21 ff.

14. This is notably the metaphysical "traffic" of Epictetus's vision of the interplay of chance and determinism in the makeup of the universe. See my "High Adventures of Indeterminacy," *Parnassus: Poetry in Review* 11, no. 1, (Spring–Summer 1983):231–63. In the last few years, John Cage spoke of "traffic" as the characteristic sound structure of contemporary life and therefore of his desire to incorporate it into the forms of his music. This was another part of his poethical imperative: to "make a piece of music in which we would be willing to live . . . a representation of a society in which you would be willing to live," *I–VI* (Cambridge and London: Harvard University Press, 1990), p. 178. This meant working within the logics of a complex realist aesthetic, one which enacts the complexity of the society in which we live.

15. John Cage, "Overpopulation and Art," this volume, ll. 624–32.

16. In 1963 Edward Lorenz published the groundbreaking paper, "Deterministic Nonperiodic Flow," *Journal of the Atmospheric Sciences* 20:130–41.

17. James Gleick, *Chaos: Making a New Science* (New York: Viking, 1987). See also David Ruelle, *Chance and Chaos* (Princeton: Princeton University Press, 1991), hereafter cited as *CC*, particularly chapters 10 and 11, "Turbulence: Strange Attractors," and "Chaos: A New Paradigm," pp. 57–72.

18. Both programs in the C language developed by Andrew Culver.

19. This difference will not be as great in a Cage performance as in the mathematical model of a weather system, and it will not necessarily undergo a progressive magnification. See note 20.

20. After a December 1992 conversation with James A. Yorke, director of the Institute for Physical Science and Technology at the University of Maryland, College Park, the mathematician who coined this current usage of the term "chaos," it seemed more accurate (within the language game of the current complex sciences) to describe the scores Cage submitted to chance operations as characterized by "deterministic randomness" (where "randomness" is the scientific term for the more colloquial "chance") than "deterministic chaos." It appears

that the critical difference between the mathematical behavior of what are currently called chaotic systems, and the notational sound elements in a Cage score has to do with the degree and nature of predictability. In models of deterministic chaos there is a high degree of short-run predictability which degenerates (rapidly) into randomness, or increasingly amplified unpredictability, over time. In Cage's scores the degree of unpredictability remains constant. There is a built-in (to the *ic* and *tic* computer programs) equal distribution of randomness. The indeterminacy included in the notation and the permeability of performances to ambient sound and individual interpretations mean, however, that butterflies are continually flying into and transforming the atmosphere of Cage's compositions when they are realized in concert. (And in some cases there may even be amplification of unpredictability in performance. See the next section of my text.) This in turn means that Cage's music, as an aesthetic of weather, is closer in its structure to our everyday experience of weather than to the computer models in the complex sciences which start with fewer variables and yield more discernible patterns. As James Yorke puts it, "Weather is wilder than 'chaos.'" Why connect Cage's aesthetic paradigm with chaos theory then? Because in many other respects, excepting those which make the difference between a complex realist aesthetics and a mathematical model of complexity, it appears to interestingly and importantly resemble this new scientific paradigm.

21. Thomas Kuhn, *The Structure of Scientific Revolutions,* 2d ed. (Chicago: University of Chicago Press, 1970). See also Kuhn's *The Essential Tension: Selected Studies in Scientific Tradition and Change* (Chicago: University of Chicago Press, 1977).

22. Counter to the cartoon tag, "Minimalist," that journalists like to use in reference to Cage.

23. I first came across this Smithson idea of "ruins in reverse" in Marjorie Perloff's *The Futurist Moment: Avant-Garde, Avant Guerre, and the Language of Rupture* (Chicago and London: University of Chicago Press, 1986), p. 199. It is from Smithson's essay, "A Tour of the Monuments of Passaic, New Jersey," published in *The Writings of Robert Smithson,* ed. Nancy Holt (New York: New York University Press, 1979).

24. In 1991 Cage published "Macrobiotic Cooking"—remarks and recipes—in *Aerial* 6/7, Washington D.C.

25. Cage, "Autobiographical Statement," Cage-Fest, 1989.

26. From "John Cage: Conversation with Joan Retallack," *Aerial* 6/7 (1991).

27. From remarks at Strathmore Hall Cage-Fest, 1989.

28. N. Katherine Hayles, *Chaos Bound: Orderly Disorder in Contemporary Literature and Science* (Ithaca and London: Cornell University Press, 1990). See her "Introduction: The

Evolution of Chaos," pp. 1–28. What Hayles is discussing in this book is structural, working definitions of chaos, i.e., methodological programs and their paradigms in the sciences and images of chaos in contemporary literature, i.e., literature envisioning and referring to elements of chaos, rather than formally exhibiting chaotic dynamics. A discussion of this latter—formal experiments embodying and enacting some of the interesting characteristics of chaos and other complex dynamics—will have to explore the contemporary avant-garde, e.g., Language poetry, and of course the compositions of John Cage. See Hayles's essay in this volume for her view of chance operations (precisely defined in several ways) in Cage's work.

29. It is interesting to note that Cage's nonperiodic music has also been seen as a "failure of the experiment."

30. What is perhaps most interesting in this is that Ruelle tells the story of Professor Chance in passing, without any of the rhetorical machinations—of, for instance, irony or allegory—one has come to expect when a stock narrative form confronts something stranger than its fictions. Either of these literary modes—irony, allegory—would empty this encounter with Professor Chance of its peculiar and complex contingency, even as it filled it with overdetermined, portentously simplifying meaning. "Professor Chance," as a character in any kind of narrative fiction—and all narratives are fictions on one level or another—would paradoxically lose his vitality as an "unremarkable" oddment of ordinary life.

31. I am relying chiefly on David Ruelle, "Information," in *Chance and Chaos*, discussions of information theory in Katherine Hayles's work, and on a conversation with Katherine Hayles at the Stanford University Humanities Center, January 1992. I hasten to absolve her of any responsibility for the way in which I construe this information on information.

32. John Cage, *A Year from Monday* (Middletown, CT: Wesleyan University Press, 1967), p. 31.

33. For example, in "Comment on the Relations of Science and Art," a paper which begins, "For reasons which will appear, the problem of the avant-garde . . . has caught my interest in unexpected and, I hope, fruitful ways," Thomas Kuhn writes, "People like [E. M.] Hafner and me, to whom the similarities of science and art came as a revelation, have been concerned to stress that the artist, too, like the scientist, faces persistent technical problems which must be resolved in the pursuit of his [*sic*] craft. Even more we emphasize that the scientist, like the artist, is guided by aesthetic considerations and governed by established modes of perception. Those parallels still need to be both underlined and developed. We have only begun to discover the benefits of seeing science and art as one," *The Essential Tension*, p. 343.

34. Douglas Hofstadter, *Metamagical Themas* (New York: Basic Books, 1985), p. 777.

35. Cage, "Autobiographical Statement," Cage-Fest, 1989.

36. John Cage, *X, Writings '79–'82* (Middletown, CT: Wesleyan University Press, 1983), p. 117. This poem on silence was written after Cage's experience in the anechoic chamber at Harvard in the early fifties, when he discovered that "silence doesn't exist."

37. Conversation with the author, April 1992.

38. See particularly D. W. Winnicott, *Playing and Reality* (London: Tavistock Publications, 1984).

Appendix

Revisions to *Overpopulation and Art*
Joan Retallack

That John Cage was open to criticism of his work until the end of his life will surprise no one who knew him. In this sense he was experimental in a way that scientists would recognize—exploring the unnoticed and the new while testing his conceptual framework against what he regarded as important "reality principles." He wanted his work to have useful consequences in the world and it couldn't have that if it was somehow off-base, inappropriate, irrelevant. In his 1959 "History of Experimental Music in the United States" Cage wrote, "I would ask this: 'Why, if everything is possible, do we concern ourselves with history (in other words with a sense of what is necessary to be done at a particular time)?' And I would answer, 'In order to thicken the plot.' . . . One does not then make just any experiment but does what must be done" (*Silence,* 68). This was his credo until he died.

When John Cage read "Overpopulation and Art" at Stanford in January 1992 it contained these lines: "the necessity tO find new forms / of liVing / nEw / foRms of living together / to stoP the estrangement between us / tO overcome / the Patriarchal thinking"; but it also contained an intermittent use of generic male nouns (man, mankind, manhour) and pronouns (he, him, himself, his). This bothered me more and more as I read and reread the "Overpopulation" manuscript in conjunction with writing my essay for this volume. I mentioned this to him at a dinner party where we couldn't really talk at length about it. He said, "Tell me how you think it can be fixed." I sent him a letter on June 10, 1992, explaining my concern more fully along with some sample revisions. In the letter I wrote, "These are the pages on which I noticed the use of 'generic' male nouns and pronouns, which are, I think, part of a language of the past (dominated by patriarchal thinking), not a healthy language of the future which should be as free as possible of all authoritarian, hierarchical, and exclusive structures/strictures. Since language is the medium in which we envision and project so much of our sense of our potential as humans, I will always opt for the most open language—the one that includes the most possibilities. 'Humanity,' 'human,' 'oneself,' 'our,' seem to me more generous, inclusive, and connective than 'Man,' 'man's,' 'himself,' 'his' . . . which (latter) I think, despite the 'higher order' logic of certain justifications, always specify and limit in the very contexts which are meant to be non-specific and non-limiting. So, thinking poethically, the textual world in which I would wish to live is a world of 'we' and 'ours' not 'man' and 'his.' This is all of course full of the breath of Wittgenstein. If you take his idea of language as a form of life seriously, then the textual—and spoken—world (the particular words and forms we choose) always have poethical implications."

Cage's response was by phone. He called to say, "I have taken benefit from your criticisms and made all the changes. I think it's greatly improved." I had given him a number of variations for each instance, some of which he used. In many cases he came up with others: "woRld us," for example, is his. In another conversation he told me he had at first thought it was hopeless because not all my suggestions had fit the lettristic rules for a 50% mesostic but then "I realized this is not a matter of vocabulary but a way of thinking and that revitalized me." He had not merely made corrections, he had revised in the root sense of re-vision as re-seeing.

One might wonder why John Cage didn't come to this sooner. But he really wasn't privy to the heart of the debate over gendered linguistic structures. He was part of an aesthetic tradition almost entirely formed by men in a time very much prior to the recent flourishing of feminist theory and he was not in touch with sources bringing him into contact with arguments for inclusive language. It is not surprising that, cut off from those lines of reasoning, and not given to being thoughtlessly "PC," he remained unalarmed about habitual, seemingly trivial "vocabulary" constructions. After our discussion and the changes to "Overpopulation," he was very concerned, inquiring several times whether all appearances of the generic male had been ex-punged. Later that summer, as we finished taping a series of conversations about his music, on an afternoon that turned out to be thirteen days before his death, he asked me to make similar changes in my transcriptions of the tapes. He said he had no doubt this was important, though force of habit in speech was hard to overcome.

This of course was/is the characteristic challenge of Cage's work—exhilarating, if not always easy, for him and us—to break out of restrictive habitual modes into revitalizing possibility. In making these revisions he was continuing to "thicken the plot," as he had in other areas of his work, to include women, by doing in 1992 "what must be done."

Line 126

> *original:* or should he Put himself aside
> *revised:* or should artists be Put aside

Line 128

> *original:* to sPeak   change himself
> *revised:* to sPeak   be changed

Line 488

> *original:* pOund kilowatt and manhour the overall
> *revised:* pOund kilowatt and workhour the overall

Line 584

> *original:* due to mankind's Vast
> *revised:* due to our Vast

Line 592

> *original:* by mAn
> *revised:* by humAn beings

Line 595

> *original:* which man invents sO that
> *revised:* which are invented sO that

Lines 609–13

> *original:* he Pleases   man's
> not needed becaUse of his
> abiLity to work
> As a slave   he's needed

                    because of his abiliTy to consume
        revised: Pleases   we're
                    not needed becaUse of our
                    abiLity to work
                    As slaves   we're needed
                    because of our abiliTy to consume

Lines 624–26
        original: of man that's now Visibly
                    dEveloping
                    is woRld man
        revised: our picture   that's now Visibly
                    dEveloping
                    is woRld us

Lines 685–86
        original: to changE not man
                    but man's enviRonment   basque friend esther ferer
        revised: to changE not us
                    but our enviRonment   basque friend esther ferrer

Lines 746–48
        original: that each peRson conceive of himself as an intelligent being
                    caPable
                    Of making his life decisions without delegating his
        revised: that each peRson is an intelligent being
                    caPable
                    Of making life decisions without delegating

Line 768
        original: authOritarian socialism anarchy seems for man's liberation
        revised: authOritarian socialism anarchy seems for our liberation

Contributors

Gerald L. Bruns, the William and Hazel White Professor of English at the University of Notre Dame, is the author of a number of books on literature and philosophy, including *Modern Poetry and the Idea of Language* (Yale, 1974) and *Hermeneutics Ancient and Modern* (Yale, 1992).

Gordana P. Crnković, assistant professor of Slavic languages and literature at the University of Washington in Seattle, has written a number of articles and is currently working on a book entitled "Eastern European, American, and English Literature against Closure: A Dialogical Perspective."

N. Katherine Hayles, professor of English at the University of California at Los Angeles, is the author of *Chaos Bound: Orderly Disorder in Contemporary Literature and Science* (Cornell, 1990) and editor of *Chaos and Order: Complex Dynamics in Literature and Science* (Chicago, 1991).

Daniel Herwitz, associate professor of philosophy at California State University–Los Angeles, has written widely on aesthetics and painting. His most recent book is *Making Theory/Constructing Art* (Chicago, 1993).

Thomas S. Hines, professor of history and architecture and urban planning at the University of California at Los Angeles, is the author of numerous books and articles, including *Burnham of Chicago* (Oxford, 1974), *Richard Neutra and the Search for Modern Architecture* (Oxford, 1982), and "Machines in the Garden: Notes toward a History of Modern Los Angeles Architecture," in *Sex, Death, and God in Art* (Pantheon, 1992).

Charles Junkerman is the associate director of the Stanford Humanities Center. He was written on contemporary fiction and documentary photography and teaches literary theory in the English Department at Stanford University.

Herbert Lindenberger, the Avalon Professor of Humanities at Stanford University, has written extensively on modern European literature, including books on Wordsworth, Büchner, Trakl, historical drama, opera, and critical theory.

His most recent book is *The History in Literature: On Value, Genre, and Institutions* (Columbia, 1990).

Jann Pasler, professor of music at the University of California–San Diego, writes on modern and postmodern music and culture. She is the editor of *Confronting Stravinsky: Man, Musician, and Modernist* (California, 1986) and the producer of the film *Taksu: Music in the Life of Bali.* She is now completing a book on music in Paris at the turn of the century.

Marjorie Perloff, Sadie Dernham Patek Professor of Humanities at Stanford University, is the author of many books and essays on modern and postmodern poetry, poetics, and the visual arts, including *The Futurist Moment: Avant-Garde, Avant Guerre, and the Language of Rupture* (Chicago, 1986) and *Radical Artifice: Writing Poetry in the Age of Media* (Chicago, 1992).

Joan Retallack, a poet and critic, is Visiting Butler Chair Professor of English, SUNY at Buffalo, 1993–94. She teaches in the Interdisciplinary University Honors Program at the University of Maryland–College Park and is an associate of the Institute for Writing and Thinking at Bard College. Her most recent book of poetry is *Errata 5uite* (Edge Books, 1993). Her book on and with John Cage, *M U S I C A G E: Cage Muses on Words, Art, and Music,* will be published by Wesleyan University Press.

Index

Adams, John, 159–60
Adcock, Craig, 124 n.17
Adorno, Theodor, 144
Arditti, Irvine, 142 n.10
Arensberg, Walter, 86, 89, 90, 105
Aristotle, 53, 215
Augustine, 52

Bach, J. S., 80, 81
Bach, Michael, 246, 247, 269 n.9
Baudrillard, Jean, 253
Bercovitch, Sacvan, 47
Bertini, Gary, 146
Bird, Bonnie, 93
Boulez, Pierre, 101, 132, 165 n.21
Bovington, John, 83
Brent, Jonathan, 94 n.3
Brown, Norman O., 8, 47, 51, 54, 57, 105
Bruns, Gerald L., 4, 9–10, 55
Bühlig, Richard, 90, 91, 94
Bürger, Peter, 113

Cabanne, Pierre, 104, 105, 114, 116, 123 n.6
Cage, John: "An Autobiographical Statement," 81, 125; *Atlas Eclipticalis*, 40; *A Year from Monday*, 48, 53; "Composition as Process," 233, 234; "Composition in Retrospect," 7, 66–67, 125–43; Concerto, 140; "Diary: How to Improve the World (You'll Only Make Matters Worse)," 229, 238; *Empty Words*, 39–40, 44, 54, 56, 60–61, 105; "Etcetera," 140; *Etudes Astrales*, 140; *Europeras*, 7–8, 144–66; "Experimental Music: Doctrine," 230–31, 234, 237; *For the Birds*, 3, 45, 48, 53–58, 61 n.6; *4′33″*, 125, 150, 161; *Freeman Etudes*, 140; "The Future of Music," 45, 191; "History of Experimental Music in the United States," 6, 275; *HPSCHD*, 52; "James Joyce, Marcel Duchamp, Eric Satie: An Alphabet," 100–101, 114, 117–22, 129, 133, 156; "Lecture on Nothing," 173; "Lecture on the Weather," 9, 194, 248, 258; *M*, 45, 54–55, 105; "Muoyce," 40, 50; "Muoyce II," 242; "Mureau," 217–18, 236; *Musicircus*, 5, 39–64, 137, 140, 162; "Music of Changes," 125; *One*^{8}, 245, 247; *One*^{11}, 242; *One*^{6}, 141; *I–VI*, 7, 9, 125, 140, 142 n.18, 194–203, 260, 270 n.14; "Other People Think," 77; "Overpopulation and Art," 2–3, 14–38, 39, 45, 55, 59, 60, 61, 139, 216, 238–40, 249, 259, 275–78; "Seriously Comma," 12; *Silence*, 8–9, 11, 53, 103, 106, 113, 167–87, 214, 215, 227–31, 236; "26 Statements Re Duchamp," 110–14; "2 Pages, 22 Words on Music and Dance," 173–

Index